KNOWING
JESUS

KNOWING
JESUS

150 Reflections *on the* Life *and* Teaching of Christ

JIM REAPSOME

BakerBooks

a division of Baker Publishing Group
Grand Rapids, Michigan

© 2008 by Jim Reapsome

Published by Baker Books
a division of Baker Publishing Group
P.O. Box 6287, Grand Rapids, MI 49516-6287
www.bakerbooks.com

ISBN 978-0-8010-1426-0
Previously published under the title *10 Minutes a Day with Jesus*

Printed in the United States of America

The Library of Congress has cataloged the original edition as follows:
Reapsome, James W.
    10 minutes a day with Jesus : growing in your love for the Savior / Jim
Reapsome.
        p.   cm.
    ISBN 978-0-8010-1307-2 (cloth)
    1. Jesus Christ—Meditations. 2. Bible. N.T. Gospels—Meditations. I. Title.
BT203.R425 2008
232—dc22   2008007346

Scripture is taken from the Holy Bible, New International Version®. NIV®. Copyright © 1973, 1978, 1984 by Biblica, Inc.™ Used by permission of Zondervan. All rights reserved worldwide. www.zondervan.com

12   13   14   15   16   17   18   7   6   5   4   3   2   1

To Mary my mother and Martha my wife,
who showed me what it means to sit at the feet of Jesus

Introduction

When I fell in love, I squeezed out every minute of spare time to be with my girlfriend. I wanted to know everything I could about her. But getting to know her in the usual way was difficult because hundreds of miles separated us. It took a lot of creative shuffling of our work responsibilities, to say nothing of some unique travel arrangements, for us to get together every month or so. When we could manage it, we spent an entire day together. Between those visits we corresponded regularly. I devoured her letters as if they were chocolate sundaes. In the end, our visits and our letters did the trick; we decided we knew each other well enough to get married.

Falling in love with Jesus is something like that. He tells us he loves us and he wants our love in return, but we are separated from him by two thousand years of history. All we have to go on are stories that his friends told and wrote about him. The Gospels of Matthew, Mark, Luke, and John are like love letters from Jesus. When we read them, the Holy Spirit informs our minds and ignites our hearts.

The incomparable beauty, strength, and love of Jesus overwhelm us. He becomes the lover of our souls and we decide

7

we want to marry him, so to speak. That's the reason, in biblical imagery, we are called the bride of Christ. Our destiny is to feast with him at the wedding supper of the Lamb (Rev. 19:7, 9).

But what do we do while we wait for that consummation? How do we keep our love aflame? We can be faithful in worship—privately and corporately—faithful in prayer, and faithful in reading the four Gospels and the rest of the New Testament. If our weekly gathering at church is just about all the devotion we give to Jesus, our love affair with Jesus will not blossom. The grave danger is that our love will grow cold. Jesus spoke about this tragic possibility: "You have forsaken your first love" (Rev. 2:4).

To develop our relationship with Jesus, we must do what I did when I was courting my girlfriend. I read and reread her letters. I could not get enough of them. Like a dog gnawing a bone, I squeezed every drop of nourishment from her words.

The apostle Paul revealed his desire to the Philippians. "I want to know Christ," he wrote (Phil. 3:10). The apostle Peter urged his readers: "Grow in the grace and knowledge of our Lord and Savior Jesus Christ" (2 Peter 3:18).

One way to do that is to set aside some time regularly to be with Jesus—at least ten minutes a day. Our goal is to experience the intimacy he wants to share with us. He promised that if we love and obey him, he and his Father will make their home with us (John 14:23). He compared our intimacy with him to that of a vine and its branches. "Remain in me, and I will remain in you. . . . remain in my love," he said (15:4, 9).

To help you start your path to intimacy with Jesus, I've looked at his story to find out more clearly how he lived. I hope some of my perspectives on his life will inspire your fresh thoughts and deeper love. Ultimately, my prayer is not only that you will love Jesus more wholeheartedly, but also that your life will reflect his values and commitments. God's purpose for all of Christ's followers is that they will become like him (Rom. 8:29).

Jesus, the Author and Perfecter of Our Faith

Colossians 3:1–2; Hebrews 12:1–2

Aspiring Olympic speedster Harold Abrams lunged across the finish line in a trial race. He missed first place by a split second. Heartbroken, he found a coach to help him win the one-hundred-meter dash. If he could learn anything that would shave even one-tenth of a second off his time, it would be worth it.

His new coach watched him run and caught him looking over his shoulder as he neared the finish line. He screamed at Harold to concentrate on the tape. You can watch this drama in the movie *Chariots of Fire*.

The Olympic race stands as a striking metaphor of the Christian life. The book of Hebrews reveals our coaching and training regimen. The writer captured the essence of what Abrams learned. He saw Christians running the race before a huge crowd of spectators. He urged them to throw away sin and other spiritual weights. As Christians pound down the track God has marked out for them, they must concentrate fully on the Lord Jesus Christ.

As the author and perfecter of our faith, Jesus stands as the only person worthy of our total concentration, loyalty, and affection. The word *author* in Hebrews 12:2 means Jesus is our leader, or pacesetter, in the race of life. He went before us and opened the way to make a saving knowledge of God possible. He invigorates and encourages us to follow him.

Perfecter means that Jesus demonstrated superlative faith from start to finish. He finished well. He won his race because he never deviated from his Father's will. When we look to Jesus, we see the purest representation of authentic faith.

The studies in this book represent a coach's manual. Whatever place we hold in the race, the winning tip is the same: fix your eyes on Jesus. We will look at Jesus from many different perspectives: the four biographies of Jesus—Matthew, Mark, Luke, and John—the prophecies about Jesus, and the apostolic teachings about Jesus.

When the coach in Hebrews counseled his readers, he knew the perils and distractions that plagued them. Many of them suffered hardship and loss because they followed Jesus. For some, the pain was too much to bear and they wanted to return to the ways of their traditional religion. Whatever the causes, the coach saw them dangerously close to dropping out of the race. "Keep going," he urged them. "Run with patient endurance. Keep looking to Jesus."

When we fix our eyes on Jesus, what do we see? We see a fellow runner, one like ourselves (Heb. 2:17–18; 4:15), who triumphantly completed his course and now rests at God's right hand. His race was unlike any other. No Christian runner will ever face and overcome the obstacles that Jesus did.

Jesus conquered his supreme test, the cross. He endured both terrible physical agony and humiliating shame. It's astonishing that he did this with joy. Neither the shame of public disgrace, nor, worst of all, the abandonment of his Father, deterred Jesus from crossing the line of victory.

Look to Jesus, whatever your test—rejection by former friends and, in some cases, family as well; turmoil at home; reversals in job and business; sudden illness; the death of a loved one; chronic pain; the toll of aging. We cannot run the race successfully unless we focus on Jesus, and when we do, he fills us with his peace and joy. Making his dwelling with us, he welcomes us when we cry out to him in prayer. Our faithful obedience delights his heart. His life in us produces fruit. When we are needy or afraid, he intercedes for us and stands guard over us. Jesus picks us up when we stumble. He forgives us so we can make fresh starts. When we get to know and rely on him, he does all this and much, much more.

It takes only ten minutes a day. Spend time with Jesus every day and you will discover what the apostle Paul called "the unsearchable riches of Christ" (Eph. 3:8).

To think about

- Remind yourself of all that Jesus has done, is doing, and will do for you.
- What distractions and "weights" do you struggle with in your race of life?

Lord Jesus, I confess that I do not focus on you as I should. Help me to think more about you, regardless of my circumstances.

Jesus, the Son of Abraham and David

Matthew 1:1–7; Luke 3:23–38

We begin our journey with Jesus by looking at his genealogy. That's the way Matthew opened his story of Jesus; Luke included it after he wrote about the birth of Jesus.

Most likely, unless you explore your own family tree, you fail to get excited about genealogies. They don't grab pressure-packed modern readers.

Matthew and Luke's contemporaries, however, read the Jesus story from an entirely different perspective than we do. Jesus had come and gone, yet the Mediterranean world stirred when the news about him began to spread. Who was he? Where did he come from? What were his credentials? The answers to these big questions shaped the New Testament biographies of Jesus.

Jewish history formed the soil in which the early church grew. The earliest followers of Jesus were Jews. Their initial proclamation of the gospel reached Jewish ears. It was imperative for Matthew and Luke to establish Jesus's family line all the way back to David and Abraham, the pillars of Jewish history and faith.

Across Israel, hope spread like a flame because people saw Jesus as King David's successor (Matt. 21:9, 15). His followers realized they could make this claim stick by circulating his genealogy. This was a critical element in their defense of Jesus and the gospel. Peter's first sermon (Acts 2:14–36) and Paul's letter to the Romans (1:3) reinforce this claim. The risen Christ declared, "I am the Root and the Offspring of David" (Rev. 22:16).

We believe rightly that Jesus was fully human and fully divine. His divine genealogy came directly to Mary from God via the

Holy Spirit. In his humanity Jesus was "made like his brothers in every way" (Heb. 2:17). Therefore he was also descended from a family tree that Matthew traced back to Abraham, the father of the Jewish nation. Matthew inserted fascinating historical tidbits into his genealogy; Luke took a slightly different approach. Because people thought Jesus was the son of Joseph, Luke started with Joseph and reached back to Adam.

Matthew's genealogy mentioned two famous mothers: Rahab, the harlot of Jericho who saved Joshua's spies, and Ruth, the refugee from Moab (Matt. 1:5). Both were Gentiles. Why did Matthew include them when most of the genealogy lists Jesus's male ancestors? Possibly Matthew wanted in a clever way to help his Jewish readers overcome some of their nasty stereotypes about women and Gentiles.

Matthew also refers to David's sins—adultery and murder—when he had Uriah killed so that he could marry Bathsheba (v. 6). He cites the captivity of the Jews in Babylon (v. 11). Significantly, when he came to Jesus (v. 16), Matthew calls Joseph the husband of Mary, not Jesus's father.

Genealogies reveal fascinating details, if we dig deeper. Stories lie behind every name. Taking the long view, these records show how God orchestrated events in the lives of people who were the ancestors of Jesus. They give us a clear road map of God's eternal salvation trail. God's love permeates these records. Jesus is one of us, and for that we are grateful.

To think about

- Why are these genealogies of Jesus important?
- How do they increase your growing appreciation of Jesus?

Thank you, Father, for showing me the humanity of Jesus in such an honest way. Thank you for substantiating his claim to be your promised Messiah, the son of David, and my Lord and Savior.

Jesus, the Significance of His Name

Matthew 1:18–25

God gave his Son the name Jesus. He "gave him the name that is above every name" (Phil. 2:9). His name is the only name whereby we can be saved (Acts 4:12). We come to our heavenly Father in the name of Jesus. We worship, witness, and serve in his name.

The name of Jesus represents who he is, God the Son, the second person of the Trinity, and God in our human flesh. Jesus is the unique Son of God, the only begotten of the Father.

The fullness of the Godhead dwells in Jesus. He is full of grace and truth. When we invoke his name, we invoke all the attributes of deity, his holiness, his creative power, his wisdom—everything that God is, Jesus is.

On the other hand, Jesus was an ordinary name, which means he is like us, fully human and susceptible to all our sins, suffering, and shortcomings. But he never sinned; he never displeased his heavenly Father. His name combines humanity and deity in one person. This incomparable person is willing to live in us.

The name of Jesus rises above all other names in the Bible and in history, just as Mount Everest surpasses all other mountain peaks. Jesus is the focal point of Old Testament prophecy, New Testament history, and apostolic preaching. Wherever we look in Holy Scripture, Jesus confronts us. Actually he is referred to by nearly two hundred different metaphors, titles, and names in the Bible.

When it was time to name him, God sent angels to Mary and Joseph. Mary learned, "He will be great and will be called the Son of the Most High" (Luke 1:32). Joseph was told, "He will save his people from their sins" (Matt. 1:21).

14

Jesus means "God saves." By this name God announced the kind of news that never before had been heard in human history. He sent his Son on a mission, so that everyone who believes in him will be saved from the consequences of their sins.

When we hear the Good News that Jesus came to save us, we choose either to accept or reject him. "To those who believed in his name, he gave the right to become children of God" (John 1:12). Our decision about what to do with Jesus determines our eternal destiny. He will save us if we confess our sins and place our trust in him. He will judge us unworthy of his kingdom if we refuse.

To think about

- What does the name of Jesus signify or represent to you?
- How can you allow Jesus to exercise his wisdom, love, and authority in your life?

Heavenly Father, thank you for sending your Son Jesus to be my Savior. May his supremacy in my life determine the choices I make.

Jesus, Son of the Most High

Luke 1:26–38

We want to discover all we can about Jesus from the angelic announcements that preceded his birth, first to Mary and then to Joseph. God sent the angel Gabriel to Mary's hometown of Nazareth with an astonishing prophecy. This young woman, perhaps a teenager, would bear a son, even though she was a virgin. She would give birth not to just a human son but "the Son of the Most High" (Luke 1:32). His name was Jesus.

What do the names of Jesus tell us? Two things: his earthly mission and his heavenly position. *Jesus* means "God saves," so we know for sure he gives us salvation. "The Son of the Most High" means that we trust him not only as our Savior but also as our Lord. He is the Son of our heavenly Father and therefore exercises divine power for us. When we confess him as Savior and Lord, we enter into a new relationship with God. He forgives us and we relinquish all our rights. We become servants of the Most High.

From Gabriel we learn that Jesus's mission and his position are tied to the Old Testament prophecies about the future of the throne of David and the house of Jacob (Israel). God keeps his promises to his people in all ages and generations, even though it may appear at times that he is doing nothing. When we join the company of Jesus's people, we share in his inheritance and enter a never-ending kingdom.

As we struggle to understand and to live in the light of the angel's stunning announcement about Jesus, we feel like kindergartners. We start by acting on the promise that whoever calls on the name of the Lord will be saved (Rom. 10:13). Jesus invites us to pray in his name, so we grow in the habit of talking to him every day. His name combines both saving and intercessory power. Jesus calls us to worship with others in his name. He tells us to serve others in his name, bringing hope and comfort to the suffering and distressed. Everything we do as Christians, in word or deed, we do in the name of the Lord Jesus (Col. 3:17).

Jesus's exalted position as God's Son guarantees our security and our freedom from worry and fear. Because he is God the Son, he lives in heaven now, preparing places for us. One day he will usher in his everlasting kingdom on earth, not as the suffering Servant but as the triumphant King of Kings and Lord of Lords.

> When he comes, our glorious King,
> All his ransomed home to bring,
> Then anew this song we'll sing:
> Hallelujah! What a Saviour!
>
> Philip P. Bliss
> "Hallelujah, What a Saviour!"

To think about

- What appears most striking to you about Gabriel's announcement to Mary?
- How can meditating on Jesus's mission and position deepen your relationship with him?

Grant, O Lord, a deeper understanding of who Jesus is and what he can do for me. Thank you for saving me by faith and giving me a place in your everlasting kingdom.

Jesus, the Bearer of Peace

·Luke 2:8–20

Perhaps the Judean shepherds ignite more nostalgia about Christmases past than any other part of the story, except for Mary and the Christ child. As we read about their finding the mother and child at the crèche, feelings of awe at the holy sight stir within us. Their gentle presence arouses hope and comfort in us.

On the other hand, how out of place these rough and ready herdsmen appear at the nativity of Jesus! Why did God choose them to give homage to his Son at his birth? Why should the angel announce to them that this baby in Bethlehem is both Savior and Lord?

As the major players in this birth drama gathered around the manger, all of them knew, via angelic messengers, that this baby was unlike any other baby ever born. God's message to Mary and to Joseph and the angels' announcement to the shepherds were the same, thus showing us how important the facts were that God revealed.

God's message shattered the past and introduced a totally new chapter in his salvation plan for the world. In essence, God entered our human experience. He became one of us to save us. He chose to do so by anointing a virgin-born child to be both Savior and Lord.

Putting the three angelic revelations together, we understand why the first believers called Jesus the Lord Jesus Christ. *Christ* is Greek for the Hebrew word *Messiah*, meaning "the Anointed One." For the believing Jews, Jesus was their long-awaited Messiah. He fulfilled their prophetic anticipations of God's entrance into their hurting world.

Of course, their world (as ours) suffered under pagan idolatry and awful cruelties. Yet under the Judean stars God announced that he was about to break the spell of human misery and depravity. Christ the Lord would bring peace, the kind of peace that comes from forgiveness and from honoring him as God's anointed one.

Just as the angel touched undeserving shepherds, so Jesus touches us at every point in our lives. While we are hard at work, or while we struggle with family and careers, Jesus comes to us and says, "Let me take charge." When we fall short of God's expectations, Jesus says, "I have paid for all your sins. Confess and let me make you clean."

The startling news about Jesus caused the shepherds to hightail it to Bethlehem. The Good News about Jesus shouts to us every day from the pages of the Bible. The Good News motivates us to crown him Lord of all. A great company of angels said it best when Jesus was born: "Glory to God in the highest" (Luke 2:14).

To think about

- Imagine how you would have felt if you had been one of the shepherds. Why would you have had these feelings?
- In one sense the aura of Christmas should brighten every day. How can this be?

O Lord, thank you for breaking the powers of sin and darkness. Grant that I might live each day in the light of the angel's message. You are my Savior and Lord.

Jesus, the Presence of God

Matthew 1:18–25

Matthew breaks into Joseph's dream, as it were, to laud the yet-to-be-born Jesus as the fulfillment of Isaiah's seven-hundred-year-old prophecy of Messiah's virgin birth. This first of Matthew's many "this took place to fulfill" explanations authenticated the necessary link between the Old Testament prophets and Jesus. Not steeped in hopes of fulfilled prophecies, as many of Matthew's peers were, we can easily miss the critical importance of these links. Fulfilled prophecy ranks at the top of God's confirmation of Jesus as his fully divine Son.

Of course, for the prophecy to come true, Joseph would have to obey what the angel told him. Before the angel intervened, Joseph had decided to divorce Mary. But following the angel's orders, he married Mary instead but had no sex with her until after Jesus was born.

Quite possibly both Mary and Joseph reflected on and discussed the marvelous mystery of how God had selected them to fulfill Isaiah's prophecy. Perhaps filled with tension, they embarked on a spine-tingling journey with God.

The remarkable prophecy about Jesus contained two stunning facts: he would be virgin born and one of his names would be Immanuel ("God with us"). God would come to earth to visit his creatures in the person of a man who would not carry the stain of the sin nature. Jesus was conceived by the Holy Spirit and thus was the only sinless person ever born into the human race. Therefore, he alone qualifies to be our Savior from sin. "God made him who had no sin to be sin for us, so that in him we might become the righteousness of God" (2 Cor. 5:21).

"God is with us" carried incalculable significance to the Jews of Isaiah's time. The hope of God's rescue sustained them through much suffering and captivity. Today the same faith anchors God's people. "I am with you always," Jesus promised (Matt. 28:20). In Christ we inherit salvation and security.

More than fifty Old Testament prophecies refer to the Lord Jesus Christ, from his virgin birth to his suffering, death, and eternal kingdom. Taken together, they provide an astonishing confirmation of his divine origin, mission, and ultimate reign. The Gospel writers and the apostles seized on this fact to buttress their appeals and arguments for the necessity of repentance and faith in Jesus of Nazareth as Lord of all.

Consequently, Jesus is eminently worthy of everything we can entrust to him. We are satisfied when we love and obey him totally. Prophets and apostles give us more than sufficient evidence to convince us to entrust our lives to Jesus.

To think about

- Why is fulfilled prophecy important to our faith?
- In what circumstances do you need assurances of Christ's love and power?

Thank you, heavenly Father, for the evidence of your sovereignty in bringing to pass all the prophecies about Jesus. Help me to reinforce my faith and my witness to others by grasping the significance of the statement "All this took place to fulfill what the Lord had said through the prophets."

Jesus, the Universal Savior

Luke 2:25–35

Presenting our children to the Lord speaks powerfully about our faith and trust in him. By doing so, we acknowledge that they belong to him and that we depend on him for their success in life. Surrounded by friends and family, we celebrate God's goodness together.

In the Jewish culture to which Joseph and Mary belonged, the law required that they present the baby Jesus to the Lord, so they took him to the temple in Jerusalem for this purpose. Unknown to them, godly Simeon went to the temple as well, responding to the impulse of the Holy Spirit.

Described as "righteous and devout," Simeon represented those faithful Jews who prayed and hoped for God's intervention and the fulfillment of the prophecies about Israel's coming Messiah. However, his prayers raced against time, because God had told him he would see "the Lord's Christ" before he died.

Somehow, by some miraculous, divine intuition, Simeon sensed that the child Jesus was "the consolation of Israel." Every day he asked God and himself, "Is this the day?" Yes, this was it.

Simeon took the child in his arms and thanked God that at last he had seen the Lord's long-awaited salvation. He declared that Jesus was God's revelation to the Gentiles and his glory to Israel. Clearly, God's saving initiative encompassed all humanity. Jesus is the world's Savior, regardless of one's ethnicity.

Then Simeon uttered a prophecy about Jesus. To Mary, he said that Jesus would cause some to fall and some to rise in Israel. His own people would not unanimously acclaim him, and some would attack him. Later on, the apostle John explained, "He came to that which was his own, but his own did not receive him" (John 1:11). Some unbelieving Jews fulfilled Simeon's prophecy.

Then Mary heard tragic words about herself. Simeon said a sword would pierce her soul. This prediction of her grief at Christ's crucifixion revealed the murderous work of those who would fall in Israel because of their unbelief.

In his brief temple encounter with Joseph, Mary, and Jesus, Simeon focused on both the coming suffering and the glory of Messiah. He gave a succinct preview of the cost of God's salvation. God's saving Light to the world would first be rejected and then killed. Simeon also demonstrated how to wait faithfully on God to fulfill our hopes. On this side of the cross we join him in waiting for Jesus to reign on earth as he does in heaven. We pray, "Your kingdom come. Come, Lord Jesus."

To think about

- What characterized Simeon's years of waiting for Messiah to come?
- How does the Bible teach us to wait for Jesus in our generation?

Thank you, Lord, for the strong example of Simeon's patient, hopeful faith. I want to be certain to embrace all that Jesus has for me, knowing that he calls me to suffering as well as to glory.

Jesus, Conceived of the Holy Spirit, Born of a Virgin

Matthew 1:18–25; Luke 1:26–38

Jesus affirmed strongly that he was the bread of life come down from heaven. His listeners stumbled over this because they knew him. He was the Nazareth carpenter, and they knew his mother and father. He must be mad to claim that he came from heaven.

Was he bread from heaven or the offspring of Joseph and Mary? Which was true? Son of God or Son of Man? Ever since Jesus offered himself as God in the flesh, people have wondered how this could be. Theological debates entangled the early church fathers, who tried to sort out the paradox, and various explanations continue to our day.

To solve what probably constitutes the greatest theological enigma, theologians answer that Jesus of Nazareth is both true God and true man. Jesus has two natures, human and divine. The apostle Paul developed this perspective, writing that Jesus was "in very nature God," but he was "found in appearance as a man" (Phil. 2:6, 8).

How was such a thing possible? Joseph could not figure it out, so the angel of the Lord appeared to him in a dream and told him that Mary had conceived a child by the Holy Spirit and, therefore, even though she was a virgin, she would bear a son. On these two pillars of truth, Christians have built their understanding of Jesus as God and man. If Jesus had somehow shown up as a stunning person in the sky, he would not be fully and truly human. Birth as a baby in the flesh was necessary.

Jesus lived a perfect, sinless life, the only person in history to do so. To be sinless, he had to be virgin born. If not, he would have inherited Adam's sin nature. To satisfy God's righteousness and justice, our Savior had to be sinless.

Christ's sinlessness stands at the heart of our salvation faith. "God made him [Jesus] who had no sin to be sin for us, so that in him we might become the righteousness of God" (2 Cor. 5:21). "You know that he [Jesus] appeared so that he might take away our sins. And in him is no sin" (1 John 3:5).

Jesus's birth without sin can be attributed only to the work of the Holy Spirit. No other explanation satisfies. In the end, we accept by faith this most profound mystery. We follow in Mary's footsteps. She also asked, "How?" The angel Gabriel explained that the Holy Spirit would accomplish her pregnancy. "The power of the Most High will overshadow you," he said, and her child would be the holy Son of God (Luke 1:35).

It's amazing that Gabriel's explanation satisfied Mary's puzzled heart and mind. She accepted his explanation. As a virgin, she gave birth to God's Son and also to the Son of Man. Two natures in one person will remain a divine mystery, requiring our faith.

Faith in a doctrine will never save us. We must place our faith in our virgin-born, sinless Savior, even though in our limited human understanding of the laws of physical nature, we cannot fully explain how the Son of God was born a human baby.

We stand with those ancient church fathers who wrote what we know as the Apostles' Creed: "I believe in . . . Jesus Christ . . . conceived of the Holy Spirit, born of the Virgin Mary . . ."

To think about

- How do you react to the angels' succinct explanations of Jesus's birth to Joseph and Mary?
- How is your faith in Jesus enlarged, knowing that as God he fully shares your humanity?

God, I accept the mystery of the incarnation of Jesus. Thank you that Jesus was made like me, except for my sin. I pray for those who stumble over this mystery, that they may come to trust Jesus.

25

Jesus, the Baby of Bethlehem

Matthew 2:1–12

The king of the universe was born in a ramshackle little town about ten miles from King Herod's capital, Jerusalem. Every December 25 we are reminded of this. In 1868 Boston clergyman Phillips Brooks penned the words we know so well:

> O little town of Bethlehem,
> How still we see thee lie!
> Above thy deep and dreamless sleep
> The silent stars go by.
> Yet in thy dark streets shineth
> The everlasting Light;
> The hopes and fears of all the years
> Are met in thee tonight.

Surely Joseph and Mary harbored no such romantic notions about the little town as they traveled all the way from Nazareth to Bethlehem, a journey of some eighty miles at a very inconvenient time. Driven to Joseph's ancestral hometown by Roman tax laws, they found there something worse than taxes: no place to stay.

So Jesus entered the world not just at an inconspicuous site but in an ignominious cattle shed, or perhaps a cave. Very poor planning, we might say. But these humble circumstances were not what Joseph planned or even what the Romans dictated; this was how God wanted it. Centuries before, the prophet Micah had revealed that the Ruler and Shepherd of God's people was to be born in Bethlehem (Mic. 5:2; Matt. 2:6).

Meanwhile, the striking appearance of a unique star had drawn Eastern astrologers to Jerusalem to worship the newly born king of the Jews. Their quest aroused King Herod and "all Jerusalem." He convened the chief priests and teachers of the law, who told him Micah's prophecy about Bethlehem. While the astrologers came to worship, Herod concocted a murderous scheme to kill all the male babies in Bethlehem, and Israel's spiritual leaders just ignored the prophecy.

Looking back, does it really make a difference where Jesus was born? The actual village itself doesn't matter, the particular stable doesn't matter, but the prophecy does. For the first time in the Jesus story, we learn that his coming was foretold right down to the detail of the site. Here is an important clue about how Jesus of the four Gospels connects to the Old Testament.

Our New Testament is packed with quotes and references to the Old Testament, and Jesus is the link between the two. God gave us these prophetic insights, providing abundant evidence for our faith in Jesus. The wonder of God's love, grace, and wisdom are revealed to us in Bethlehem, an ordinary but very special town.

When we meditate on the place and circumstances of Jesus's birth, we see the obedience of his poor parents and their humiliation. But we also see in the infant Jesus the fulfillment of prophecy. Jesus had to be born in Bethlehem. Our faith journey with him begins in a most unlikely place, but it ends with the glory of heaven. We walk with him from a cattle shed to the new heavens and new earth, where we shall reign with him forever.

To think about

- Why did the star of Bethlehem attract Eastern astrologers and King Herod but not Israel's religious leaders?
- How can you make your next Christmas a time of growing devotion to Jesus?

Thank you, Lord Jesus, for coming to earth in humility and not in pomp. Help me to appreciate the exactness of your prophetic Word. May I grow in confidence and trust in you.

Jesus, the Child Prodigy

Luke 2:41–50

Jesus established strong spiritual roots in his childhood. Although the Gospel writers give us just one story about Jesus as a boy, that is enough. His parents, Joseph and Mary, both walked in vital faith in the Lord. They obeyed God implicitly under the most demanding circumstances.

Before Jesus was born, Joseph was given a supremely painful task. He could have chosen to rid himself of pregnant Mary. However, when the angel told him not to do this, he listened and obeyed.

When Mary could not understand how she could be pregnant while still a single woman, God told her how, not in medical but in spiritual terms. God's Holy Spirit had impregnated her with his Son. Then Mary willingly submitted to the Lord.

Given these facts, it is safe to assume that Jesus assimilated strong faith as a child and youth. Luke's brief conclusion tells us all we need to know: Jesus grew up with such unusual wisdom that he confounded the temple teachers. Beyond that, even at age twelve, Jesus was known to walk favorably with God and the people—his brothers and sisters and the neighbors and friends of Joseph and Mary.

Because his parents were devout Jews who scrupulously kept the laws of Moses, Jesus learned the basic truths and duties of a God-fearing family. This included not only the regular religious observances but also the practices of prayer, giving to the poor, and serious study of the holy Scriptures. Later on, his knowledge of the law stumped his critics.

Parents are responsible to teach their children the gospel and biblical values and habits. Learning to walk in godly ways from earliest childhood brings untold blessings throughout a person's life.

Our opportunities and advantages for building strong faith in childhood far surpass those that Jesus had. He was limited to synagogue school and services. Today through our childhood and youth, we have not only church and Christian education programs but also a host of specialized activities led by people with advanced professional training. Camps and retreats help us to learn how to live the Jesus way.

However, our children face many more distractions than Jesus did as a boy. No one led him into a regimented sports program, for example. Television was not a staple of his daily routine, nor were pop music, computers, the Internet, and entertainment fads of all kinds.

Our children need the same wholesome upbringing that Jesus had. Our children's spiritual growth and development must rank in importance ahead of other activities. Academic excellence is a worthy goal, but attaining God's wisdom as a child is much more valuable and important. Joseph and Mary taught the child Jesus not just the laws of Moses but also the intensely practical wisdom of the Proverbs. Living the Jesus way as a child includes both welcoming him as Savior and learning the godly lifestyle detailed in Proverbs.

To think about

- What do you think was included in Jesus's daily routine when he was a child?
- How does this brief story about Jesus in Luke 2:41–50 help us know how to train our children spiritually?

Lord Jesus, help me to exemplify the best spiritual values for children. May I be a beacon of truth and righteousness for all children in my spheres of influence.

Jesus, the Carpenter

Mark 6:1–6

Vocational opportunities were scarce for Jesus. He had no guidance counselors in the synagogue to suggest possible career paths. In that day it was assumed that the eldest son would learn his father's business or trade, and that ended the discussion. So Jesus did what was expected of him and became a carpenter because that was Joseph's trade.

Jesus did not resist his calling. He followed the natural contours of his family, culture, and religion. For Jesus, this was a carefully circumscribed route, and yet it was entirely wholesome and pleasing to God.

Historians suggest that because the city of Sepphoris, the capital of Galilee, had been destroyed by the Romans and was being rebuilt, carpenters would have been in great demand, including those living in Nazareth, four miles away. Joseph and Jesus may well have made a daily trudge to work at the site.

Of course, when that project was completed, father and son returned to their regular tasks of operating a home carpentry shop, mostly crafting chairs and tables. Jesus continued this practice until he was thirty years old, most of those years by himself, because the absence of Joseph's name in the stories about Jesus after he had grown up suggests that Joseph did not live to a ripe old age.

Was it drudgery for Jesus to do this work? I doubt it. He learned contentment in a somewhat menial task. Following Jesus in our formative years means that we learn to accept the role God gives us, working cheerfully and expertly because this is what pleases him.

This model stands out in church history. For example, God sent early Moravian missionaries—carpenters and others—to plant the gospel in the West Indies and India. God took one of the world's greatest evangelists, D. L. Moody, from a shoe store to pulpits around the world. Moody preached like he sold shoes, with energy and zeal, which took him from Boston to Chicago in search of customers. God does the same today, using what we learned as youths to open doors for ministry.

Visiting a university campus one day to help establish a student witness there, I met one of the resident dorm leaders who asked me about the students I was meeting. When I mentioned the leader's name, she was shocked. "How could he lead your group?" she demanded. "He does not do his cleaning job here in the dorm very well." People watch us, perhaps not paying attention to our preaching but noticing how we handle our everyday tasks.

Following Jesus, we do our best every day, no matter how unexciting the task may be, because that is what he did for many, many years in a tiny Galilean town, far from the world's limelight. He did not achieve fame or wealth. No structures were named after him. But Jesus pleased God, his family, and his community. That's what counts.

To think about

- What questions may have arisen in Jesus's mind during his carpentry years?
- What steps can you take to transform your work into a God-pleasing ministry?

O God, forgive me for thinking my vocation is useless in your kingdom. Give me a positive perspective that will help others see that I serve you in my work.

Jesus, the Obedient Son

Luke 2:51–52; Matthew 3:13–17

Early on, Jesus knew that God had a special role for him. His contemporaries affirmed his knowledge, wisdom, and grace when he was twelve. Beyond that, however, his biographers do not record anything Jesus did for the next eighteen years until he reached the age of thirty.

Perhaps we can fill in the blanks in a general way. Jesus lived in a social environment that was radically different from ours. Parents kept a tight rein on their children, even deciding whom they should marry. Synagogues served educational needs. Family circumstances limited career choices. Money, investments, and retirement did not come into play at all. Most people lived day to day on the produce of the land and the income from their trade or business.

Jesus obeyed his parents and became a skillful carpenter. He prayed, worshiped, and studied the Scriptures. Scholars think Joseph died while Jesus was still at home, so Jesus would then have cared for Mary. He also interacted with his siblings.

But one day Jesus knew he had to leave home, family, and vocation. The Gospel writers do not tell us how Jesus knew it was time for his ministry to begin, but he left his family and never returned to a settled home and job again.

Jesus had learned how God had called Israel's prophets to take up their missions as his spokesmen. In the same way, some inner voice convinced Jesus to join a group of repentant sinners being baptized by John in the Jordan River. John tried to dissuade Jesus from being baptized, but by this time Jesus had clearly understood and accepted God's call. To obey his call meant that he must first be identified with sinners, even though he had no sins to confess.

Publicly God affirmed Christ's obedience by thundering his words of approval and love from heaven (Matt. 3:17). This divine imprimatur launched Jesus on his mission of teaching and healing and in the end led him to his death and resurrection.

After Jesus's baptism Satan severely tested his commitment to obedience. Firmly resisting him, Jesus pushed ahead, but Satan kept on pestering him for the next three years (4:13). The general lack of response to Christ's teachings and the open enmity of the religious leaders mounted the pressure on his obedience. He held firm to his calling in spite of all, including poverty and a hand-to-mouth existence.

Later, on leaving the upper room, he told his disciples, "The world must learn that I love the Father and that I do exactly what my Father has commanded me" (John 14:31). He told his Father, "I have brought you glory on earth by completing the work you gave me to do" (17:4).

Finally, as he prayed in the Garden of Gethsemane, Jesus confronted the ultimate test of his obedience. The looming cross drove him to ask for a way out. In the end, Jesus "learned obedience from what he suffered" (Heb. 5:8).

His example stirs us to deeper levels of obedience, regardless of the cost. Jesus followed his Father's will to the cross. We have to ask how our obedience to our Father measures up to his.

To think about

- What do you think Jesus may have struggled with before he knew it was his time to serve his Father's will?
- Consider all the things that get in the way of your desire to obey God in the way that Jesus did.

Heavenly Father, I want to know and obey your will. I ask for courage and faith when I have to make hard choices. Help me to say yes to your good and perfect will.

Jesus, the Eternal Word

John 1:1–5, 14

There is no more fundamental truth at the heart of our Christian faith than the person of Jesus Christ. *Person* means who he was and his relation to God the Father. If Jesus was not in some unique sense the Son of God, then he was simply another great man whose teachings and example inspire us.

The apostle John wrote a deeply profound description of Jesus. He called him "the Word." He clearly identified "the Word" with Jesus by saying, "The Word became flesh and made his dwelling among us" (John 1:14).

John used the Greek word *logos* for "word." It carries the idea of a thought or concept and the expression or utterance of that thought. Jesus is the physical expression of who God is. "He is the image of the invisible God" (Col. 1:15). "The Son is the radiance of God's glory and the exact representation of his being" (Heb. 1:3).

Succinctly, John revealed the timelessness of Jesus, his relationship to the Father, and his inherent deity. Jesus had no temporal beginning as we understand time. Jesus existed from eternity past. There never was a time when he did not exist. He had a beginning in the flesh, but his existence in the triune Godhead knew no such beginning.

How can we picture the relationship of the Father and the Son? "The Word was with God" (John 1:1). Jesus gave a brief glimpse of their relationship when he prayed, "Father, glorify me in your presence with the glory I had with you before the world began" (17:5). Mystery confronts us and we accept the fact by faith, even though we cannot precisely describe the details. The unique relationships in the Trinity defy human analogies. Rather than dismiss this concept because we cannot get a physical handle on it, we bow with our finite minds and give praise to God for the stunning beauty of this eternal relationship.

The inherent deity of Jesus bursts forth with greater glory than the most magnificent sunrise: "the Word was God" (1:1). Jesus is truly and completely God, not some caricature of deity. In the flesh he voluntarily relinquished some of his divine attributes (Phil. 2:6–8), but at all times he was fully God.

Christ, the eternal Word, activated creation and brought light and life to the world. He bridged the gap between heaven and earth. Even though the Godhead's internal affairs may seem out of reach, anyone can now reach Jesus, anyone who chooses to commit himself or herself to him. Ignorance of God is no excuse, because the Word has spoken and we are responsible to listen.

God spoke his Word in the person of Jesus. Knowing Jesus gives us access to the full knowledge of God. Because he is "full of grace and truth" (John 1:14), Jesus takes us by the hand, as it were, and ushers us into God's presence. By his grace he loves and forgives us; by his truth he guides us unerringly in the right path. No wonder the apostle Paul said we have "unsearchable riches" in Christ (Eph. 3:8).

To think about

- What does the picture of Jesus as the Word bring to your mind? Why?
- How can you keep on growing in the grace and truth of Jesus?

> *Lord Jesus, thank you that you are the eternal Word. Help me understand and appreciate everything this means. Grant me confidence in your truth and rest in your love.*

Jesus, Loved by God

Mark 1:9–11

Through his childhood, youth, and adult life, there was no need for Jesus to be baptized. He was quite familiar with this religious rite and custom because the Jews baptized their Gentile converts. Suddenly the news spread across Galilee from the Jordan River that a prophet named John, a cousin of Jesus, was baptizing Jews, not Gentiles.

From all over Palestine, including Jerusalem, the seat of religious authority and power, people flocked to John. They confessed their sins, and John baptized them in the river. The leading clerics came to check this out and John called them a "brood of vipers" (Matt. 3:7), sensing their hypocrisy.

John urged people to repent because that was the way to get ready spiritually for the coming of the Messiah. The writers of Scripture called him the forerunner of Jesus, the one who was called to dig up the hard soil and soften it in preparation for Jesus and his mission.

Imagine John's amazement, then, when one day he looked up and there stood Jesus with a crowd of confessing sinners, asking to be baptized. John was so humbled that he said he needed to be baptized by Jesus. However, Jesus insisted, saying his baptism would be a sign of God's righteousness—despite the fact that he had never sinned in thought or deed. He did not stand on his prerogatives.

When John consented, Jesus plunged into the Jordan River along with a crowd of lawbreakers convicted of their sins. Then God sent an impressive message to assure the prophet that he had done the right thing. In the form of a dove, the Holy Spirit came over Jesus, and his Father's voice was heard to declare: "You are my Son, whom I love; with you I am well pleased" (Mark 1:11). From that moment Jesus was thrust into his mission. Thus his baptism stands both as the symbol of full identification with humanity's unrighteousness and as a divine seal of God's approval.

Contemporary church culture reveals an astounding array of theologies and methods of baptism. Such a simple act has produced not only differences of opinion but also heated arguments and in some cases the founding of different denominations. Generally it is agreed that baptism is a command of Jesus, but questions of who, how, and why tend to divide us. It's sad that some people drift through life without taking Jesus's command seriously.

Our focus must not be on doctrinal disputes but on our Lord himself. Church and family customs can be of no lasting value if we do not repent and confess our faith in Jesus. If the holy Son of God humbled himself and walked into the Jordan River, we must allow his Spirit to challenge us, lest we be sidetracked by controversies.

To think about

- Why do you think Jesus was baptized?
- What does your baptism signify?

Thank you, Lord Jesus, for accepting John's baptism. Your decision to stand with repentant sinners encourages me to make a public profession of my faith. I want my faith to be a witness to my family and friends.

Jesus, Student of Scripture

Luke 4:1–13; 24:25–27

A well-known painting of President Abraham Lincoln shows him perched on a stool near the fireplace in a darkened cabin, reading by candlelight. It teaches the importance and value of earnest study, regardless of the circumstances. No such picture of Jesus exists, but it's not hard to imagine him doing the same throughout his childhood and youth and into his early adult years.

We may mistakenly assume that the Holy Spirit implanted all of Jesus's Bible knowledge in his mind at birth. After all, Jesus was the Son of God, so he knew everything and therefore he did not have to study the Scriptures. I believe such an assumption is false, because the Bible tells us that Jesus took on our flesh and blood, experienced everything we do, and was willing to call us his brothers.

I'm much happier with a Jesus who studied than with one who did not have to, one who could march around the house, flaunting his superior knowledge among his sisters and brothers. He sat with them day by day, patiently learning the Old Testament's teachings and prophecies.

He studied earnestly so that by age twelve he confounded his superiors. His knowledge of the Scripture was so thorough that he was called at various times teacher, rabbi, and master. Perhaps his most dramatic display of scriptural knowledge came when he repulsed the temptations of the devil by quoting Bible verses (Matt. 4:1–11).

On other occasions he replied to questions and criticisms with appropriate Scriptures. He challenged and rebuked the Sadducees for their lack of scriptural knowledge and understanding. After his resurrection, he chided the walkers on the Emmaus road for not knowing the prophets.

Jesus packed his teaching with words from the Old Testament, surely the fruit of years of study. When Luke noted that Jesus grew in wisdom (Luke 2:52), we can be sure that foremost in his mind was the wisdom that comes from diligent study.

To follow Jesus, it is essential that we be filled with profitable, soul-satisfying adventures as we soak our minds, hearts, and wills with Scripture. There are no shortcuts here. We have to go deeper than, for example, lifting a quick fix off the Internet. The daily discipline of Bible reading, study, and meditation is the only way to walk in the footsteps of Jesus. Since he needed to do that, we certainly need it much more.

To think about

- Why did Jesus need to study the Scriptures?
- What changes do you have to make in your life to become a more faithful student of the Bible?

God, you know I need discipline to study your Word. I confess giving other things priority. Give me a strong desire to meet you every day.

Jesus, the Mightier Baptizer

Matthew 3:1–12; John 1:6–8, 15–37

John the Baptizer took Jerusalem and Judea by storm. He shot out of the desert wearing simple clothes and eating simple food as he called the nation to repent. Fulfilling Isaiah's prophecy about Messiah's forerunner, he declared that God's kingdom was approaching. Crowds of people believed him, and he baptized them in the Jordan River.

In the midst of this national revival, however, he refused acclaim. In fact the people wondered if John was indeed the Christ (Luke 3:15). But he knew that his role, in spite of its strategic importance, was secondary to that of Jesus. He acknowledged his place in God's salvation economy by explaining that he wasn't fit to tie Messiah's sandals.

Such humility befits those who really understand who Jesus is. Clearly, John's startling cry gave Jesus priority. To receive Jesus and the kingdom of God, one had to repent and confess sins. Jesus was not the latest model in the prophetic line; he was the culmination, the summit, the epitome of God's message to the world. No one surpasses Jesus.

John warned the people that his baptism was nothing compared to what Jesus would do. John used a powerful metaphor to illustrate the future work of Jesus. He compared him to the wheat thresher who keeps the grain but burns the chaff. This was Messiah's work of baptizing with the Holy Spirit and with fire (vv. 15–17).

John also revealed the supreme paradox in God's kingdom plan. The King would be killed before he would reign. Such news did not sit well with the people then and it does not sit well today. The promised Messiah was also God's sacrificial Lamb, who had to die for the world's sins. This news is a major stumbling block to some, but to those who are wise

40

enough to see the enormity of their sins and its consequences, it stands as the best news ever revealed to the world.

John's conclusion was that Jesus is both Judge and Savior. He pointed the way for those who flocked to hear him, so that they might fully grasp the meaning of Jesus's mission. He shows us how to know the joy and freedom pictured in Isaiah's ancient prophecy (Isa. 40:3–5).

To think about

- Why do you think people flocked to hear John tell them to confess their sins and repent?
- Reflect on all it means that Jesus is your Lamb of God.

Thank you, God, for John's faithful, powerful witness to Jesus. Help me to be as bold as he was in pointing my friends and family to Jesus.

Jesus, the Faithful Worshiper

Luke 2:41–42; 4:15–16; Mark 1:21

Worship was an integral part of Jewish family life in the days of Jesus. It was not optional. You couldn't say, "I'll go to temple if I feel like it." Every Jew was obligated to observe the Sabbath for the reading of the scrolls. Special feast days called for appropriate ceremonies and sacrifices. All of life centered on the Jewish religious calendar, first given by Moses and then affirmed by the prophets and teachers. Along with this allegiance to worship, many religious duties had been added over the centuries, so that Jesus found certain laws and traditions bound the people to ritual and led to self-righteous pride.

Jesus went to the temple in Jerusalem as a boy of twelve with his parents, Joseph and Mary. The occasion was the highlight of the Jewish religious calendar, the Feast of Passover, which commemorated God's deliverance of the Jews from four hundred years of slavery in Egypt. Luke emphasized that the family did this every year (2:41).

After this account of the trip to Jerusalem when Jesus was twelve, the Gospel writers skip the next eighteen years of Jesus's life, to focus on his final three years of ministry, suffering, death, and resurrection. However, they repeatedly told stories about his synagogue experiences. According to local custom, Jesus was often invited to teach.

Synagogues were primarily community places of worship, prayer, and study. Services were led by priests or local teachers. Traditionally, they taught the children and often expounded the Old Testament.

Although Jesus saw through contemporary hypocrisy, he never turned his back on worship. He did not leave the synagogue because some worshipers and their leaders lacked sincerity or because they failed to grasp the full meaning of the Old Testament prophecies. Instead, he worshiped and sought to teach a higher level of morality and the necessity of repentance and faith, admonishing the people that God's new kingdom was at hand.

Following Jesus demands that we worship faithfully, as he did. He declared that his house was a house of prayer (Matt. 21:13), and he met God there. So must we, week in and week out throughout the year. As we worship, we understand more fully what it means to follow Jesus. Without faithful worship, our profession of faith is hollow mockery.

To think about

- How do you think Jesus kept his focus on worship?
- What are the values of faithful worship for you and your family?

Thank you, heavenly Father, for the priceless privilege of worship. May my heart be true to you always and free of idols.

Jesus, Victor over Temptation

Matthew 4:1–11

Having heard his Father's approving voice from heaven at his baptism, Jesus soon received another message. The Holy Spirit directed him from the Jordan River up into the mountains of the Judean desert, a starkly forbidding area of rocky, desolate outcroppings. No one went there for spiritual renewal. Travelers from Jericho to Jerusalem crossed it with fear and trepidation because its caves hid bands of robbers.

Nevertheless, Jesus obeyed the command of the Holy Spirit. He took no provisions with him, despite the fact that there was nothing to eat in the mountains. Rather, he endured a forty-day fast. With astonishing understatement, Matthew simply said that at the end of forty days, Jesus was hungry.

That moment, when Jesus was most vulnerable, the devil challenged him to turn the stones into bread. Nothing could have been easier for the divine Son of God, but Jesus refused, in spite of his intense desire for something to eat. He reminded Satan that we do not live on bread alone but on God's Word—every utterance from God's mouth (Matt. 4:4).

Next, the devil appealed to pride and power. He quoted the Bible and challenged the deity of Jesus. If he was the Son of God, he could throw himself off the temple and survive the fall. Again Jesus turned back the devil with a biblical reminder that we are not to test God (v. 7).

Finally, the devil offered Jesus the world's kingdoms if he would worship him. Jesus drove him away with the scriptural command to worship and serve God only (v. 10).

Jesus emerged victorious from the kind of spiritual warfare we know little, if anything, about. Satan's plot was a monstrous scheme to frustrate God's saving plan for the world.

He knew that Jesus was the centerpiece of salvation and stood as the ultimate block to Satan's powerful sway. Three times Jesus refused to give in to the devil, so that he could accomplish his mission to redeem us.

Here we see authentic spiritual power and integrity at its best. At the outset of his ministry, the incomparable Christ defeated Satan. Everything depended on his successful repulsion of Satan's attack.

Since Jesus defeated Satan, we know he can defeat him in our lives when we are tempted to sin and dishonor God for selfish ends.

In one way or another, we all face what the apostle Paul called the cunning and fraud of Satan (see Eph. 6:11). He uses every possible avenue to subvert our faith, not just to lead us into some terrible sin, but also to feed us lies and distortions about God and his saving grace. When Satan attacks, we repel him the same way Jesus did—with God's authoritative words.

Jesus was "tempted in every way, just as we are—yet was without sin. . . . so that we may receive mercy and find grace to help us in our time of need" (Heb. 4:15–16).

To think about

- To what did Satan appeal in each of his temptations of Jesus?
- How does he appeal to you?

Thank you, Lord Jesus, for defeating Satan in the hour of your temptation. I confess my need of your strength to resist him when he tempts me. I want to be faithful to you, to feed on your Word, and to love God supremely.

Jesus, Preacher of Repentance

Matthew 4:12–17; Mark 1:14–15; Luke 13:5

Jesus, the thirty-year-old carpenter from Nazareth, took up a new calling. God's voice of approval at his baptism signaled that it was time for him to declare heaven's message. God's one-two punch, starring John and Jesus, delivered a stunning blow to the people of Israel. John and Jesus urged the same action: repent.

According to God's eternal timetable, Jesus entered the scene when the time was ripe (Gal. 4:4). This was not something Jesus decided on his own initiative. No public relations focus group told him that the people were now ready for him to go public with his message.

On the other hand, Jesus did not begin to preach until John had tilled the soil, preparing the way for him. John made "straight paths" for Jesus (Matt. 3:3). John could have shared the limelight but, instead, he humbly confessed of Jesus, "He must become greater; I must become less" (John 3:30).

Jesus preached indoors and out-of-doors. Synagogues, village streets, and mountainsides rang with his words. He shaped his sermons to his audiences, addressing special needs, answering questions. Hard questions demanded forthright answers. People soon recognized that he was no ordinary preacher. They said he did not waffle like their own preachers but spoke with authority (Matt. 7:28–29).

Jesus was the Word of God in our flesh. He is called the Word, so when he preached, not only did he verbalize the truth, he *was* the truth. Such a model of preaching eludes us, because not one preacher exists, or has ever existed, who is flawless. Jesus was what he preached.

Heaven was his home and heaven was his message. Gaining heaven comes by repentance, meaning that we acknowledge

46

the wrong things, bad things, and transgressions of God's holy laws that we've done, making us ineligible for heaven. We admit our pride and rebellion. Therefore we must listen and obey when Jesus tells us to repent.

He sends his messengers with the same proclamation in our time. Jesus speaks through what the apostle Paul called "jars of clay" (2 Cor. 4:7), but regardless of the fragility of the vessel, God requires us to pay attention. "Repent!" sounds forth clearly and powerfully from the printed Word of God, from a host of media outlets, and from the lips of faithful preachers and all Christian witnesses.

Jesus the preacher expects us to believe his words and to trust him. No other words offer us eternal life (John 6:68).

To think about

- Can you picture Jesus preaching? Think about the way he delivered his message.
- How can you prepare to hear and obey God's Word?

Thank you, Lord Jesus, for your faithful obedience to God's call to preach. I confess my need to repent of my sins. May the power of your words inform my mind, control my will, stir my heart, and change my conduct.

Jesus, Preacher of Good News

Matthew 4:12–17; Mark 1:14–15; Luke 4:43–44

Gospel is the word traditionally used to describe what Jesus talked about and what the apostles later preached. Newer translations and paraphrases tell us that he preached the Good News, giving us a more modern concept, helping us understand the word the writers used who wrote the original Jesus stories.

The New Testament writers took a commonly used word and gave it a Christian spin. It was a Greek word used when someone ran into town and said the army had won a battle. Amplified, it became any message of joy or good news.

So Jesus launched his career by coming to Capernaum with Good News or gospel. Why did the writers describe his message in such glowing terms? Jesus did not come to town to announce that the Roman conquerors had been defeated. In fact he reiterated again and again that his Good News was not earthly but heavenly. It was about God's kingdom not man's.

His proclamation was good news because he announced liberation from sin, God's forgiveness, and a new community of faith and obedience that lived by standards completely different from those of the world. Contemporary religious, social, and political culture was turned upside down by such news, especially because the one who brought it claimed that he had come from heaven. Good News from Jesus meant bad news for the religious hierarchy and hypocritical, self-righteous people.

But Jesus completely reversed the common understanding of things when he explained that the Good News from heaven would cost him his life. The kingdom way was the way of the cross, not the way of political, military, and religious power.

However, in the towns and villages and along the highways and byways, many people did in fact rejoice because Good News had arrived from heaven. People of faith looking for God's promised Messiah welcomed him. Jesus's news reverberated in their hearts with a heavenly beat.

Followers of Jesus are called to be bearers of Good News. Jesus lived, died, and rose again to open heaven's gates to all who believe. Our Christian lives are meant to be billboards announcing Good News. Our words are intended to instruct others in how to find the key to heaven. Like Jesus, we must make the words of eternal life available to all.

To think about

- In what sense was the gospel Good News to the people of Jesus's time?
- What are the different ways in which you can be an announcer of Christ's Good News?

Thank you, Jesus, for your Good News that gives me forgiveness and eternal life. May I be a consistent bearer of your Good News to those who are defeated and discouraged.

Jesus, the Light of the World

John 1:3–9; 3:19–21; 8:12

Jesus, the light of the world, lit up the land, just like the prophet Isaiah said he would (Isa. 9:2). Isaiah's poignant words sharply identified the prevailing darkness when Jesus began to preach. John, in his Gospel, cast Jesus's entire mission in terms of the battle between light and darkness.

In his prologue, John chose not to detail what he meant by darkness, but the entire story line of the Bible concerns people falling into moral darkness because they refused to follow God and his ways. Brilliant flashes of light occasionally interrupt that story line. We see faith and obedience to God as light in the lives of Abraham, Jacob, and Joseph, for example. People like Samuel and David brightened their days through faith, as did the prophets, such as Isaiah and Jeremiah.

But none of these worthies claimed to be the world's light. In Jesus, light became life. Jesus did much more than illuminate his territory. He delivered such intense pure brilliance that it was the essence of life itself.

Light dispels darkness. In the moral and spiritual realm, however, darkness did not comprehend the light of Christ. Even though Jesus epitomized light and holiness, the world did not recognize him. More than ignoring Jesus, the religious leaders demanded his crucifixion and the political leaders acquiesced to their cries.

But the light-giving Jesus was not suppressed. He still gives true light to everyone. Jesus the Creator established the parameters not only of the physical world but also of the moral and spiritual worlds. He alone determines what is true, beautiful, and good. His moral excellence—his sinlessness—authenticates his claim to be the true light.

It's astonishing that Jesus brings light to all. Because he does so, he creates the moral imperative of either receiving or rejecting his light. Anyone can, if they so desire, switch off Christ's pure, searching, powerful light.

He promised that those who open their lives to him will not stumble about in darkness, which in the end leads to death. Instead, they will receive true light, or life. Jesus opened the unheard-of possibility of living above the inroads of sin and selfishness. His light is our only source of truth and life. His light shines on our pathway so that we can clearly see how to direct our lives.

Coming to Jesus means living in the light, as he is in the light. It means living in fellowship with him and with our fellow believers. We are secure with God and with one another because the blood of Jesus purifies us from our sins (1 John 1:5–7). To cite one example, John wrote that if we hate our brother, we live in darkness, not in the light (2:9–11). This shows that Jesus intends to make a difference. His light in us brightens the people around us. Thinking of him as the light, and seeing how he not only lived but also taught the true light, we are empowered to do the same.

To think about

- How does Jesus compare to light?
- In what dark places in your life do you need the light of Jesus?

Thank you, Jesus, for bringing light and health to my soul. Help me always to follow your light for my own good and for the good of my family, church, and friends.

Jesus, the Interpreter of the Law

Matthew 5

Old Testament laws, interpretations, and traditions tightly regulated the lives of the people in the community where Jesus grew up. Jealously, specialists in these laws and traditions protected them and rigidly enforced them. More than once Jesus got into trouble for crossing the specialists.

Jesus never broke any of God's moral commands, but in his heart he knew how much the people suffered under the religious police and the chief priests and lawyers who laid the foundation for incredibly intense legalism. Rather than giving people freedom, they increased their oppression. One religious party, the Pharisees, prided themselves on scrupulously obeying the minutia of the laws and traditions.

When Jesus announced that God's kingdom had arrived, he knew that he had to teach the moral and spiritual principles of his new reign. When he delivered what we know as the Sermon on the Mount, he taught an entirely new way of looking at the old laws.

Unerringly Jesus bore to the heart of the monumental laws regarding murder, adultery, divorce, oaths, and revenge. For example, he taught that personal hatred equals murder, that a lustful look equals adultery, and such truth cut through the smoke screen produced by outward conformance to the laws.

Jesus never taught that God's original laws were shaky. Rather, he proved that these laws did not go far enough. Speaking to the crowds around him on the mountainside, Jesus stunned them with the clarity of his moral vision. "You have to do better than the Pharisees and the teachers of the law," he said (see Matt. 5:20).

Jesus directed them to look beyond the letter of the law to the deeper core of what God's laws really meant. Brilliantly he set the stage for the righteous way to live in the kingdom of heaven. Not only did Jesus expose the fatal flaw of self-righteousness, he produced a totally new way to look at moral and ethical conduct. The Sermon on the Mount stands unchallenged as the best there is in defining human moral behavior.

Seeing Jesus this way, we confess his moral and spiritual superiority and our own abysmal failure to come close to what he had in mind. Jesus is the only one who slashes through external religion and demands an inner change of heart. His interpretation of the law cuts the ground out from under anyone who thinks law keeping is the route to heaven.

Jesus raised the bar so we can understand clearly the kind of life that rules in his kingdom. This provocative Jesus brings us to our knees. No one can stand up to Jesus and claim goodness of their own in the face of his kingdom's moral imperatives and glory.

Jesus demonstrated powerfully his right to interpret the law by asserting at each juncture, "But I say to you." If we quarrel with his interpretations, we quarrel with him personally. He is the King of God's new kingdom. Anything that falls short of total homage and obedience insults the King.

To think about

- Why did Jesus interpret the old laws in a new light?
- How do his fresh insights challenge your thinking about your own moral code?

Thank you, God, for everything good and true that Jesus taught about his kingdom. I confess that I fall far short of his incomparable standards. I want to make a fresh start toward greater conformity to his kingdom principles and values.

Jesus, the Fulfiller of the Law

Matthew 5:17–20

Picture yourself perched on eighteen inches of rocky ground on a hillside in northern Israel. From your right and left, people squash you, but your discomfort does not prevent you from listening to the new prophet from Nazareth and Capernaum.

You've heard reports of what he did to the hawkers in the temple courts at Jerusalem (John 2:13–22). Wow! But the news gets even more dramatic. People say this Jesus has healed the sick, cast out demons, and cleansed a leper.

Now he's here and you've heard the most amazing stuff: the poor, the meek, the grief-stricken will somehow be made happy. Even the persecuted will be blessed because they own the kingdom of heaven (Matt. 5:1–12). But listen to this: now you hear him claim that he has fulfilled the law and the prophets!

That's a tall order. The teachers of the law were just that: they taught the laws but they never had the audacity to claim that they kept the laws perfectly. By this time in his address, Jesus had already stood the crowd on its head. What the people anticipated and what Jesus said were radically different.

Jesus knew he had to prepare his audience for what was coming. He was about to dig behind the externals of the law and expose the inner core. After hearing what he said about murder, adultery, divorce, false witness, revenge, and relations with one's enemies (vv. 21–48), the people could easily think that Jesus had come to abolish the law.

To head off that possibility, Jesus said, "Not so." In effect, he said he came to show what the laws really mean. But explanations were insufficient. Imagine your Sunday school teacher or pastor saying, "Now, I'm going to explain what this command of God means. But before I do, I want you to know that I personally am the embodiment of what it means. Look at my life if you really want to know what it means."

Yes, that is preposterous, but that is exactly what Jesus did—regarding not just the Old Testament laws, mind you, but all the prophecies too. Now, if you are still sitting down on your hard seat on the hillside, you are about to jump up and cry, "Fraud! Faker! Impossible!"

To put it mildly, Jesus grabbed your attention. To fulfill the law means to keep every one of its requirements. Jesus is the only one who has ever done that. He kept not just the letter of the law but the spirit as well. Add to this his stupendous claim that all the Old Testament prophecies point to him. New Testament writers took great pains to point out even the tiniest of details about Jesus that connected with the prophets.

The apostle Paul rattled his readers when he said Jesus is the end of the law as a way of our attaining righteousness in God's sight (Rom. 3:21–31). When we receive Jesus as Lord and Savior, he comes to live in us and his perfect righteousness becomes ours as well. We enter his kingdom on his merits not ours.

God counts our faith in Jesus Christ as righteousness (4:22–25). Therefore we live to please Jesus. We are set free from the burden of impossible law keeping, but motivated to live according to his perfectly holy, true, and good will for our lives.

To think about

- Describe how you would have felt if you had heard what Jesus claimed.
- How can you grow in your obedience to Christ without falling into the trap of legalism?

Lord Jesus, you are the embodiment of everything God demands of me. I confess that many times I have tried to please you by keeping religious rules. Grant me both the freedom and the impulse to love and obey you totally in all I do.

Jesus, Lord of Nature

Mark 4:35–41

Pressed by throngs of Galileans eager to hear what he had to say, Jesus retreated to the water's edge of the Sea of Galilee (Mark 4:1). Seated in a boat, he told stories to illustrate basic spiritual principles. By nightfall, exhaustion had overtaken him and he asked his disciples to row him the eight miles across the lake.

They agreed, taking him "just as he was" (v. 36) and joined a flotilla of other watercraft. A nice evening cruise would give them some relief and relaxation. Apparently the phrase "just as he was" meant Jesus was so tired that he immediately fell asleep in the boat. He was more than ready for bed, once again revealing how human he was.

Suddenly a furious storm attacked the boats. The wind whipped the waves so ferociously that the disciples thought they were doomed. While panic and fear gripped them, Jesus slept undisturbed. On the verge of going down with their boat, the disciples aroused Jesus and cried out, "Don't you care if we drown?" (v. 38).

Somehow, they sensed that Jesus could save them, though he had never plucked them out of physical danger. They had seen him heal sick people, but what could he do about a life-threatening storm? They were experienced fishermen, but Jesus was a carpenter. When they left their nets to follow him, he gave them no assurances that he would protect them.

The disciples were about to go down. Impulsively they appealed to their Teacher's love and care. "Don't you care?" seems a ridiculous question to us. Of course Jesus cares. But facing imminent death, while Jesus slept peacefully, it appeared to them that Jesus did not care if they drowned. They could have shouted something like, "Jesus get up! Our boat is sinking!" Such a plea would have showed that they feared Jesus would drown too.

The floundering fishermen, the debilitated disciples, suddenly heard and saw something that terrified them as much as the storm had. Their Teacher subdued the wind and the waves with his words. His voice replaced howling winds and monster waves, and peace and calm reigned on the sea.

Quick to seize the teaching moment, Jesus chastised his men for their lack of faith. Fear had pummeled them. But weak as their faith was, it had driven them to Jesus for rescue from certain death.

Then the men asked the most fundamental question of all about Jesus: "Who is this?" (v. 41). The utter impossibility of such a thing happening did not fit their scheme of things. No one had ever squelched a Galilean storm, least of all by commanding wind and waves to be quiet. Little did they know that the man sleeping in the storm-tossed boat was also the man who had created the world and keeps it running (Col. 1:16–17). We can excuse them for not knowing that.

But there are no excuses for us. In the Gospels it seems as though we're watching a video of Jesus, who is Lord of nature, commanding the wind and the waves. In the public arena people pay homage to Mother Nature. But when we see Jesus in action, we must ask, "Who is this?" Since he is the Lord of nature, he is my Lord as well, and therefore I do not need to collapse in fear when storms blow into my life.

To think about

- Why do you think the disciples' faith deserted them in the face of the storm?
- When situations appear hopeless, how does your faith in Jesus give you hope and courage?

Lord Jesus, forgive my feeble faith. I'm with the disciples on this one. Help me to trust you completely in all circumstances.

Jesus, the Conqueror of Demons

Mark 5:1–20

Demons knew who Jesus was (Mark 1:23–24; 5:7–8). The apostle James explained that demons believe in one God and "shudder" (James 2:19). Therefore it should not surprise us that Jesus battled Satan and demons. Their battle raged on two levels, the cosmic and the human. When Jesus became flesh, he entered the arena against demons who lived in people, bringing all kinds of afflictions.

Demons terrorized people of that time. Into this intense fear, anxiety, and spiritual warfare, Jesus came with the compassion and strength to deliver people from their demonic oppressors. The demonic and the divine locked in combat when Jesus came. His encounters with demons tested his divine power and gave people hope for deliverance.

The demon-possessed man epitomized the public's worst fears about demons. Jesus stepped into the picture with compassion and composure. Rather than turn aside from this beaten, bleeding man, Jesus accepted him, knowing full well that demons were causing his suffering.

Jesus delivered the man by his forceful command, "Come out of this man, you evil spirit!" (Mark 5:8). With the same divine power by which he created the world, Jesus conquered the evil spirit.

Expecting torture, the man pleaded for mercy. Lovingly Jesus asked for his name. Because so many demons oppressed him, he said his name was Legion (or we might say, "Mob" or "Thousands"). He begged Jesus not to disperse them but to send them into a nearby herd of pigs, which he did.

The man's deliverance astonished the townspeople as much as his terrible condition had. In their fear they pleaded with Jesus to leave. Later on, the Pharisees—the strict enforcers of the religious laws—accused Jesus of casting out demons by the power of the prince of demons (Matt. 9:34).

The man had received mercy from Jesus and that was his story. Jesus delivered a man from the impossible tyranny of demons. The before and after pictures of the man show vividly the difference Jesus makes in the lives of human sufferers of all kinds. After he was delivered, the Bible says the man "was dressed and in his right mind" (Mark 5:15).

Jesus's power extends even to the realms of the demonic. Martin Luther caught this fact in his hymn "A Mighty Fortress Is Our God." He wrote:

> And though this world, with devils filled,
> Should threaten to undo us,
> We will not fear, for God hath willed
> His truth to triumph through us.

No matter how hazardous our spiritual journey may be, Jesus living in us overpowers our demonic foes. He knows our physical and our spiritual afflictions. We need not live in bondage to fear. Demons may assail us in one way or another, but Christ in us meets the enemy and defeats demons. He liberates us from spiritual attacks because he loves us and because he came to conquer death and the devil. We walk safely through life with him.

To think about

- Why do you think Jesus bothered to heal the demon-possessed man?
- In your mind's eye, how do you picture Jesus overcoming your spiritual foes?

I praise you, Jesus, because you loved a horribly afflicted man and freed him from his legion of oppressors. I praise your compassion and your power. I ask for your special protection when I am experiencing doubts and spiritual attacks.

Jesus, Embodiment of Prophecy

Luke 4:16-21

Probably nothing Jesus did at the outset of his ministry staggered the people of Nazareth like his claim that he was the embodiment of Isaiah's prophecy about Israel's Messiah.

In other places people followed Jesus enthusiastically. They praised him everywhere, especially in their synagogues. In Mark 1 we read a kind of synopsis of the things Jesus was doing that made his popularity grow like wildfire. He drove the evil spirit from a man in the synagogue in Capernaum. He drove out many demons and healed many sufferers of various diseases. The crowds flocking to Jesus prevented him from entering towns openly, so he retreated to isolated places. "Yet the people still came to him from everywhere" (v. 45).

Imagine the enthusiasm, then, when Jesus returned to his hometown of Nazareth and stood up in the synagogue to read the scroll of Isaiah 61:1-2. This prophecy gave glowing, triumphant hopes to the people of Israel. Everything a subjugated people might long for is included.

Jesus did not give a lecture on the meaning of the prophecy. Rather, he said something that shattered the boundaries of traditional religion: "Today this scripture is fulfilled in your hearing" (Luke 4:21).

Who would dare to make such an astonishing claim? What kind of a person would publicly say, "I am the one Isaiah talked about seven hundred years ago?" Such audacity was unthinkable in the synagogues of Jesus's day. In fact it was close to blasphemy.

The Nazarenes knew this man. He was a carpenter in the house of Joseph. They knew about his Galilean miracles, but they did not recognize who Jesus really was. Through his statement Jesus claimed, "The Spirit of the Lord is on me" (v.

18). God had anointed him and God had sent him to preach Good News, cure the blind, and offer hope and freedom to the prisoners and the oppressed.

Everything the people desired stood in front of them in the flesh. They looked at God's Messiah and after a brief flurry of approval, they tried to throw him over a cliff.

This scene reveals God's majesty and grace in his ability to bring to pass exactly what the prophets had foretold. Jesus's reading of the scroll drove the people back to their own Scriptures. In this segment we see what kind of a person Jesus was and what his mission was. In Jesus were united love, mercy, grace, forgiveness, and peace. He is God's anointed to bring these blessings to all, including the poor, whom the rich and powerful excluded. He came to touch the blind and free the prisoners.

What power, love, and glory are manifested in this magnificent prophecy! The parameters of this prophecy did not include all that Jesus would do. For example, Isaiah also foresaw Messiah's suffering and death (53:1–2).

This synagogue encounter instructs us to be sure we look at all of Scripture to get the whole story about Jesus. We see him here inextricably rooted in the Old Testament prophecies, revealing that he did not appear from out of nowhere. Jesus knew where he came from, so he could boldly testify to his deity before his own countrymen.

To think about

- What picture of Jesus does the prophecy in Isaiah give you?
- What hopes for your own future are tied to Jesus?

Lord Jesus, you are the one anointed to fulfill Scripture. I want to enlarge my faith and understanding, so that you can accomplish your good and perfect will in my life. Thank you that you are more than a carpenter.

Jesus, the Lamb of God

John 1:29, 36; 1 Corinthians 5:7; 1 Peter 1:19

If we were to choose an image for our spiritual leader, we would not choose a lamb. We think of sheep as pretty much stupid and helpless, wandering over fields and hills. Sheepdogs nip at their heels and shepherds whack and guide them with their staffs. One day they are manhandled and shorn of their wool. After that, well, lamb chops.

But if we had been steeped in the culture and literature of the Old Testament, we would have grown up with a much different perspective. The people of Israel were shepherds and they had spent centuries depending on sheep for their sustenance.

During their four hundred years of slavery in Egypt, the Egyptians despised them because they were shepherds (Gen. 46:34). Nevertheless, when God chose a symbol to depict his liberation of his people from bondage, he chose a lamb. From then on the Israelites sacrificed their lambs to God to commemorate their glorious release and freedom (Exod. 12:1–11).

In addition to their Passover history, the Israelites knew the vivid imagery of Psalm 23, their picture of God providing care and protection to his flock. They also knew the dramatic prophecy of Isaiah 53:7, 11.

This prophecy gave John's declaration its most powerful impact, because John said Jesus would take away the world's sins. That could be accomplished only by his sacrificial death, according to Isaiah 53. That's the reason the apostle Paul declared later on, "For Christ, our Passover lamb, has been sacrificed" (1 Cor. 5:7). Peter emphasized that Jesus fully met all the requirements of the Passover lamb, since he was "a lamb without blemish or defect" (1 Peter 1:19). In the book of Revelation, the apostle John revealed not only the Lamb's sacrificial death but also his ultimate victory.

Therefore, we can well imagine the astonishment that must have greeted John the Baptist's declaration that Jesus was the fulfillment of everything the Passover depicted—redemption by the blood of the Lamb. His blood had to be shed to secure our salvation.

In John's story of Jesus, this declaration happened before Jesus had invited anyone to join his team. From the outset, his looming sacrifice stood front and center. These men were willing to join someone who would be a sacrificial lamb not a conquering lion.

The figure of the Lamb of God sends strong messages about the nature and character of Jesus. He was God before time began. But in the flesh he assumed the role of a sacrificial lamb. Willingly Jesus accepted his role in God's eternal salvation plan, but not without inner struggles and agony. He knew well what it meant to be God's Lamb.

The role of the lamb speaks of humility and utter helplessness. For Jesus this meant divesting himself of certain divine prerogatives so that we might see in him our only hope of salvation and our only sure guide to successful living.

Jesus the Lamb set the tone for the way his followers should think of themselves as living sacrifices (Rom. 12:1). God calls the followers of the Lamb to divest themselves of all pretense of power and glory. Like sheep, we have all gone astray (Isa. 53:6), but Jesus, "like a lamb to the slaughter," brought us back to the fold (v. 7).

To think about

- What does John's imagery of Jesus suggest to you?
- In what issues of your life do you need to follow Jesus's example like a lamb?

Thank you, Lord Jesus, for being my Passover Lamb. I confess it is hard for me to yield myself the same way you did. Give me grace and strength to be a living sacrifice for you.

Jesus, Cleanser of Lepers

Mark 1:40–45; Luke 17:11–19

Clusters of lepers dotted the Palestinian countryside. They embarrassed healthy people, who ostracized and ignored them. According to Old Testament laws, their repulsive skin disease meant they had to be quarantined (Lev. 13:45–46).

One day when Jesus was traveling, a leper broke into the crowds and crept close enough to worship him. Overcome by the power of his incurable disease and his own helplessness, he begged Jesus to heal him.

What drove him to such a risky venture, breaking the religious and social taboos? Perhaps he had crouched on the fringes of the crowd listening to Jesus elucidate the principles of his kingdom (Matthew 5–7). He had grasped enough about Jesus so that, throwing caution to the winds and keeping clear of other people, he made his way into Jesus's presence.

Jesus had healed "many who had various diseases" (Mark 1:34). Doubtless such news rang through the camps of the lepers. Here was a new prophet who exhibited compassion and power. What did the leper have to lose?

On another occasion, ten lepers appealed to Jesus, calling him "Master." No one had yet addressed Jesus as Lord, and, significantly, he did not disavow the honor attached to this title.

The lepers used the title in the common way, meaning "master." However, New Testament writers used "Lord" or "Master" as a divine title more than 650 times. They translated the Hebrew *Jehovah* as "Lord." They used it most often as the divine title of Jesus, identifying him with the God of the Old Testament.

In Mark's story, without delay or questions, Jesus touched the leper and cleansed him of his horrible, incurable disease. Jesus proved his power and his love in a nanosecond. As quickly as the man asked, so quickly did Jesus heal him. He broke the Levitical law and shocked the onlookers who were revolted even by the mere thought of touching a leper.

For some reason—possibly to avoid a premature rush of public enthusiasm—Jesus told the man to be quiet and to follow Moses's prescriptions of showing himself to the priest and making sacrifices (Mark 1:44). This would be a sign to the priests of Jesus's divine power.

Jesus calls us to worship and prayer even when we are helpless. Because he is Lord of all, we bow before him whether we have critical needs or not, but often it takes a serious problem or illness to cause us to fall at the feet of Jesus.

The Master welcomes us into his presence. He does not chide us for our weaknesses. He desires and welcomes our appeals for his assistance. When we bring to him even what seem to us to be trivial matters, we respond to his matchless love.

We worship him not because we are clean, but because we are unclean and need his healing, cleansing power. We worship him in our weaknesses, not in our pride and strength. And Jesus lovingly puts his hand on us, no matter how despicable or revolting our condition may appear.

To think about

- Why do you think the leper ignored the social and religious taboos to confront Jesus?
- What sometimes keeps you from approaching Jesus with your needs?

Lord Jesus, thank you for breaking barriers to touch an incurably ill man. Touch and cleanse me, I pray. And may I reach out and touch the untouchables with your love.

Jesus, Recruiter of Disciples

Matthew 4:18–22; Mark 2:14

At the outset of his ministry, Jesus gathered a team of fellow missioners—the twelve apostles. Did he need a team to accomplish his work? Not in the ultimate sense, of course. He could have worked alone, but for the sake of the spread of the gospel and the establishment of the church after his ascension into heaven, Jesus needed to build a team.

Early on, he confronted a number of undistinguished men—men whom we would most likely not have recruited according to our standards of success. The Gospel writers tell us their names and, in the case of five of them, their occupations. Four were seasoned fishermen; one was a hated tax collector—not a likely pool of talent for a worldwide mission. One of them is identified as a thief and traitor.

In spite of their apparent lack of qualifications, Jesus wanted their friendship and companionship during three years of homelessness and loneliness. He wanted their help in his preaching, teaching, and healing. Eventually, it turned out that they were the corps God used to spread the gospel.

We look for clues about how Jesus trained these men. Basically, he wanted them to learn to live by faith. He wanted them to focus on God's kingdom, not the anticipated earthly kingdom of the Jews. Naturally, his team was alternately confused, surprised, disappointed, and defeated. Despite their lack of understanding about his mission, Jesus never gave up on them.

Jesus was not a Lone Ranger evangelist, teacher, and healer. He needed a team, and so do we, though for different reasons. We must learn to work with and depend on others for our spiritual growth. Through a team we learn patience and forgiveness and how to trust people with our needs and problems. And like Jesus, we need the friendship and companionship of others. We are not in the game of life alone. We can't run through all the opposing tacklers without some blockers. It's for our good that God puts us on teams—our spouses and children, fellow church members, and people in the community.

To think about

- Why do you think Jesus chose the men he did to be his disciples?
- How can you better relate to your fellow believers on your church's team?

God, help me to be a team player for Jesus. I want to join my heart and hands with those who love you, that together with them I might be stronger in my Christian faith and work than by trying to stand by myself.

Jesus, Hometown Reject

Luke 4:23–30

Murder by a mob rocks our souls. The mob decides the guilt of the victim and takes justice into its own hands. Incredibly, that's what happened one day in Nazareth when its citizens tried to kill Jesus. How they could do such a thing cries out for explanation.

Jesus, fresh from triumph over Satan, enjoyed the praises of his audiences in the Galilean synagogues. The Sabbath day in Nazareth followed the usual routines. People went to their synagogue to worship and to hear the Old Testament Scriptures read and expounded.

The members extended to Jesus the courtesy of reading God's Word. He read Isaiah 61:1–2 and then stunned the people by claiming that the prophet was talking about him. He said, in effect, "I am the fulfillment of this prophecy" (Luke 4:21).

At first, the members applauded his words, but they were confounded because they saw Jesus not as the fulfillment of Isaiah's prophecy about the Messiah but as the son of Joseph the carpenter. The claim and the claimant did not compute. To their minds, something was terribly wrong.

Jesus knew this. He knew they were expecting him to perform miracles like those that had already made him famous in Galilee. Seeing into their rebellious hearts, he pronounced the most damning judgment possible: God had rejected them and had chosen to bless Gentile believers, even as he had done several times in their history. Such a judgment was like tossing a lighted match into a tank of gasoline. Fury enveloped the synagogue worshipers and they tried to throw Jesus over a cliff, but he walked away from them.

This episode recalls Simeon's prophecy about Jesus: "This child is destined to cause the falling and rising of many in Israel" (2:34). The people of Nazareth exemplified how some people in all generations would respond to Jesus. "You, an ordinary carpenter, claim to be the Messiah? Preposterous!" Not all who refuse to believe try to kill Jesus, of course, but in their hearts, minds, and wills they try to get rid of him.

Knowing how his hometown would treat him, Jesus courageously stood on the authority of God's Word. He knew that by applying Isaiah's words to himself, he was claiming to be God's Messiah. This incendiary application lit the fires of rebellion, putting his life in jeopardy.

When we stake our destiny on Jesus, we align ourselves with his claims. He fulfilled ancient prophecy and there's more to come. Just as Nazareth failed to dispose of Jesus, so will all those who war against him fail.

We may have supreme confidence in Jesus who boldly stood for truth and righteousness. We cannot see into human hearts like he did, but we can assert that his lordship extends to all creation. This may be a costly business for us, as it was for him.

To think about

- Why did the people of Nazareth reject Jesus? How do you explain rejections of him today?
- What sometimes hinders you from being forthright about the claims of Jesus?

Lord Jesus, I admire your courage, your integrity, and your willingness to stand for truth. You are God's anointed one. You are the one Isaiah predicted would come. Thank you for coming to redeem me.

Jesus, Our Creator

John 1:2–3; 1 Corinthians 8:6; Colossians 1:15–16; Hebrews 1:1–2, 10

Our most familiar titles for Jesus are Christ, our Lord, and Savior. Frequently he called himself the Son of Man. He did not directly refer to himself as our creator, but the New Testament writers did. By this means they established his eternal deity and they defined his unique role in the Godhead.

They also enlarged the scope of our understanding about Jesus so that we might see him in an entirely different perspective from what we see in his everyday encounters up and down Galilee, Judea, and Jerusalem. Could the person who labored with a team of ordinary fellows be their creator? Could the one who encountered both physical and spiritual disease in the throngs of people who followed him also be their creator? Could the entire universe actually be the work of his hands?

This enormous, almost unbridgeable gap perplexes us at first glance and calls for our understanding and appreciation. How could the agent of creation be the same person who came and lived among us in the flesh? How could the One who made the world allow himself to be executed?

This picture of Jesus exalts his power, majesty, and humility. If by some strange quirk I were given power like that by which Jesus made the world, would I ever, ever consider becoming not just part of that world, but also becoming that world's suffering savior? Not likely. In the hands of humans, power leads to self-gratification and self-glorification, not humble service.

Jesus, our Creator, calls for our worship and our humility. We confess our finiteness in the face of Jesus. We confess our limitations in knowledge and wisdom. We confess our spiritual deficits before the One who made us for his pleasure and glory.

Not only did Jesus make the world, he loves it and keeps it going. Creation and love unite in Jesus, so we can be absolutely sure we are in good hands. His power extends to our salvation and to our spiritual prosperity as we walk with him.

Our Creator stands against the efforts of unbelievers to usurp his role as Lord of the universe. The kingdom Jesus created is both physical and spiritual. Therefore, when we confess Jesus as our Lord and Savior, we also confess that he created and controls the universe, even while we see him revealing more and more of the secrets of the universe to human investigators.

Each new discovery should cause us to praise and thank Jesus with full humility, knowing that without him we can do nothing. What humanity does with its discoveries depends on the outcome of spiritual battles between the rules of God and the rebellion of humankind.

As we follow Jesus in the pages of the Bible, and in our own faithful obedience, we learn to bless him for his creation. We also learn to pray for the fulfillment of his creation in the new heavens and new earth to be revealed at his second coming.

To think about

- Contrast the roles of Jesus as Creator and Redeemer.
- How does your hope as a Christian affect your understanding of creation's "groaning" (Rom. 8:18–22)?

Lord Jesus, I praise you for creating me for your purposes and glory. May I fulfill all you had in mind when you made me.

Jesus, the Life and Death Authority

John 3:35–36; 1 John 5:11–12

Jesus spells the difference between life and death. God handed to Jesus the authority to determine who receives eternal life and who is sentenced to eternal death. Because he holds this divine prerogative, we are enjoined to enter a personal relationship with Jesus Christ. To choose Christ is to choose life now and forever. To refuse Christ means temporal and eternal loss.

Looking at Jesus in this light brings a sobering dimension to our consideration. The New Testament records concerning Jesus reveal his commanding presence in a host of excruciating circumstances: sickness, grief, death, paralysis, demon possession, blindness, leprosy. Add to this his invitations to repent and his condemnations of inner rottenness and hypocrisy and you confront a person who compels thoughtful responses. Then we see him manhandled, unjustly condemned, and finally crucified. The climax of the Jesus story is his resurrection and ascension.

Such are the basic facts about Jesus, Son of God and Son of Man. You can gather the same essential facts about other prominent historical figures, from Julius Caesar to Winston Churchill. But no matter how much we know about history's heroines and heroes, none of these persons has the authority to declare, "You have life in me now and forevermore." Regardless of our deepest respect for them, they can never give us eternal life.

When God gave all authority to his Son, he elevated Jesus to be the supreme Judge of everyone. Secular authorities and their minions often decide who lives and who dies, but their authority extends only to this life, not to eternity. That's the reason Christian martyrs went fearlessly to the stake. They knew that their eternal destinies were in the hands of Jesus, not the Roman emperors. The same is true of thousands of Christian martyrs in more recent times.

Jesus overshadows all human authorities and powers. He alone rules and judges. Because the Son has received this authority from the Father, he commands our faith, trust, honor, worship, obedience, service, and respect. He holds everything in his hands, most important of which is our destiny.

The facts we believe about Jesus constitute the foundation of our faith. We must believe the testimony—the record—about Jesus. However, the facts about Jesus do not save us. We gain eternal life by saying yes to Jesus as Lord and Savior and inviting him to be the controlling person in our lives.

Therefore, the authority of Jesus consoles us and relieves us of our internal pain and emptiness. He provokes the fundamental question of our religious quest, how to find and enjoy his eminently satisfying quality of life.

Standing before Jesus, I want to hear him say, "Well done, good and faithful servant. Enter the joys of my kingdom." I want to settle for nothing less. His authority releases me to claim this hope, so I do not quake before the supreme Judge of the universe. I thank him because he is the only fair, unbiased Judge of my soul.

To think about

- What do you think about God's life or death options, according to Jesus, that leave no middle ground?
- How does the authority of Jesus make you a better person?

Lord Jesus, I confess your authority in all things. Thank you for giving me abundant life now and life for all eternity. May I live securely in your authority and your love.

Jesus, the Son of Man

Matthew 8:18–20; 16:13, 27–28; 17:9–12

Jesus referred to himself as the Son of Man about eighty times. Thus he affirmed beyond all doubt that he is one of us. Or, as we might say, he stands as the model of all humanity, male and female. Or he is the representative human being. By calling himself Son of Man, Jesus also laid claim to the fulfillment of Daniel's prophecy (Dan. 7:13).

Jesus did not shrink from becoming one of us. The Bible argues strongly that he became the Son of Man so that he might die and taste death for us and destroy Satan, who held the power of death.

Jesus also became the Son of Man to prove that he knew how to be a merciful, faithful high priest for us. "For this reason he had to be made like his brothers in every way" (Heb. 2:17).

In the nomenclature of Jesus, Son of Man joins Son of David, his distinctively Jewish name, and Son of God, his divine name. In a striking way, Jesus called himself the Son of Man to point to his mission, which transcended Jewish expectations. So he used it in connection with his teaching about his death and resurrection and his second coming. To the Son of Man, God has committed universal judgment (John 5:26–27).

In light of Matthew's startling reference to Isaiah's prophecy about Messiah's suffering (Matt. 8:17), it seems fitting that he should add what seems like a footnote to the life of Jesus in the flesh. After leaving the carpenter's shop at Nazareth, Jesus never had a place to call his own. This divine person possessed nothing. Jesus was born in a stable, and he was buried in someone else's tomb. Jesus lived at the mercy of the land and his few friends.

That's why as the Son of Man he uniquely identifies with the poor, the homeless, the exploited, the dispossessed, the refugees, and the landless peasants of all time. *Son of Man* expresses not only who he is but how he lived in sharp contrast to the rich and powerful.

Son of Man also says he was not ashamed to mix with ordinary sinners. He rubbed shoulders with the lepers, the demon possessed, the despised tax gatherers, and women of the streets.

Son of Man proves that one man could take the worst that wicked people could do to him and thus become our fully qualified representative before a just, holy God. Adam was our representative sinner, and Jesus is our representative Savior (1 Cor. 15:45–47). Adam is from the earth; Jesus is from heaven.

Although he came from heaven, the Son of Man knows all about our human frailties. In some way beyond our comprehension, he knows what it is like to suffer spiritually and physically in all respects as we do. Not one thing that we experience is beyond his knowledge, understanding, and compassion.

The Gospel writers do not glorify the fact that Jesus lived like an itinerant pauper. They made it part of the record to encourage us to relate to Jesus on a human as well as a divine level. The Son of Man was poor but powerful. He owned nothing but he made the universe and owns everything in it. Without anything of this world's goods to offer us, he gave us himself, what the apostle Paul called his "unsearchable riches" (Eph. 3:8).

To think about

- Why does *Son of Man* seem an appropriate name for Jesus?
- How does this name help you to develop a deeper relationship with Jesus?

Lord Jesus, I confess that rarely do I call on you as the Son of Man. I need humility to put myself in your shoes when you lived here. Make me more appreciative of what this cost you and what you can do for those who have little of this world's wealth.

Jesus and His Priority Diet

John 4:27-42

Out of seemingly innocuous situations, Jesus derived profound truths, exposing the essence of what he believed and the reasons he did what he did. I call this his priority diet, not because of what he ate but because he selected food as an appropriate metaphor for his divine mission. By so doing he set himself apart from his disciples and the rest of his would-be followers.

Before he got to his supper menu, on the road from Judea to Galilee in hostile Samaritan territory, Jesus interviewed a licentious woman by Jacob's well and eventually she confessed that he was indeed the Messiah who was to come. Because of her confession, the whole town came to believe in Jesus.

Meanwhile, his disciples had been in town shopping for supper and when they returned, they urged Jesus to eat something. As educators say today, a teachable moment presented itself. Jesus was not interested in eating supper, he said, because he thrived on an entirely different God-given menu. In effect Jesus said, "You men don't know what I'm having for supper."

Dumbfounded, the disciples looked around for another parcel of food brought by someone else to feed Jesus. Then Jesus explained his priority diet: to do God's will and finish his work.

God's will and work for Jesus meant "harvesting" people for God's kingdom. His disciples were oblivious to what had been going on at Jacob's well and in town. They had been shocked at the sight of Jesus talking with a Samaritan woman. Their "diet" prevented them from seeing the souls of the despised Samaritans as priority meat and drink.

Jesus jumped on the chance to explain that even in Samaria the fields were ripe for harvest. If his disciples could penetrate the ethnic and religious barriers of their time, they would see all people as prospective followers of Jesus.

His priority diet meant that for Jesus people of all kinds were his obsession. No one should be automatically excluded from his mission of love, forgiveness, and salvation. Those followers of Jesus who choose his diet will engage in completing God's mission as Jesus did.

Rather than rest and wait for supper, Jesus talked with a solitary social outcast, gaining her trust and that of her village. Rather than look at Samaria as too tough to reach, Jesus saw the territory as a place ripe for spiritual harvest. Having the right diet sustained Jesus on his divine mission.

When we adopt Jesus's priority diet, it sharpens our spiritual focus and commitment. It determines our interests and how we use our time, money, skills, biblical knowledge, and service. The joy of filling our bellies pales in comparison with doing God's will even in hostile environments. Supper can wait if we obey a higher calling.

Jesus's priority diet improves our vision and nourishes our endurance. The more we give ourselves to doing our Father's will, the stronger we grow in spiritual muscle. Like marathon runners, we shed fat and run with singleness of purpose.

To think about

- Why do you think Jesus refused the food that his disciples brought?
- Is your spiritual diet compatible with accomplishing God's will and mission? Why not? What can you do to change it?

Heavenly Father, help me to order my life so that doing your will becomes my top priority. I confess it is hard to keep a sharp focus on the people ripe for harvest. Show me who they are and how I can reach them.

Jesus, Disturber of the Peace

Matthew 10:34–39

Having carefully outlined to his team what the fight would be like on the world's spiritual battleground (Matt. 10:1–33), Jesus thrust himself into the engagement by saying that he would inspire trouble, not serenity. Those who grapple with the life and death issues of the gospel would agree, experiencing opposition, even in their own families.

Jesus compared his role to that of a sword-bearing soldier. Rather than bringing peace, he would bring strife. Metaphorically speaking, the struggle over who Jesus is and what he came to do amounts to armed conflict. In some families and groups, civil war erupts over Jesus.

Can this be the same Jesus who also promised to give us his peace (John 14:27)? Well, yes. But we rarely discuss the side of Jesus that brings discord. In Matthew 10 he speaks to men preparing for spiritual warfare. In his love and wisdom Jesus wants his disciples to know what the fight will be like when they take the gospel to the towns and villages of Israel. In John 14 he speaks to the same men, preparing them for his imminent arrest and crucifixion.

Whenever the gospel is preached, the battle for hearts and souls is joined. This is not a battle for lightweights. Gospel proclamation arouses the powers of darkness. Tough bearers of the gospel must be prepared, because Satan's agents will try to deflect and stamp out the Good News.

What is welcomed as Good News by some will be rejected by others, even within the same families and communities. That is the undeniable record ever since Jesus came and returned to heaven. Some people love him; others hate him.

This is the reason the prophet Isaiah warned that Messiah would be like a boulder in the road over which people would stumble (Isa. 8:13–14). The apostle Paul explained that the wise men of the Greeks would decry the gospel as foolishness, while the Jews would see it as a stumbling block (1 Cor. 1:23).

So that his disciples would not misunderstand or be fearful when they encountered such divisiveness among their hearers, Jesus explained that it would be inevitable. Following Christ brings division. He gives his peace to those who believe him, but for some believers their faith costs them their family and friends.

In fact Jesus said that if a prospective convert is not prepared to sacrifice his family, he is not worthy to be Christ's follower (Matt. 10:35–37). Jesus compared this sacrifice to taking up the cross and losing your life for his sake (v. 38). Jesus bears a sword that cuts deeply. It may separate us from those whom we love best.

The Good News is that Jesus makes clear how to gain life by losing it. In that sense, his sword is essential to our finding eternal, satisfying, fulfilling, abundant life. If for the sake of keeping the peace, we reject Christ's lordship, we will lose our lives. On the other hand, the same cross that brings strife also brings everlasting peace to our soul.

Therefore, as his followers, we boldly proclaim, "Christ died for our sins," knowing that this is offensive to some listeners, but to others it brings the hope they so desperately need.

To think about

- Why do you think Jesus was so blunt and honest about how he divides people?
- Of what value is it to know how costly it is to follow Jesus?

Lord Jesus, this is a hard teaching, and I confess I would rather ignore it. I pray for families split over you. I ask that those who resist you would repent, believe, and bring peace to their family.

Jesus, Searcher of Hearts

Mark 2:8–12; John 2:23–25; 4:27–30

In Psalm 139 King David described God's all-encompassing knowledge of him. There was nothing about him that God did not know; God knew not just his ways but also his thoughts. "O LORD, you have searched me and you know me," he cried (v. 1).

Jesus Christ, God's Son, exercised the same divine power. As our colloquial expression puts it, Jesus sees right through us. Every thought and intent of our hearts are exposed to his search. He knows what is in us.

The writers of Jesus's story give us brief glimpses into certain situations where it was necessary for them to explain the reason Jesus did what he did. For example, Jesus refused to be taken in by the popular acclaim accorded him in Jerusalem early in his ministry because he knew the fickle hearts of the people and the ephemeral nature of political enthusiasm for someone who performed miracles.

When he encountered the hard-hearted Pharisees, who challenged his authority to forgive sins, Jesus knew what had inspired their anger. Their bluster and presumed defense of God's name did not fool him. Their phoniness was apparent to Jesus like the pages of an open book. He knew the text.

The adulterous woman at Jacob's well was mystified because Jesus knew her past. Rather than flee, she admitted courageously to her neighbors that Jesus knew all about her sordid past. Eventually her confession moved the whole town to believe in Jesus.

We can choose to recoil in fear because Jesus knows us or we can enjoy the security and comfort of his acceptance of us in spite of who we are. On the human level, we would be devastated if anyone really knew all there was to know about us, including our thoughts. Such fear of being exposed is one of the consequences of sin. Adam and Eve fled from God's presence after they had sinned.

However, realizing that Jesus knows all about us drives us to confession and repentance. Every day, in one way or another, we fall short of God's glory, and we can never make up this enormous debt. Jesus knows it all and he still paid our debt in full.

Each day he gives us new opportunities to thank and praise him for accepting us just as we are. The apostle Paul's terse statement, "While we were still sinners, Christ died for us" (Rom. 5:8), sums up brilliantly the nature of our spiritual transaction with God. Happy are those who accept Christ's knowledge of their condition. Such acceptance is necessary to healing and wholeness.

When illness strikes us, we first desire a clear, accurate diagnosis. Without it, we cannot start treatment and eventually be healed. In his days on earth Jesus went about telling people their true condition. Now he continues that work by means of the Holy Spirit.

Jesus sees us, knows us, and loves us, in spite of everything disclosed by his searchlight. Day by day we move on, not in terror that we will be found out, but in relief, praise, and thanksgiving because Jesus welcomes us into his arms.

To think about

- Why do you think Jesus did not come right out and tell his critics, "I see right into your hearts and heads"?
- How does the fact that Jesus knows all about you help you move from pain to healing?

"Search me, O God, and know my heart; test me and know my anxious thoughts. See if there is any offensive way in me, and lead me in the way everlasting" (Ps. 139:23–24).

Jesus, the Judge

John 5:17–30

The apostle Paul's address to the philosophers of Athens drew a variety of responses: scorn, procrastination, and belief (Acts 17:16–34). The mockers scoffed at the idea of resurrection. Without naming Jesus, Paul identified him as the one who would judge the world because God had raised him from the dead.

When Jesus tangled with his critics who conspired to kill him because he claimed equality with the Father, he asserted boldly that God had entrusted eternal judgment to him. *Blasphemy!* they thought. But Jesus explained why he was the Judge and on what basis he would issue his verdicts.

Jesus decides who gains eternal life. As the Son of God, he alone possesses life-giving power. As the Son of Man, Jesus has been given the right to pass judgment. Therefore, everyone should believe him and honor him. There is no higher court to which anyone can appeal. When Jesus the Judge pronounces life or death, his sentence is final and eternal.

The outcome of the trial, so to speak, hinges on the character of the judge and the nature of the charge against the defendant. Although some human judges are corrupted by bribes, Jesus is incorruptible. Nothing can influence his decisions one way or the other. Jesus is beyond the reach of any outside influences or persuasions. He said his verdicts are just because he does not do his own will but God's.

In our courts, judges often rule on various procedural issues, even though a jury may determine the final verdict. In many cases, defendants face a bench trial before the judge. All in all, judges require great wisdom, especially when it comes to sentencing. Judges hear appeals. They decide when people are telling the truth or lying. Even our most qualified and experienced judges are fallible.

Jesus is uncompromisingly fair and infallible. He is the wisdom of God totally without any gaps in his knowledge. No lawyer, no defendant can argue Jesus into making a wrong decision. All of his judgments are perfect all of the time.

In his debate with the Jews who were trying to kill him, Jesus confronted them forcibly with the truth that only by believing in him could they escape eternal condemnation. Jesus did not quibble with them about obscure, irrelevant points of law. There is only one way to escape judgment and gain eternal life. It is through faith in Jesus, our Judge.

Our Judge decides who passes from death to life. Not only does our Judge decide who gains life, he possesses life in himself. Judges often rule on capital cases. However, no judge but Jesus has ever said that he is the life.

The sentence to eternal condemnation falls on those who reject Jesus, the righteous Judge. Those who receive Jesus as Lord and Savior—although they deserve the death penalty because of their sins—will not be sentenced to eternal death.

When we recognize that Jesus is the God-appointed Judge of all the earth, we welcome the opportunity to repent, confess, believe, and obey him. To do anything less courts disaster.

To think about

- How does Jesus qualify to be our Judge?
- What is it about Jesus as Judge that changes your attitude toward him and toward those who as yet have not trusted in him?

Lord Jesus, I confess my sins and agree that my only hope is your mercy and forgiveness. Thank you that you are life and the giver of life to all who believe in you.

Jesus, the Focus of the Old Testament

Luke 24:44–49; John 5:31–40

Because our Bible comes to us in two parts, the Old and New Testaments, and because Jesus Christ our Lord is the centerpiece of the New, we sometimes forget that he is also the focus of the Old. Much of the New Testament, especially the Gospels and Acts, is easier to read than, say, Leviticus, in the Old Testament, or is more understandable than trying to figure out the messages of the prophets.

But if we listen to Jesus, we discover that he bridges the Testaments. The Old Testament writers, inspired by the Holy Spirit, wrote more than they knew. Jesus gave their writings God's full authority. They wrote God's words.

Jesus's contemporaries held the Old Testament as sacred, some of them devoting their whole lives to its study. They were convinced that their Scriptures held the key to life's meaning. However, despite their fervid searches, they missed the testimony that their Scriptures gave to Jesus. Because they did not see Jesus there, they did not welcome him when he appeared to them in the flesh, claiming to be the One to whom the Old Testament points.

Jesus scolded his critics, who looked to Moses as their final authority. He explained that if they really believed Moses, they would also believe him. In effect, he said, "It was about me that Moses wrote. But if you do not believe what he wrote, how are you to believe what I say?"

Jesus placed himself on a par with Moses. That presented a painful dilemma to the Jews. Could Jesus of Nazareth actually be as authoritative as Moses? Did Moses actually write about Jesus?

Perhaps some of them went away, determined to scour Moses for every possible crumb of information about Jesus, because when the apostles preached Jesus in Jerusalem after his resurrection, many priests believed in him. In the end Jesus's diagnosis of their spiritual blindness to the Old Testament bore fruit.

If we can put ourselves in the shoes of Jesus's listeners, we can imagine how hard it would have been to find signposts in the Old Testament that pointed to Jesus. Even Christ's disciples found this to be an insurmountable task. They believed Jesus, but they missed those Old Testament signs. Especially hard for them to understand was how Jesus's suffering was foretold in the Old Testament. For this reason Jesus took them aside and explained everything to them. He gave them a global positioning satellite, as it were, on the Old Testament so they could find him there.

We have the benefit of both Testaments, so we can see how Jesus links them. But even so, it requires much diligence and discipline if we are to see how the Old Testament testifies to Jesus. Walter Elwell's *Topical Analysis of the Bible* devotes ten pages to signs of Jesus in the Old Testament and ten pages of Old Testament prophecies of Christ (Grand Rapids: Baker, 1991, pp. 69–88).

Our faith walk with Jesus will be immeasurably enriched if we study the Old Testament diligently for its testimony to him. We cannot expect to enjoy the magnificent riches of Christ if we fail to see his glory in Moses's writings, the Psalms, and the prophets' messages.

To think about

- Why do you think Jesus's contemporaries were not able to find Jesus in their Scriptures?
- How is your understanding and appreciation of Jesus increased by studying him in the Old Testament?

Heavenly Father, I praise you for making one picture of Jesus in both the Old and New Testaments. Help me to grow in my love for Jesus and in my faith and obedience to him because of what I see of him in the Old Testament.

Jesus, the Serpent on the Pole

John 3:13–17; Numbers 21:4–9

Nicodemus got much more than he bargained for when he praised Jesus for his miracles (John 3:1–2). Contrary to the majority in the Jewish council, he was willing to seek truth.

Jesus gave him an enigmatic answer about the necessity of spiritual rebirth, which Nicodemus could not grasp. Seizing the moment, Jesus divulged important facts about himself, which probably also stunned Nicodemus, although we have no record of his response. However, after the crucifixion of Jesus, he brought a lavish gift of spices to anoint his body.

As Jesus continued to talk with Nicodemus, he shifted the subject to heaven with the astounding news that it was his home (v. 13). He said that he left heaven to come to earth, where he would be lifted up (crucified) to give eternal life to all those who believe in him.

Undoubtedly, Nicodemus understood the reference to the serpent that Moses lifted up on a pole, but did he understand the import for all humanity of what Jesus was saying? At the time of Moses, God judged the rebellious spirit of the Jews by sending poisonous snakes among them, and many had died. After the people confessed their sin, God provided a way to escape death. The people had to look at the bronze serpent on a pole that God had told Moses to erect.

How is this bronze snake an object lesson pointing to Jesus? What do we learn about him from this sorry episode? Here it is in a nutshell: Jesus gives eternal life to those who place their faith in him, in the same way that those Israelites were saved when they obeyed God and looked in faith at the bronze snake.

To us this is perhaps a crude object lesson but nevertheless penetrating, because death stalks behind the serpent and hovers over the cross of Jesus. Just as the Israelites were dying because of their sins, all humanity lives under a death sentence because of sin. No one is exempt, no matter how good or religious he or she is.

God gave the Israelites a way of redemption, and God gives us redemption through the sacrifice of Jesus on the cross. The analogy fits. Jesus knew that only by going to the cross could he save those who believe in him, and he was willing to leave heaven for this purpose.

The truth of John 3:16 fits the Israelites in the wilderness. God loved them so much that he saved anyone who would look at the bronze snake on a pole. This is a picture of what God did for us. He allowed Jesus to hang on the cross so that we would not die but have eternal life by believing in him.

Inevitably sin brings eternal death; looking to Jesus brings eternal life. In effect, God placed Israel's sins on that bronze serpent. God places our sins on Jesus; he made Jesus to be sin for us (2 Cor. 5:21).

Nicodemus must have reeled at the thought of a crucified Messiah, but the truth is that unless Jesus is lifted up to die for us, we have no hope. Therefore, if we are to live and be saved from God's judgment, we must fling ourselves totally at the feet of our crucified Savior.

To think about

- Why was it hard for Nicodemus to understand Jesus's purpose and mission on the cross?
- How does this object lesson help you understand and appreciate the theology of the cross?

Lord Jesus, I marvel at your forthrightness and the clarity of your words. May I have your courage to affirm the necessity of your death on the cross for my sins. Thank you for leaving heaven to take my sins on yourself.

Jesus, Full of Grace and Truth

John 1:10–18

How can it be said of anyone that they are "full of grace and truth" (John 1:14)? These are the very qualities of character that we need most. Admittedly, grace and truth are theological doctrines, but the words also powerfully convey character. In our Lord Jesus Christ, character and doctrine unite.

Jesus brought to earth the visible demonstration of God's grace. To say that Jesus brought grace to the fullest possible degree proves that human beings stand in great need of his grace. We stand before God as helpless beggars because we have miserably failed to love him totally and because we have committed atrocious sins. Further, we have failed to show justice and love to our neighbors. We have failed to walk humbly before God and other people. Jesus said we're supposed to be as perfect as God is (Matt. 5:48), and no one in his right mind claims to be so. Therefore, we desperately need God's grace.

"Full of grace" means that Jesus offers God's forgiveness to all of us. It means that no matter how reprehensible the record of our behavior may be, we stand acquitted before the bar of God's justice. The righteous Judge condemns us, but Jesus pleads grace for us because of his blood shed to atone for our sins. "From the fullness of his grace we have all received one blessing after another" (John 1:16).

"Full of grace" also means that Jesus is gracious in his character and conduct. The record of his life explodes with grace toward all kinds of people. His graciousness attracted people to him like bees to a dripping honeycomb.

Jesus is also "full of truth." He said, "I am . . . the truth" (14:6), not truth in the abstract but truth in the flesh. Jesus taught the truth and lived the truth. Because God is true, his

88

Son declared the truth about God and his kingdom. Truth came through Jesus to make the Father known.

This fact presupposes that we live in the domain of darkness and error. We are born in darkness regarding the truth. Sin blinds our eyes to the truth about God and about ourselves. Jesus dispelled our spiritual ignorance. He promised that our knowledge of the truth would set us free (8:32).

Consistently, patiently, and lovingly, Jesus expounded the truth. He was perfectly truthful in everything he did. Not an iota of falsehood or deceit ever came from his lips. He did the truth and spoke the truth.

Grace and truth merged in Jesus so that those who lived with him saw God's glory. God's glory had been revealed to Moses (Exodus 33–34). Now the disciples of Jesus saw God's glory in him, a living person. Jesus did not simply expound a set of ideas or a philosophy, he exemplified God's attributes in himself, and so he could say that anyone who had seen him had seen the Father (John 14:9).

Seeing Jesus as "full of grace and truth" reveals to us how much we lack and compels us to confess our own need of grace and truth. We worship Jesus, not just as the truth about God, but as God's truth in the flesh. We praise him because he freely offers us the grace we need.

To think about

- Why do you think that both John the apostle and John the Baptizer (John 1:15–18) were so impressed by the grace and truth in Jesus?
- Under what circumstances do you particularly need grace from Jesus? Why? Under what circumstances do you particularly need truth from him? Why?

I worship you, Lord Jesus, because you embody grace and truth to the fullest. I want to know the power of your grace and truth to make a difference in my life.

Jesus, Feeder of the Hungry

Matthew 15:32–39; John 6:1–14

Thanks to television, we have seen mobs of hungry people fighting for food that has been thrown to them from helicopters and trucks. In well-fed America we wince at the plight of these desperate people, and many of us give generously to feed them.

Starvation was not endemic to the Palestine of Jesus's day. He did not confront long lines of thousands of people standing forlornly with their bowls, waiting for something to eat. On the other hand, there were no soup kitchens or food pantries for those who were hungry. They were left to fend for themselves, sometimes eking out a sparse existence because of droughts and crop failures.

Jesus was well acquainted with these people because he traversed the hills and valleys and could identify with them; he lived a hand-to-mouth existence as well. Jesus and his disciples knew what it was to be hungry (Matt. 12:1). He knew poverty firsthand, not theoretically. He understood the difficulty of farming hard soil and the apparent capriciousness of rain and plentiful harvests. The poor and hungry flocked to Jesus because they sensed that he cared and that he was one of them.

When a large crowd had gathered to follow Jesus and listen to his teaching for several days, Jesus knew they were hungry. He confronted his disciples with their responsibility to feed the people, but the disciples were helpless. They lacked the cash needed for such emergencies. All they could find was a lad with some bread and fish, a rather pathetic dinner for thousands of men, women, and children.

Rather than send them away, Jesus fed them. He accepted what the disciples brought from the boy, blessed it, and turned it into a satisfying meal with abundant leftovers. He

90

fed them by his unique power, satisfying their physical needs; his teaching had already satisfied their spiritual needs.

Sometimes we forget that when Jesus performed his miracles, he did so because of his compassion and not simply to prove that he was the promised Messiah from heaven. Jesus knew that hunger hurts. He also knew the hunger gnawing at the hearts and souls of the crowd. He alone satisfies both kinds of hunger.

Of course Jesus was well aware that not all of those whom he fed were also spiritually hungry. In fact he told a crowd of seekers that he knew they were following him simply because he had fed them (John 6:26). Their bellies were full, but their hearts were hard. When Jesus turned up the heat on them, they turned aside (v. 66).

Mixed motives snare many people who want what Jesus offers but who are not prepared to commit themselves to him. Jesus fed people like this anyway, showing that his love carried no price tags. Neither should ours. We feed the hungry as Jesus did, simply because they need food.

What amazing opportunities we have to follow Jesus by helping to feed the hungry nearby and around the world. We have more than enough to eat, apparent by the contents of our garbage cans. Therefore it is imperative that we follow Jesus and model his love by feeding the hungry. In this way we show not only that we care but also that Jesus cares, opening the way to provide food for their hearts and souls as well.

To think about

- What goals do you think Jesus had in mind for the people when he fed them? Why?
- How can you keep from being desensitized by the enormity of world hunger?

Heavenly Father, when I thank you for my food,
help me to understand that millions go hungry every
day. Show me what to do and how to do it. Use me
to offer both food and Jesus to needy people.

Jesus, the Bread of Life

John 6:30-58

Old Testament miracles reverberated in the minds and hearts of Jews. Of course the most magnificent miracle of all was the one that gave birth to their nation—their liberation from Egypt. This miracle led to a succession of miracles under Moses's leadership on their forty-year trek across the desert to Canaan.

The miraculous milestones of their history comprised benchmarks against which all successive events and leaders were measured. Therefore, when some people in the crowd of five thousand whom Jesus had miraculously fed demanded a sign, they pointed, as an example, to God's provision of manna in the desert (Exod. 16:4–35).

Quoting Scripture boomeranged on them, however. Jesus seized their history and turned it upside down so violently that many who had been following him now deserted him (John 6:66). Yes, it was a miracle that the people ate manna every day for forty years, but they died eventually. By way of sharp contrast, Jesus promised that those who ate the bread from heaven that he brought would live eternally.

Both the manna and Jesus came from heaven, but manna satisfies for a day, while Jesus offers bread that satisfies spiritual hunger for all time. His provocative reinterpretation of Jewish history sparked their curiosity and they asked Jesus for this new heavenly bread.

"I am the bread of life," he told them and they were stunned (v. 35). "Come to me," he said, "and you will never be hungry." He went on to explain that as living bread he would give his life for the world.

Jesus climaxed his offer of eternal life by comparing the living bread to his own flesh. They had to eat it. "The one who feeds on me will live because of me" (v. 57). He was telling the crowd that, to be saved, they must eat and digest Jesus himself. This was more than they could stomach, and Jesus knew they were shocked.

They could not assimilate the concept of faith as an intimate union with a person. Using their history, Jesus pointed to a radical turn in God's dealings with humanity. With the coming of Jesus, salvation depends on integrating one's life totally with him.

Physically, bread represents everything our bodies need for satisfactory health and nourishment. Spiritually, Jesus represents everything our souls need for eternal life. Therefore, unless we feed on Jesus, we are doomed to starve spiritually. Metaphorically, his flesh provides all we need to live now and forever.

When Jesus instituted the Lord's Supper, he took bread and said it was his body. Because he alone is the bread of life from heaven, we are fools if we seek satisfaction in anyone or anything else. Jesus holds exclusive rights to the bread of life.

Eating Jesus equals believing in him, trusting him, and obeying him. We eat our first meal of the bread of life when we make our initial commitment to him and confess him as our Lord and Savior. We keep on eating every day, because, unless we savor every meal, our souls will suffer from malnutrition. His supply of living bread is inexhaustible. When we eat Jesus, so to speak, he dwells in us and we dwell in him.

To think about

- Why do you think Jesus chose a metaphor like eating his flesh to make clear the meaning of believing in him?
- What kind of spiritual diet best satisfies your needs for growth in Christ?

Lord Jesus, I confess that at times I do not feel intimately connected to you. You are my living bread. Help me to know what that means in terms of my life in the world, so that I can grow stronger in you.

Jesus, Attested by God

Mark 9:1–8; Luke 3:21–22; John 6:26–27

The Good Housekeeping Seal of Approval has been a marketer's dream for a long time. When a product has this seal, the buyer can rest assured that it's worth the price. Lacking the magazine's seal, other companies seek to promote their products with the testimonies of famous people. For example, athletes endorse everything from gym shoes to pain medication, reaping millions of dollars.

Now suppose someone claimed theirs was a God-given product? It's unlikely anyone would believe the claim. But when it comes to power over people, leaders down through history have claimed God's endorsement. Historians call this the divine right of kings. Claims of possession of religious authority from God have ensnared millions in cults and false religions. So when Jesus appeared on the scene, saying that he had come from God in heaven, how were people supposed to know if that was true? To prove his claim, Jesus appealed to both his teachings and his miracles (John 14:10–11).

Jesus was not alone in asserting that he was sent from God. The Father himself spoke his authentication of Jesus at his baptism and at his transfiguration (Matt. 3:16–17; 17:5). God's authoritative voice made clear that Jesus was his Son and that the people could believe and trust him.

Later Jesus was standing on the same truth when he promised the gift of eternal life to all who believe him. He could do this, he said, because he possessed the seal of his Father's authority.

The prophet Isaiah pictured Jesus as a servant who pleased God. He gave Jesus his authority by placing his Spirit on him (Isa. 61:1–2). Preaching on the day of Pentecost, Peter declared that Jesus, approved by God, was not another in a long line of false prophets (Acts 2:22). Jesus was the real thing.

In his second letter, Peter recalled what he had heard on the mount when Christ was transfigured. God's voice from heaven attested to his pleasure in Jesus (2 Peter 1:17–18). What a remarkable affirmation this was for the benefit of Peter and the others! They had left everything to follow Jesus and wondered if he really was the promised Messiah. Could they trust him completely, this humble carpenter from Nazareth? How could they be sure?

When they heard the words of God, his voice made it unmistakably clear: Jesus is my Son and he carries my full authority. Then they knew that they had no choice but to follow him and do all that he said.

The issue of authority remains a powerful challenge. When Isaiah described our condition, he said we act like willfully independent sheep, going our own way rather than following the shepherd (Isa. 53:6). When we reject Christ's authority, it is because we think we know better than he does. We find it painfully difficult to live by the dictates of another. But this is exactly what Jesus demands. Fully attested by God, Jesus is our way to truth, to God, and to eternal life. Following anyone else leads to disillusionment and disaster. Jesus alone merits our unrivaled, pure trust.

To think about

- Without hearing a voice from heaven, how do we know Jesus is truly the Son of God?
- What does it cost you to follow Jesus unequivocally? Why?

Thank you, heavenly Father, for your seal of approval of Jesus. I need your grace to enlarge my confidence in him. Help me to pass on my confidence and faith to others.

Jesus, Man of Prayer

Luke 4:42; 5:16; 6:12; Matthew 6:9–13; 26:36–44

Anticipating an earthly kingdom, the disciples of Jesus wanted action. But Jesus knew that his kingdom was not of this world and he relied on prayer for daily guidance. Finally, one day the disciples asked him to teach them to pray.

Jesus had grown up in a religious culture of prayer. Some of it was hypocritical, but a godly remnant of Jews prayed with faith in their hearts. They pleaded with God for Messiah to come. Jesus knew the heart's cry of these people.

The entire Jewish tradition of prayer covered every detail of life. The Old Testament stories frequently include prayers in a multitude of circumstances. Many of the Psalms are prayers, reflecting a deep piety among the Jews. The people prayed often, not just for the sacrifices on feast days as prescribed by Moses. By the time of Jesus, however, prayer seems to have become part of the legalistic framework by which one sought to earn God's favor and blessing.

Jesus radically transformed both the spirit and content of prayer. Most dramatically, he addressed God as Father. When he prayed, "Our Father in heaven" (Matt. 6:9), he thrust aside obligatory, rote prayers. Prayer became the heart's reflection of a personal relationship with God, whose name the Jews would not say.

Jesus also changed the practice of prayer. He did not limit prayer to formal times of worship or to special events. He knew and said that the temple was a house of prayer, but many times he went off by himself into the hills to pray, to commune with his heavenly Father. For Jesus, prayer was a vital element in making God's power available to people in need.

The four Gospels depict Jesus as a man of prayer in a host of circumstances. Not only did he give his disciples a model prayer, he also prayed for them and with them.

It is not difficult to summarize the reasons Jesus prayed. Jesus prayed when unbelieving people confronted him. After his lengthy teaching session with his disciples, Jesus prayed. His longest recorded prayer (John 17) occurred when he faced separation from his disciples. With the cross looming before him, he prayed in Gethsemane. Hanging on the cross between two thieves, Jesus prayed. At the end, as his life ebbed away, he prayed.

Whatever else we may gain from his example, we cannot overestimate the priority Jesus gave to communion with his Father. Prayer sustained him in his daily routine of doing good and engaging critics.

If we follow Jesus, we will pursue persistent, disciplined, prevailing prayer. Difficult as it is to find the time and place to pray, we cannot hope to become more like Jesus if we do not pray. Prayer must saturate the family circle. It must encompass church, community, and worldwide needs. Without it, we are empty vessels, driven to and fro by our culture.

To think about

- How did Jesus revolutionize prayer?
- What is your greatest hindrance to consistent prayer?

Heavenly Father, how good of you to desire to hear my prayers. Fill me with intensity in praise, thanksgiving, and intercession for others.

Jesus, the Revealer of God

Matthew 11:25–27; John 1:18; 14:9–10; Hebrews 1:1–2

Perhaps one of the most revolutionary ideas that Jesus introduced is that God is knowable and could actually be seen in the person of Christ. Nothing in religious history prior to Jesus even faintly suggested this possibility. Idols and spirits are not knowable as persons. People lived in dread of their gods. Since familiarity breeds contempt, they thought it better to keep the gods at arm's length.

Even the Old Testament worthies, although women and men of remarkable courage and faith, did not relate to God as a knowable person. God was on their side and he could be trusted, but everything in the Mosaic system suggested that you must stay far away from God. Even Moses was shielded from God's presence. When Isaiah caught a glimpse of heaven, his immediate response was humbly confessing his sinfulness.

In the prayers of prophets and psalmists, we see intensely personal dealings with God, yet these prayers never even broach the possibility of actually seeing God and knowing him as a person. Pictures of God's holiness abound in the Old Testament. God appeared to humans in dreams and visions and by angelic messengers. Somehow, God spoke and people heard his voice. The prophets cried, "Thus says the Lord." But that was it.

Then God sent his Son, Jesus, to make himself known. That was a revolutionary departure from the way he had communed with his creatures in the past. The Creator of the universe came to earth in the person of Jesus, and now we can finally see him. God spoke in the past in prophetic words; now he speaks in his Son, the Lord Jesus Christ.

Still, when he came, it was very difficult to really see and hear with spiritual vision and hearing. Thousands of people saw Jesus, but they did not recognize that he was God. Even one of Jesus's closest associates uttered the desperate cry, "Show us the Father and that will be enough for us" (John 14:8).

Jesus understands his role. His mission is to show us God. He takes away the blinders from our eyes and unstops our ears, so we can see and hear God. When we look at Jesus and study the accounts of his life, we do much more than study history. We confront the personal, knowable God. God is not uncaring and distant from us. He engages us in the deepest part of our heart, mind, and soul so that we worship him in spirit and in truth.

Our only access to God as our Father is through Jesus Christ. Searches for other ways to God always end in failure. There is no other person through whom we can approach God and secure forgiveness and eternal life (Acts 4:12).

Do you want to see and know God? Look to Jesus. He reveals God to us in all his majesty, love, power, and glory. Jesus is the full, final, and complete revelation of the living God in heaven. We know God as much or as little as we know Jesus.

To think about

- Why do you think it was hard for people in general and the disciples in particular to see God in Jesus?
- What are ten things about God that you have learned from Jesus?

O God, I have barely scratched the surface in knowing who you are. I confess my lack of interest in knowing more. Help me to plunge into the depths of the knowledge of you that is available to me in the Lord Jesus Christ.

Jesus, Healer of the Paralyzed

Mark 2:1–12

Paralysis has long been mankind's scourge. I lived through the dreaded epidemics of what was called infantile paralysis in the 1930s and 1940s. One of my cousins was struck down by the disease and remains severely crippled to this day. All of America heaved a huge sigh of relief, and many thanked God, when Dr. Jonas Salk developed the first polio vaccine in 1955.

People in Jesus's day knew nothing about vaccines. Whatever the cause of their crippling diseases, no cures awaited them. They suffered humiliating poverty and public abuse along with their physical pain and limitations. Their only hope was a miraculous cure, and many healers came to town offering such cures.

It appeared to some that Jesus of Nazareth was another one of these miracle workers. So when the word got around that he was teaching in a certain house in Capernaum, they jammed the place to hear him. Seizing the opportunity, four men brought their crippled friend to the house, carrying him, bed and all, to the place where Jesus was.

However, their mission was temporarily thwarted when they discovered that they could not get their friend into the house. Undeterred, they carried him up the outside stairway to the roof, which would have been made of branches and reeds laid over beams and layered with dried mud. Picking apart the roof, they made a hole large enough to lower the man and his mat into the crowded room right in front of Jesus.

Success at last! The paralyzed man had reached the miracle worker. But what would Jesus do? How would he react to this rude and crude interruption? Would he ignore the needy man or berate his friends for their audacity and lack of manners? Perhaps he would tell them to take the man away and come back later after he had finished his teaching.

Jesus would do none of these. He pulled a magnificent surprise out of his hat. Rather than heal the man, he told him that his sins had been forgiven. Forgiven? Only the priests could forgive someone in God's name, and then only after the obligatory sacrifices had been made. According to the Pharisees, Jesus's words were outrageous blasphemy.

Jesus knew what they were thinking and in response healed the crippled man. Thus he demonstrated that he was God. The Son of Man has the authority to forgive sins and to heal physical ailments.

Jesus healed both physical and spiritual infirmity, bringing wholeness, joy, and peace to the paralyzed man. Now able to walk, he walked away a forgiven man. We can imagine how he and his friends celebrated that night.

Sometimes people attribute to good luck what actually comes from Jesus. But in God's love and wisdom, there is no such thing as luck. The Holy Spirit draws people, sometimes out of dire circumstances, and drops them in front of Jesus. Often he uses the friends of those who are crippled in body and soul to bring them to Jesus. When this happens, Jesus reaches them. He is not put off by what seems to be the impossible. As the Son of Man, he hurts with us; he knows all about chronic pain and incurable diseases. Whatever the case, his love brings healing, not always of sickness but always of our sins.

To think about

- Picture the scene of the crippled man being lowered in front of Jesus as it might be depicted on television. What stands out in your mind? Why?
- What has Christ's forgiveness done for you? How can you help someone else find the way to Jesus?

Thank you, Lord Jesus, for your healing love and for your forgiveness. Touch those who ache in body and soul. Use me to bring peace and wholeness.

101

Jesus, Forgiver of Sinners

Matthew 9:2–8; 26:28; Luke 7:36–50; 23:32–43

Jesus commanded his disciples to announce astounding news after his resurrection and ascension. Repentance and forgiveness of sins would be preached in his name to all nations. Jesus made forgiveness possible by suffering crucifixion, thereby atoning for the world's sins.

In our social sense, forgiveness assumes that someone has done something personally harmful and needs us to say it's okay. In the divine order of things, we have broken God's laws and failed to do what is right, true, and good, thus offending God's holiness, justice, and righteousness. Because we are sinners by nature and practice, we need God's forgiveness before we can meet him personally.

Looking at the Jesus story before the cross, we see him offering forgiveness. He modeled God's forgiveness and demonstrated that as God's Son he had the right to forgive people.

He forgave the paralyzed man, even though apparently he had made no previous confession of his sins to Jesus. His friends carried him to Jesus seeking physical not spiritual healing. In the end, the paralytic received both.

When Jesus's authority to pronounce forgiveness was challenged, he healed the paralyzed man to prove his right to forgive sinners. Jesus forgave one sinner out of many in the house that day. When the man got up and walked away, Jesus had demonstrated the best news possible, namely, that sinners can be forgiven. That news shattered all preceding religious formulae and duties. The false gods might be temporarily placated by sacrifices, but they never forgave anyone.

One day a real live "sinner" worked her way into a dinner party so that she could worship Jesus by wetting his feet with her tears and drying them with her hair. Such appalling behavior aroused the host's indignation, but Jesus rebuked him for his failure to do what was socially acceptable for guests—the host had failed to wash Jesus's feet.

Then, metaphorically, Jesus socked the Pharisee between the eyes. He told him that the woman's "many sins have been forgiven" (Luke 7:47). The sinful woman's humble deed proved her great love for Jesus and her compelling desire for his forgiveness of her sins.

By forgiving her, Jesus executed God's plan to save anyone who repents. The woman confessed, not in words but in deeds, seeking Jesus and his forgiveness. His forgiveness of this outcast of society proved that he will forgive anyone.

During Jesus's dreadful crucifixion, there are two heart-rending examples of Christ's forgiveness. He asked his Father to forgive his executioners. The only explanation why he could do this is his incomparable compassion and sympathy for the soldiers. The second incident of Jesus's forgiveness while on the cross was of the one repentant thief.

To make absolutely certain that we do not miss what happened on the cross, Jesus explained that his blood secures our pardon and forgiveness (Matt. 26:28). Whatever our deeds and failures, the blood of Jesus covers them all.

To think about

- Why do you think the people who heard Jesus say, "Your sins are forgiven," resented it?
- How do you show your appreciation to Jesus for forgiving you?

Lord Jesus, I praise and honor you for forgiving my sins. Thank you for your blood shed on the cross. Keep me looking to you on the cross when the enemy of my soul makes me doubt that you could forgive me.

Jesus, the New Wine

Luke 5:36–39

Communications theorists expend countless hours and millions of dollars to find out how and why people change. Politicians and marketers alike try to fathom this mystery, because the answer produces votes for the politicians and dollars for the marketers. Their selling strategies try to overcome both our comfort with the old and our resistance to the new.

Jesus lived in a religious environment that resisted anything new. He brought fresh ideas into the arena of religious thought and practice. Rather than be open-minded toward the miracle-working prophet from Galilee, the authorities, with their deeply entrenched ideas, steadfastly resisted Jesus and his innovative teaching.

For the teachers of the law and the Pharisees, the laws of Moses were the last word from God, and it was dangerous and heretical to think that anyone would want to supplant Moses. Adding one word to it or subtracting one word from it was a mortal sin. That's why they tried to protect the law by going beyond it and adding their traditions and interpretations to it. Like barnacles on a pier, these human accretions often vitiated the law's purity and provided a fertile ground for hypocrisy.

Jesus punctured their deeply ingrained resistance to change by pointing out two facts of everyday life. It would be stupid to try to patch a hole in an old pair of pants with new material that had not been first washed and shrunken. Likewise, anyone who poured fresh wine into an old wineskin courted disaster. Fermenting new wine gives off a gas that puts pressure on the wineskin. Old wineskins, previously stretched to the limit, would explode. A new skin is more elastic and can expand.

When Jesus brought the Good News of the gospel, he brought new wine into the marketplace of ideas. As a teacher, he did not fit the rigid concepts of the past. He taught revolutionary, explosive ideas that shattered hundreds of years of traditions. If his new wine were to be preserved, new receptacles were required. People had to change.

Jesus preached repentance of sins. He explained the laws of Moses and taught that transgressions of the heart were just as deadly as outward transgressions. Repentance implies change. The penitent person changes his or her mind about self, his or her ways, and God. The repentant person accepts God's verdict and opens his or her heart and mind to the Jesus way of faith and righteousness.

Jesus's teachings were shocking to people in towns and villages and in the den of thieves in Jerusalem's temple courts. This new wine enraged the religious establishment because he threatened their power. Essentially the Jesus wine offered a new kingdom of heaven, available only to those who repented and followed the Jesus way. It was intoxicating for some, sickening to others. Those who could not swallow it determined to kill Jesus.

New wine demands new wineskins—the hearts and minds of people prepared to make Jesus Lord and to obey his good and perfect will. The Jesus wine is everlastingly new. It never grows sour or bitter. Every generation must decide to change and live or to resist and die.

To think about

- Why was it so difficult for people to accept the new ideas Jesus introduced?
- What keeps you from enjoying the full taste and power of the Jesus wine?

Heavenly Father, too often I have found it hard to change my habits, some of which keep me from growing spiritually. Make me open and receptive to all that Jesus wants to do for me. Make me alert to everything he wants to teach me.

105

Jesus, Our Strength

John 15:1–5; 2 Corinthians 12:7–10; Philippians 4:10–13

Astrong sense of foreboding gripped Jesus's disciples when they gathered around the table in the upper room in Jerusalem. Da Vinci's *Last Supper* fails to adequately portray their dismay, fear, and discouragement. Their dreams were shattered by the impending doom of the one on whom they had pinned their hopes for the restoration of Messiah's kingdom. Instead of freedom from Rome, they now anticipated their own arrest and probable death.

Having departed their secret meeting place, they ventured cautiously through the streets of Jerusalem toward the Garden of Gethsemane. On the way Jesus explained graphically a way to look at their unique relationship. Comparing himself to the vine, he said they were his fruit-bearing branches.

Under the present circumstances, it seemed unlikely that they would ever be able to bear fruit. However, Jesus explained the key to their success: maintain their vital faith union with him at all costs. How does a branch bear fruit? Through the intimate connection with the vine that circulates all the essential nutrients. How could the disciples be strong in the face of imminent disaster? By nourishing their hearts, souls, and minds on Jesus's life-giving provision. They were weak; he is strong. Their strength, courage, and hope depended on their dwelling in him and his living in them.

The apostle Paul gathered strength by the same principle. Chronic illness plagued him. He prayed and prayed for relief. God answered his prayers in a surprising way. He did not heal Paul but he told him that his weakness would be perfected in Christ's strength (2 Cor. 12:9).

106

Paul received a miraculous transfusion that radically changed his outlook on his various weaknesses. Somehow, Jesus injected his strength into Paul's veins. Instead of complaining, he rejoiced. Instead of giving up, he bragged about his hardships so that Christ's power could be seen in him.

Later on, while he was imprisoned in Rome, Paul wrote to his friends in the church at Philippi about this time of weakness, but again Paul rose above it. In both good and bad times, he could do everything in the strength of Jesus. Such strength far surpassed his physical needs. Jesus made him strong in soul, mind, and spirit so that Paul found contentment "whatever the circumstances" (Phil. 4:11). Paul lived in such intimate fellowship with Jesus—as a branch on the vine—that his attitude toward his circumstances was transformed.

Earlier in his letter, Paul told the Philippians that he desired to know the power of Christ's resurrection in his own life (3:10). Every ounce of our spiritual strength and nourishment comes from Jesus who lives in heaven. Abiding in him, we feed on his strength. Without his power, we are doomed to spiritual sterility.

We do not have to be weak, powerless Christians. In tightly bound union with Jesus, we enjoy all the strength we need. His strength produces our fruit.

To think about

- In what circumstances did Jesus's disciples and the apostle Paul feel weak?
- In what areas of your life do you feel your greatest need for Christ's strength? Why?

Heavenly Father, I confess my spiritual weakness. I confess a lack of consistency in seeking closeness to Jesus. Show me how to grow stronger in my relationship with him.

Jesus, the Exposer of Hypocrisy

Matthew 15:1–9; 23:1–33

No one ever called Jesus a hypocrite. People called him a drunkard and some said he was crazy. Others charged him with being Satan's tool. The top religious rulers accused him of the capital sin of blasphemy. But they never accused him of failing to live up to what he taught.

On the other hand, Jesus came down especially hard on hypocrisy and hypocrites. His strongest condemnation of any sin was reserved for hypocrisy. His harshest criticisms and judgments were levied against hypocrites—the religious leaders of Israel.

Why did hypocrites so disturb him? Because their self-righteousness and religious double-dealing posed such a tragic peril for ordinary people who were trying to please God. Among other things, Jesus compared the religious leaders to whitewashed tombs, brilliant on the outside but corrupt on the inside (Matt. 23:27). Since this was true, what would become of their followers?

God's true righteousness was at stake in Israel. The people could not be prepared to receive the Good News of God's kingdom if their leaders betrayed them. Therefore, Jesus exposed their nitpicking, faultfinding behaviors, helping people understand clearly what God expects.

Because our values are not the same as his, we may wonder why Jesus was so critical of the hypocrites. He cared supremely about people and knew they were being led into the abyss because they were following blind, hypocritical guides. This may not bother us, but it bothered him because he knew what was at stake.

Critics of the church complain that it is full of hypocrites. Never mind that hypocrisy is rampant elsewhere in our society—one need only inspect the realms of politics and business to find many examples. Many people's lives have been shattered when they discovered that a trusted friend or colleague was living a double life, saying one thing and doing the opposite. Children find it hard to follow moral and spiritual guidelines when they see their parents failing to live up to their professions of faith.

To love Jesus means we must first check our own conduct and attitudes and root out hypocrisy unmercifully. As standard-bearers for Jesus, we are called to inspect ourselves. If we find just a "speck" in our eye—just a hint of wrongdoing—we must get rid of it (Matt. 7:3–5). As we grow closer to Jesus, he will let us know what hinders our walk with him. Then we shall be in a position to expose hypocrisy wherever it rears its ugly head.

To think about

- When religious leaders are hypocritical, how does this endanger their followers?
- How can we shed the hypocrisy that we've allowed in our lives?

Lord Jesus, root out any hypocrisy in my heart and soul. I want to be your true, authentic follower, not a phony.

Jesus, Author of the Words of Life

John 6:58–71

Frequently cartoonists address the theme of how and where lost souls can find wisdom. The usual drawing depicts a beleaguered man wearily trudging up a mountain peak to find the guru who holds the secret meaning of life. Of course the guru, with a long, scraggly beard, carries a staff and wears sandals and a tattered shirt and pants.

Humorous as this scene is, it reflects a profound yearning for something more soul satisfying than all the wealth and the wisdom of the world put together. God, who created us to find our satisfaction in fellowship with him, knows all about our search for something to fill the void in our hearts. That's the reason he sent Jesus to offer words of life.

Many times, however, Jesus's words proved too tough for many seekers of wisdom and life to follow, and often they decided to abandon Jesus. Somehow Peter grasped that there is no other source of truth and life. When Jesus asked if the disciples would leave him too, Peter confessed that Jesus alone offered words of life (John 6:67–68).

Jesus speaks words of life because he alone is God, was with God, and came from God. He alone existed from eternity past. He alone knows what the future holds. He created and sustains the universe. No earthly guru possesses the credentials of Jesus, Son of God and Son of Man.

Jesus is the exclusive author of life because he holds eternal life in his being. He entered the world as a human being and he died, but death did not conquer him. He is the resurrection and the life. He is the only teacher who has ever overcome death. All the wise men of the world, many of whom claimed to have the keys to life, have perished and are still in their graves.

Jesus speaks words of life because he personifies supreme wisdom. Only Jesus knows our hearts. Only Jesus knows what we need. Only Jesus loves and cares for us, in spite of our lame efforts to be good. He knows we are dead in our trespasses and sins and that we desperately need his life in us.

Jesus authors words of life because he knows that we do not live by bread alone, but by every word that comes from God. He knows that without God's truth we starve to death, frantically looking for happiness and fulfillment everywhere but in him. We struggle to feed on his words, because so many attractive alternatives appeal to us. Sometimes we feel like the cartoon character struggling up the mountain, and our struggles are doomed to fail, unless we seek Jesus who tells us what eternal life is all about and how to achieve it.

The life of faith is not easy. It will involve trial and testing. Though Peter knew that Jesus was the only way to truth and he trusted him, he also failed him when he was severely tempted.

We can prepare for such tests of our faith and commitment by nourishing our heart, soul, and mind on the words of life that Jesus gives us. He speaks his words to us in our personal readings of Scripture, when we worship, when we are taught his truth, and in our listening to his voice and the voices of our Christian friends through prayer and fellowship.

To think about

- Why do you think many people turned away from following Jesus?
- How can you sharpen your spiritual appetite for Jesus's words of life?

Thank you, Lord Jesus, for your life-giving words. I have not consistently fed my soul on your words. Please keep on speaking to me and feeding me. I need the special quality of life your words bring to me.

Jesus, Magnanimous to His Betrayer

John 6:66–71; Matthew 26:20–25, 47–50

A teenage girl betrayed her parents when she became pregnant. The executive of a Christian organization betrayed the staff, donors, and board when she misappropriated capital campaign funds. Another mission agency executive betrayed his wife, friends, and staff by engaging in adultery. A pastor betrayed his wife, children, and the members of his congregation when he ran off with another woman.

To describe how the wives, children, Christian workers, church members, and board members handled these betrayals would require many pages. One word sums up their feelings: pain, not ordinary pain but intense pain, bitterness, frustration, and anger. This kind of pain does not submit to Tylenol. To say that they all forgave their betrayers would not be the truth. Some did, but not quickly.

Keep looking to Jesus, the Bible tells us, but our look at how Jesus handled Judas his betrayer both astonishes and rebukes us. It is a mysterious puzzle, and we simply cannot put all the pieces together.

The first piece is why Jesus chose Judas in the first place, since he knew in advance that Judas would betray him. Was Judas supposed to be the most vivid example of total hypocrisy? Is he a warning to us? Did Jesus choose Judas to show us the perfidy lurking in our own hearts? Are we all potential betrayers of Jesus? Was there a possibility that if Judas confessed and repented, his conversion would speak powerfully to anyone who has committed such treachery?

None of us would ever choose a spouse or a board member or an executive if we knew that person was a traitor. So we fall on our face before Jesus and humbly confess that we're not sure why he picked a traitor to be one of his companions, and the treasurer to boot. We must continually search our own heart for any hints of betrayal and confess those times when we have betrayed our Lord.

The second piece, and equally astounding, is why Jesus called Judas his friend in the hour of his wicked deed. I suspect that I would have screamed, "Traitor!" at Judas. I knew the culprits in the examples I cited at the beginning of this piece. As I heard of each betrayal, my pain was so intense that I felt like someone had stabbed me in the belly with a hot knife. At that moment, "Friend" was not in my heart or on my lips.

So when I look at this snapshot of Jesus, not just in Gethsemane but throughout his three years of fellowship with Judas, I see only a vast chasm between Jesus and me. I admit hatred and anger, not tenderness and forgiveness, toward people who have betrayed me or others.

Jesus is so different from me. He handled betrayal with patience and forthrightness during his work and at his last supper with his disciples. He did not fire Judas for stealing their money (John 12:4–6). Jesus never flinched in the face of the traitor, even when it meant exposing him to his inner circle. He kept the door open for Judas to repent.

Jesus handled betrayal with exceptional grace and magnanimity as his betrayer confronted him. By so doing he set the highest standard for all who profess to be his followers.

To think about

- Why do you think Jesus chose Judas as one of his disciples?
- What seeds of betrayal do you see hiding in your heart? Why?

Lord Jesus, I confess that I fall far short of your example. It is so difficult to deal positively with betrayal. Your powerful grace is my only hope. Stir my heart to be more like you and weed out all seeds of betrayal.

Jesus, Man of Fellowship with God

John 1:1–2; 5:17–23; 8:54–56; 14:9–11; 17:1–5;
Mark 14:32–42

Somehow, in the mysteries of eternity past and the unique relationships within the Godhead, the man Jesus of Nazareth knew incomparable fellowship with God the Father. Theirs was a Father-Son relationship like no other. It was so intimate that from a human standpoint we can say that it broke the Father's heart to send his Son, Jesus, to earth to die for our sins.

Whatever it was like, it continued during the lifetime of Jesus on earth. As a twelve-year-old he talked about being in his Father's house (Luke 2:49). The people, even his parents, did not understand. As far as they were concerned, for the next eighteen years his "house" was that of Joseph and Mary. But their understanding of his place exploded one day at the Jordan River when a voice thundered from heaven, "You are my Son, whom I love" (Mark 1:11).

From that moment on, the disciples and friends and followers of Jesus knew that he enjoyed a distinctive fellowship with the God of the universe. He saturated his teachings with references to his Father in heaven. He buttressed his claims to deity by declaring that he and his Father are one, that his Father sent him, and that he did the works and will of his Father. Their unique relationship changed forever our understanding of God and his desire to enjoy our fellowship as well.

Temporarily Jesus laid aside his heavenly prerogatives (Phil. 2:5–11). He became a servant but he energized his servanthood by constant, unbroken fellowship with his Father.

The thought of their special Father-Son relationship so angered the Jews that they condemned Jesus to death for daring to call God Almighty his Father. "Blasphemy!" they screamed.

As his cross loomed in the near future, Jesus tested the depths of his fellowship with God the Father by asking him to find another way to accomplish universal salvation. His agonizing prayers in the Garden of Gethsemane expose the incredible depths and intimacy of their fellowship.

Jesus's special fellowship with his heavenly Father was poignantly ruptured on the cross when he cried out in bitter anguish to his Father, "Why have you forsaken me?" (Matt. 27:46). In one disastrously dark moment, it seemed, Jesus lost what was most precious to him—fellowship with his Father and partnership in a world-saving mission conceived in eternity past. But resurrection power restored that fellowship. Jesus now sits at his Father's right hand.

Walking with Jesus takes us into the deepest secrets of the Godhead. Nothing in human wisdom and experience can match such intense personal fellowship. No mystery religion, no cult, no occult practices can take us into God's heart. Although our fellowship with our heavenly Father may never plumb the depths of Jesus's special Father-Son relationship, God calls us his children and bids us to call him our Father. Because of Jesus, we enjoy fellowship with God now and forever. Nothing surpasses the supreme value and blessing of knowing God on the most intimate terms.

To think about

- How did Jesus maintain fellowship with God? Why did he insist on publicly declaring their special relationship?
- What value do you place on your fellowship with your heavenly Father? Why?

O Lord, may fellowship with you be my extreme passion. I confess to not loving you totally with heart, mind, and soul. Refresh me with your presence every day.

Jesus, Our Source of Peace and Rest

Matthew 11:28–30

"Come to me," Jesus said. Nothing could be clearer and simpler. However, we have to admit that responding to his invitation often appears to be difficult for us. Too often, it seems, we are prone to accept other invitations first.

Our work gets hard and our load gets heavy. These apt descriptions make clear the emotional, spiritual, and physical price we pay for just being human. Sources of weight and pressure mount steadily as we encounter family and professional demands, plus the responsibilities we accept in our community and church. Issues of marriage and money often conspire to make our life burdensome.

If we discard some of our baggage, we still carry what the Bible calls the heavy load of sin. We try hard to do what is true, right, and good, and to measure up to what we believe God requires of us. In spite of our best efforts, sin jumps up and bites us more often than we would like. Our guilt adds another ton to our load.

Under such pressure, we seek relief. Many options stare us in the face. Some of the cures for our hard work and heavy load are delusions and snares. Some are addictive. Many are dangerous and destructive panaceas. Books and television shows tell us how to get rid of our burdens; seminars and retreats give us a temporary respite. As we seek answers, we may happen onto some new formula for success with others and with God, but its help is transitory.

Jesus says, "Come to me." Why should we go to Jesus? Because he alone knows and understands the full extent and the toll of our hard work and heavy load. He grasps completely what we endure and is not impatient with us because we may have made some wrong choices. Even though our pain may be self-inflicted, Jesus is sufficiently wise and loving to offer us relief.

"I am gentle and humble in heart, and you will find rest for your souls," he promised (Matt. 11:29). Jesus possesses infinite wisdom, power, and love. He lacks nothing that we need for healing. Plus, he heals us gently and with humility. Jesus is never overbearing. His personality compels us to say yes to him.

We go to Jesus to make our initial confession of faith in him. We keep on going to him, daily and many times a day. "Come" means he welcomes us and listens to us at all hours of the day and night.

"Take my yoke upon you and learn from me" implies humility on our part and a willingness to be taught. Going to Jesus demolishes our pride and self-sufficiency. "My yoke is easy and my burden is light" (v. 30) means that Jesus does not put an onerous list of religious duties on our back. He gives us himself. He gives us wholesome satisfaction. "My peace I give you," he promised (John 14:27).

When we go to Jesus and give him our burdens, our actual load does not disappear, but he takes away the destructive pressure and pain the load can cause. Then we do much more than survive, we thrive in the power of his mercy, love, and grace.

To think about

- What kinds of hard work and heavy burdens did Jesus have in mind when he told us to come to him for rest?
- What keeps you from transferring your burdens to Jesus? Why?

Thank you, Lord Jesus, for inviting me to come to you with my burdens, fears, worries, and frustrations. I want to be satisfied with all that you give me. I want to talk to you every day and transfer my load to you.

117

Jesus, the Publicity Man's Nightmare

John 7:1–9

J esus was a publicity man's nightmare. Rather than capital-
ize on his growing fame, Jesus shunned public acclaim.
How out of step this is with the accepted notions of our
time! Publicity and marketing, even in the realm of religion,
dominate our media. The spirit of saturating and selling the
public on one's idea or product prevails. Advertising covers
virtually every available blank space in our environment.

Jesus used none of the public relations approach to winning people to his cause. But his brothers thought he should.
They challenged him to go to Jerusalem and make a show
of himself. What better opportunity than the great Feast
of Tabernacles? Why stay in seclusion in the backwoods of
Galilee?

At the outset of Jesus's ministry, Satan had offered him all
the kingdoms of this world, but Jesus refused that tantalizing
opportunity. Now, after Jesus had taught and done miracles in
Galilee, it appears that Satan tried to ambush Jesus through
his brothers, who were not believers.

Satan knows that the public limelight draws people like
moths to a lamp. Popularity and fame lure us, even in small
ways. The good feelings of acceptance pander to our pride.
Praise goes to our head, yet Jesus, though able to do wonderful things, resisted the temptation to be puffed up.

Jesus's brothers threw out enticing bait: "Your fans in Jerusalem would love to see some of your miracles," they said,
in effect. "Don't disappoint them." How often has a subtle
argument such as this trapped us?

Apparently Jesus's brothers missed the significance of
his warnings to those whom he had healed. "Don't go and
tell anyone," he said to them, but of course they did (Mark

1:44–45). From the beginning, shunning publicity dominated Jesus's thinking, but his brothers were completely out of step with his mission and his approach to the kingdom.

Jesus accepted fully his Father's timetable for his mission. He knew that winning people to the kingdom of heaven does not rest on advertising, popularity, and salesmanship. Jesus refused his brothers' suggestions because by nature he was a humble servant, not a publicity hound.

Of course his brothers may have pictured Jesus in the role of his people's conquering king. They may have hoped to see him ride the tide of popularity and they may have expected to share in Jesus's acclaim. Or, as some have projected, they may have hated him so much that they knew he would be killed if he went to Jerusalem. Whatever their motives, Jesus resisted the tug of their appeal. Their thinking was totally inconsistent with his call to discipleship and with his own lifestyle.

We too find it easy to get out of step with Jesus. We succumb to temptations to put ourselves forward and to put our churches forward. "Look how great we are," we crow. Jesus would have none of that.

To think about

- Why did Jesus's brothers want him to go to Jerusalem? Why did he refuse?
- In what guises does the temptation to be popular appear to you? How do you respond?

Lord Jesus, thank you for resisting the appeal of public acclaim. Thank you for modeling humility and what it means to be an obedient servant of the Father. Give me strength and courage to turn away from ungodly appeals to my pride.

Jesus, Rejected by His Brothers

Mark 3:20–21, 31–35; John 7:1–9

Given all the evidence they had, based on what they had seen and heard, Jesus's brothers faced the same dilemma that challenged all the other witnesses: should they believe Jesus or reject him? For up to thirty years his brothers had lived and worked with him in Nazareth. They had seen nothing that led them to suspect he was their Messiah.

Now here he was, abandoning his home and family to preach repentance, claiming to be Israel's Messiah, criticizing established religion, casting out demons, and healing the sick and crippled. He called God his Father and said that God gave him the words to say and the works to do. James, Joseph, Judas, and Simon (Mark 6:3) stumbled over his claims, and others probably asked their opinion about them.

However, they could not deny that Jesus was a lightning rod. People jammed the villages and packed into houses to hear this new miracle worker and prophet from Nazareth (3:7–8). He was so overwhelmed with people at all times that Jesus's family decided enough was enough. We assume the brothers took charge of the rescue mission to save Jesus from himself.

They were inspired by reports that Jesus was out of his mind. Jerusalem's doctors of the law determined that Jesus was possessed by Beelzebub, the prince of devils. Whatever the problem, Jesus had to be brought home. If the charges spread, the family would be humiliated and Jesus would be liable to prosecution by the religious authorities for misleading God's people.

Of course Jesus refused to go home with Mary and his brothers. More than that, he firmly cleared up matters by explaining that his real mother and brothers and sisters were those who obeyed God's will.

120

During the following year, we might imagine that Jesus's brothers pondered his new definition of "family." But apparently nothing budged them from their resistance to their brother, because the next reported incident shows them trying to persuade Jesus to go to Jerusalem. "Go and show off to the crowds in the city for the big festival," they seemed to tell him. Sarcastically (I believe), they added, "Show yourself to the world" (John 7:4).

John, the writer of the Gospel, demystified their urgent appeal by saying Jesus's brothers were not believers. That was their tragedy. To be so close to Jesus and yet to miss who he was and what he came to do seems virtually impossible to us. However, the four men serve as prototypes of others who, even in the face of the evidence, refuse to believe Jesus. Their story warns us that the evidence about Jesus may leave people unmoved.

Our look at Jesus reveals how he resisted pressure from an unexpected source—his own family. His physical brothers were not his spiritual brothers. That was painful. He labored on without them at his side. Think how they might have supported their brother. Instead, they stumbled over him, following the lead of their fellow townspeople.

After Jesus's resurrection, James became a believer and a leader in the Jerusalem church. Some scholars think that the author of the Epistle of Jude was brother Judas. Joseph and Simon disappear from the record.

To think about

- Why did Jesus's brothers reject him?
- What issues do you face in choosing to join Jesus and be a member of the family of God? Why? What does belonging to his family mean to you? Why?

Heavenly Father, the brothers' rejection of Jesus saddens me because I know how much I need support. I pray for believers whose faith in Jesus has cost them their families.

Jesus, Hated by the World

John 15:18–25

Jesus brought light, truth, hope, peace, forgiveness, and eternal life to people and showed us the way to God. He offered satisfying water and bread to the thirsty and hungry. He healed the sick, welcomed sinners, and raised the dead. He taught magnificently and gave the world's most profound spiritual, moral, and ethical guidance. He lived selflessly and sacrificially.

Facing his cross, Jesus declined to soft-pedal what lay ahead for his disciples. He told them the unsettling news that his persecutors would persecute them as well. The haters of Jesus had determined not just to kill Jesus, but also to eradicate his followers and therefore his teachings.

The world of Jesus's contemporaries hated him. He was light, "but men loved darkness instead of light because their deeds were evil" (John 3:19). He told his brothers that the world hated him for exposing the wickedness of its ways (7:7).

The world's hatred sprang from their refusal to believe in the light and hope that Jesus announced. They made a fatal choice, loving darkness and wickedness more than the purity and forgiveness of Jesus. If they chose Jesus, they would have to abandon their evil ways. The cost of discipleship was too steep and severe for them.

Because his disciples bore the unmistakable imprint of Jesus, they would be vulnerable to attack. By following Jesus they had moved from darkness to light, from the world to the kingdom of heaven. The world persecuted Jesus, and unbelievers would also persecute his disciples. Bearing Jesus's name would be enough to bring down the world's hatred, which originated in the people's ignorance of God the Father. Hatred of Jesus equals hatred of God.

The world received light from both the teachings and miracles of Jesus, and people had no excuses for rejecting and hating him. Evidence to condemn the world's unbelief is overwhelming. Those who hated Jesus did so for no good reason (another fulfillment of prophecy).

Since the coming of Jesus, the supreme exposer of wickedness, many evil powers have conspired to eradicate his name and his followers. Despite wiping out millions of people, these tyrants have never extinguished the flame of Jesus and his church.

Paradoxically, when he is hated and his name maligned, his power reigns in his kingdom people. The strong name of Jesus prevails over wickedness even as it exposes it. Therefore, although his followers can expect the same treatment as Jesus received, they know that by his grace and strength they can conquer the world's sin and evil. We are more than conquerors (Rom. 8:37).

Hatred of Jesus is not necessarily expressed through wicked violence. This hatred appears in many different guises even in sophisticated societies. Intellectuals often sneer at his name. Power brokers stiff-arm Jesus. Without firing a literal shot, they attempt to annihilate him nevertheless.

Meanwhile, his followers bear his stigma without fear or apologies. Difficult and painful as it may be, Christians refuse to knuckle under to the world's hatred, whether it is subtle or overt.

To think about

- Why did people hate Jesus in his time? Why do they hate him now?
- What has your allegiance to Jesus cost you? In what ways have you been persecuted for bearing his name?

Lord Jesus, I confess I have often failed to stand up for you publicly for fear of ridicule or worse. I want to be liked not hated. Give me the courage and wisdom to bear your name without apology.

Jesus, the Sent One

John 8:12–18, 23–30

John's Gospel could very well be called the Gospel of "the sent one." He recorded at least forty times when Jesus answered challenges by claiming that his Father had sent him. We find extended interchanges in chapters 5, 6, 7, 8, and 12, plus the Lord's Prayer in chapter 17 in which Jesus indicated the supreme importance of believing that God had sent him.

Two basic truths emerge: Jesus had a mission to fulfill, and God's full authority backed his mission. Therefore, as Christians, we emphasize that Jesus, although born in the flesh, lived and died for purposes that were not of his own choosing but of God's. He was not a misguided zealot who died for a noble cause.

Sometimes people use Jesus to promote revolution and liberation. On many occasions he is held forth as a wise, godly person who gave us some good advice. Such evaluations of Jesus completely miss the point of his mission and his authority.

Of course, as John's accounts show, Jesus's contemporaries demanded regularly that he prove his right to demolish their accepted religious traditions. They were not prepared to move in a new direction until they were positively sure that this Galilean prophet would not lead them astray. So, in effect, they kept on asking, "Who are you? Who gave you the right to tell us what to do?"

Their questions stand as the fundamental questions of our day. It's not that the public wants to abolish Jesus. The old musical hit *Jesus Christ, Superstar* expresses adequately the opinion of many people. But to confess Jesus as the God-sent Lord and Savior of all who believe in his name requires much more than adulation.

Jesus prayed for his disciples because they believed that God had sent him. He prayed for unity among his followers so that the world might believe that God had sent him. We have faith in Jesus because we know where he came from. To say that Jesus was sent means that he existed in the Godhead from all eternity past. He enjoyed a special relationship with his Father. He left heaven and that relationship to come to earth, accepting a unique mission from God the Father.

Our confession of our sins and our trust in Jesus arise from the fact that we know why he came. We know that his mission was to save us, forgive us, and give us a place in his eternal kingdom. All people need to know and accept Christ's mission in this light. That is why Jesus prayed for us to be united in our witness and testimony. People want to see us live what we believe about Jesus.

We can only ponder what it cost Jesus to be sent from heaven to redeem us. Jesus knew what his mission would bring, and he came despite knowing that it would mean rejection, misunderstanding, humiliation, and crucifixion. He lost everything we count valuable. To accept a mission on such terms is unthinkable to us.

Remember, then, that Jesus said: "As the Father has sent me, I am sending you" (John 20:21). His mission becomes ours when we trust and obey him.

To think about

- Construct an imaginary conversation between the Father and the Son about Jesus's mission. What facts would you include? Why?
- What convinced you that Jesus was sent from God? How does that fact influence your walk of faith and obedience?

Thank you, heavenly Father, for sending your Son to die for me. I praise you, Lord Jesus, for accepting your Father's mission so that I might enter your kingdom as a forgiven sinner.

125

Jesus, Authoritative Teacher

Mark 1:21–22; Luke 4:22–37; John 7:14–17

People look for religious authority anywhere they can find it, from books, sermons, videos, sacred scriptures, personal gurus, and holy women and men. Confusion reigns in the search for truth. Wars based on different religious authorities mar the records of human history.

Within the relatively small circle in which Jesus traveled and taught, authority rested pretty much with the established Jewish experts and their interpretations of the laws of Moses and traditions handed down over hundreds of years. Yet even within this sphere, there was no unanimity of thought, so many debates raged over minute matters. Jesus charged the leaders with straining gnats and swallowing camels (Matt. 23:24).

Ordinary folks, used to the teaching of the Jewish experts, woke up one day to find a new kind of teacher in their midst, a man who spoke with authority. Jesus did not hem and haw. He did not say, "Rabbi so and so says this, but rabbi so and so says that." He spoke directly without equivocation or theological subtleties. The temple guards told the chief priests and the Pharisees that no one ever spoke like Jesus (John 7:46). His hometown folks marveled at the words of grace that fell from his lips. The authority and power of his words amazed onlookers, who asked, "Where did he get these words?"

He confounded the experts because he had not studied at their rabbinical schools. They challenged Jesus to reveal the source of his authority. If it was from heaven, they were in trouble. Jesus answered them with a question of his own, but they refused to answer, because no matter what they said, it would give Jesus the upper hand, and above all they

126

could say nothing that would acknowledge his deity (Matt. 21:23–27).

Jesus knew that people suffered from this kind of rigid, overbearing spiritual leadership. Coming from heaven, his teaching offered relief and hope for people who were spiritually strangled to death. Today it is still possible, of course, to miss the import of what Jesus says by adhering dogmatically to what others have handed down. We may have to take an unpopular stance on the issue of religious authority. We listen and learn what we can about different religions, without compromising the truth about Jesus and his teachings.

The issue between Jesus and the experts was not just academic debate. He knew their hearts. Since they failed to acknowledge his lordship, they had to find some way to dodge his teachings. He told them that the key to finding truth was choosing to do God's will.

Because Jesus is the truth, he spoke the truth. God authorized what Jesus said. God spoke from heaven and told people to listen to Jesus. Then, as today, some people refused to believe and obey Jesus. Because he was authoritative, so must his followers be, albeit with grace and love.

To think about

- What was so different about Jesus's teaching? What effect did this have on people?
- How has Jesus's authoritative teaching influenced your life? What steps are you taking to learn more?

Lord Jesus, I want to be as authoritative as you were, in the best way, so help me to grow in both your grace and knowledge. Help me to engage others lovingly and truthfully for your sake.

Jesus, Man of Compassion

Matthew 9:36–38; 14:13–14; 20:29–34; Luke 7:11–17

Compassion was Jesus's indelible mark. For him, compassion far surpassed the customary feelings of sympathy or pity. His compassion moved him to do things that changed people's lives.

The psalmists praised God for his compassion (see, for example, Pss. 111:4; 145:8–9). For them, God's compassion brought mercy and life's daily necessities. In Jesus we see God's compassion personified in deeds of kindness and mercy. When we read about Jesus's deep compassion for people in the Bible or experience his boundless love and mercy ourselves, we are moved to love him.

It is sometimes difficult for us to appreciate the depth of Jesus's emotions. We experience hurt and pain when others suffer. So did Jesus. But for him, compassion went so much deeper. The Greek word used for *compassion* describes powerful feelings from deep within one's inner being. Literally the word means "to have bowels of yearning." What was it that aroused such feelings in Jesus? Basically, it was the tragic spiritual condition of his people. When he surveyed the crowds following him, he compared them to harassed, helpless sheep without a shepherd (Matt. 9:36). What an apt picture of our generation. His compassion moved Jesus to appeal to his disciples for more workers. Only by knowing the truth about Jesus could helpless sheep be rescued. So we continue to pray for many more compassionate workers.

Likewise, people's physical needs aroused Jesus's compassion. His heart went out to the sick and hungry. He healed the sick and told his disciples to feed the hungry. They lacked the needed food, so Jesus multiplied the loaves and fish and fed five thousand men, plus women and children (14:21).

Moved by the plight of two blind men sitting by the roadside, Jesus heard their plea and restored their sight (20:34). Walking down the road one day with his entourage, Jesus encountered a grief-stricken widow en route to burying her only son. Stirred by the magnitude of her condition, Jesus comforted her and raised her son (Luke 7:14–15). Deeds of mercy accompanied our Lord's compassion. He changed the lives of those who suffered.

To help us understand true compassion, Jesus told stories about people who exercised it in everyday life. In one story, a king responded to a debtor's pleas with compassion and canceled his debt (Matt. 18:23–27). In another, the father of the prodigal son welcomed him home because he was filled with compassion for him (Luke 15:11–24).

Following Jesus, the Man of compassion, calls us to emulate both the intensity of his feelings for people and his actions to help them. The need for people of compassion to serve in God's harvest fields remains critical. We need to let others know, though they may feel like harassed and helpless sheep, there is One who will be their true shepherd, leading them to safety.

To think about

- In what different settings did Jesus display his compassion openly?
- How do you move from sympathy and pity to compassion? What makes the difference? How do you respond differently?

Lord Jesus, I praise you for who you are, the flawless example of compassion in action. I confess my lack of love for others and my little concern for their needs. May your grace move me to change my attitudes and my actions.

Jesus, Healer of the Sick

Matthew 8:5–13; 14:34–36; 15:29–31; Mark 5:21–34; Luke 17:11–19; John 9:1–12

Our culture confronts sickness with an overwhelming array of weapons and treatments. New technologies, equipment, and drugs are developed virtually every day. The costs of healing the sick mount accordingly, so many people face astronomical medical bills.

Stories about health and health care have seized the media like an onslaught of locusts, and when we look at the Jesus stories, we find something just like our contemporary media frenzy. People flocked to Jesus for healing, as if he were the latest cancer cure.

Today purveyors of food, natural remedies, and drugs vie competitively for our dollars, but in AD 30 no such plethora of expensive treatments existed. People were at the mercy of practitioners of all sorts of alleged cures. They crowded after miracle workers. They flocked to waters that supposedly had healing properties. Many received treatment for years without results.

Jesus entered this miserable scene like a laser beam, drawn to the sick and needy. Moved with compassion, he healed by word and touch a dazzling array of illnesses and ailments, from leprosy to blindness. He healed people who had suffered for a lifetime. He healed people because he loved them and hurt for them. Seeing their terrible needs and sometimes the evidence of their faith, he restored their health and strength. Consequently people thronged around him, wanting to touch him.

For some reason, two groups of sufferers drew the most attention from the writers: lepers and the blind. This might be because they were so totally helpless and their healings were more striking. Perhaps also Jesus was trying to tell us something beyond the physical healings. Sin defiles us, as leprosy

130

did in those days. Sin causes blindness; spiritual blindness afflicts everyone until Jesus gives us our spiritual sight.

At the same time, certain cases impress us, such as the long-distance healing of the centurion's servant (Matt. 8:5–13). Jesus also healed the woman who had sought help from doctors for years and had sufficient faith to believe that if she just touched Jesus's cloak, she would be healed (Mark 5:21–34).

Jesus was never far from crowds of suffering people. His mission included healing as well as teaching. He explained to unbelievers that his deeds done in his Father's name were his credentials (John 10:25). He told his disciples that his miracles proved his deity (14:11). Raising Lazarus from the dead proved that the Father had sent him (11:42). Jesus honored God; he did not seek honor for himself. He never told the crowds, "Look what I did!"

Following Jesus compels us to serve and comfort the sick. We can be Jesus for many people who need emotional and spiritual wholeness as well as physical healing. Jesus calls all of us to find his touch because it opens doors to God's love and care. In a world surrounded by medical technology and professionals, the personal touch is often the key to physical, emotional, and spiritual healing.

To think about

- How would you describe the scope and the purpose of Jesus's healings? Why do you think healing was such a large part of his ministry?
- How has your reflection about Jesus as a healer influenced your opinion of him? In what ways does he minister to you because of this?

O Lord, open my heart to the needs of the sick and chronically ill. May I respond with love and care to those in hospitals, to people taking cancer treatments, and to those confined to nursing homes.

131

Jesus, Friend and Enabler of the Twelve

Matthew 10:1–42

Jesus chose twelve men to leave their work and follow him, promising them new careers. Most of them were fishermen, and they would become fishers of men.

Why did these men leave everything for Jesus? The story writers do not tell us, so it surprises us that—at least on the surface—their decisions seem to have been made without much prior thought. That may be misleading. Probably these men had heard Jesus teach and had witnessed some of his miracles before he called them. Luke described a fishing miracle that certainly caught their attention (Luke 5:1–11).

Did Jesus really need these men to accomplish his mission? (See "Jesus, Recruiter of Disciples," p. 66.) In one sense no, because he was strong enough to do what needed to be done. Why, then, did he pick them? They were not legal experts in the law. Later, their enemies ridiculed some of them as ordinary, uneducated men (Acts 4:13).

First of all, Jesus picked his disciples because God's harvest was ripe and he needed workers, so Jesus commissioned them to preach, heal, and cast out demons. Mark added a second reason: Jesus desired their companionship (Mark 3:13–19). Jesus saw the necessity of having both helpers and friends.

With the Twelve at their last meal together, Jesus drew both ideas together. He called them his friends whom he had chosen to go and bear lasting fruit. He washed their feet to show how much he loved them. As their teacher, he had told them everything he had learned from his Father, and he planned their eternal companionship (John 14:1–3)

Jesus trained the disciples to do the needed work. Matthew detailed their curriculum. It was both practical and frightening. Jesus prefaced his overview of their mission by

132

giving them his authority. Only in his name could these men hope to accomplish their difficult assignment. He told them to copy his lifestyle and leave behind their money and extra clothes. They would have to live off the land. While some homes and villages would welcome them, others would not. Aptly Jesus compared them to sheep among wolves. He told them to be both wary and guileless.

Jesus refused to entice the disciples to follow him and accept his mission by offering appealing results. Instead, he told them that as they fished for people, they would encounter serious opposition. But in times of difficulty, God the Father would tell them what to say. Not only that, Jesus encouraged them not to be afraid because God knew all about them and loved them beyond measure, counting them worth more than sparrows, which received the Father's daily care (Matt. 10:29–31).

Their work amounted to cross bearing for Jesus. As they suffered for his name, people would believe their message. They would stand in the place of Jesus, so that, in effect, those who received his apostles received Jesus and his Father.

The men Jesus chose would be the backbone of his new community, the church. But when he called the Twelve, they did not know this. In some ways we are like them. We step out in faith to follow Jesus, not knowing what lies ahead. We go, just like the Twelve, because something powerfully attractive about Jesus compels us to say yes.

To think about

- After their first lesson, why did the Twelve agree to accept Christ's mission?
- What changes do you see in your life as a result of following Jesus?

Thank you, Lord Jesus, for calling me your friend and helper. I want to know you more intimately as your friend. I want to bear more fruit for you. Keep me faithful to the end.

Jesus, Battler for the Truth

John 8:12–47

Jesus said he was the truth, but the majority of his listeners ridiculed him and refused to take him seriously. Most notably, the chief priests, Pharisees, and doctors of the law opposed Jesus steadfastly and sought to put him away. They tried character assassination—calling him a friend of sinners, a wine bibber, and demon possessed—and used epithets to impugn his heritage—Nazarene, Galilean.

The prevailing popular and scholarly view held that truth had been handed down from God to Abraham and then to Moses. Of course God's Old Testament revelation was true. Jesus never argued that point. But neither Moses nor Abraham possessed the whole truth. God's salvation program did not end with them.

So it is quite easy for us to understand why certain of the Jews attacked Jesus like a swarm of hornets. As we read the dialogue, we are enveloped by the overpowering scent of spiritual warfare like smoke over a battlefield. They battled for the truth because eternal destinies were at stake. Theirs was not a polite academic discussion.

The Pharisees attacked Jesus's credibility because he testified on his own behalf. They missed the essential truth that God had sent Jesus into their midst. Because they did not know God, they turned their backs on Jesus.

Their desperate cry to Jesus, "Who are you?" pains our hearts (John 8:25). We wonder how they could possibly fail to grasp the truth about Jesus. Challenging some who had responded favorably, Jesus said their ongoing discipleship hinged on their obedience to the truth. Knowing the truth would bring them spiritual freedom.

134

Further acrimonious debate ensued, especially when Jesus questioned their Abrahamic paternity (vv. 39–41). Their failure to live up to Abraham's saving faith was truth that cut them to the heart, so they tried to kill Jesus, the bearer of the truth.

Not only did Jesus tell them their father was not Abraham, he told them who their father was: the devil (v. 44). Ouch! Their spiritual DNA test proved that they followed the devil while rejecting the truth Jesus brought. His words are true and those who are children of God believe him.

Jesus's courage, boldness, wisdom, honesty, and forthrightness shine brilliantly on this truth encounter. Steadfastly he refused to accommodate his challengers, not giving an inch because truth hung on the scaffold. In the face of this bitter onslaught, Jesus did not offer some mushy defense, such as, "Well, okay, if that's what you want to believe." Jesus was the battler for truth. It was not okay for people to believe falsehoods, but they would never find the truth if they persisted in rejecting him.

The father of lies and the Father of truth engage in warfare for our souls. Followers of Jesus commit themselves to him and to his truth. As they do, they stand up courageously like Jesus and accept the same kind of criticism and insults that he did.

The old hymn expressed it best: "Give of your best to the Master; . . . join in the battle for truth" (Howard B. Grose).

To think about

- Why did the religious authorities reject so violently the truth Jesus brought?
- What truth encounters do you face? Why? How do you handle them?

Lord Jesus, help me in my battles for truth to be honest and courageous. Forgive me for shaving the truth sometimes so that I won't be ridiculed. May I always respond winsomely, so that people will see you in me.

Jesus, Subject of Rome

Luke 2:1–7; Matthew 17:24–27; 22:15–22

The Romans controlled the world into which Jesus was born. At that time, for some reason, Emperor Augustus felt it was time to order a tax census of his subjects, making a long, arduous journey necessary for Mary and Joseph. So our Lord was born as a subject of Rome, growing up, working, and obeying God's mission under a repressive regime.

However, the writers of his story seldom trace any intersections between Jesus and Rome prior to his trial before Pontius Pilate. We simply cannot paint a portrait of Jesus as a revolutionary in the political sense, although he preached an extraordinarily revolutionary message.

When Jesus's Jewish critics tried to nail him for some false step, they began by accusing him of breaking their own traditions and laws. For instance, he was a Sabbath breaker, they said. But that line of attack never amounted to much with the people, so someone thought they could get Jesus into trouble with the Romans on the issue of paying taxes.

As far back into history as we can peer, taxes have been a sore subject for most and a cruel burden for many. When ancient Israel demanded that the prophet Samuel give them a king, he warned them that a king would levy onerous taxes.

Skip a thousand years and you find God's people still chafing under taxes, this time they were exacted by their Roman overlords. The Romans fixed taxes every fourteen years, based on the census.

According to our tax laws, Jesus could easily have been tax-exempt. He definitely met the requirements of a not-for-profit charity. After leaving his carpenter's job, he could have pleaded poverty. There's no reason to think that he had squirreled away a nest egg in Nazareth.

Despising the hated Romans and their taxes was an article of faith among the Jews. Their Messianic hopes centered on deliverance from such burdens. When Jesus stepped into this hostile milieu, his critics tried to trap him. If they could get Jesus to say that he supported taxes, he would be a traitor to his people. If he spoke against paying taxes to the Romans, they would arrest him.

Jesus neatly sidestepped his critics' hypocritical question (Matt. 22:17) and showed that, although he came from heaven, he would subject himself to the Romans. In this case, the tax issue provided another glimpse into the kind of man he was. Not only did Jesus exude wisdom, he did so with humility.

Living as a subject of Rome, he did not raise his voice against the ruthless dictatorship. As he later said to his Roman judge, Pilate, his kingdom had nothing to do with political empires. But Jesus did authorize paying taxes, thereby showing us how to be good citizens.

We may regard our tax rates as unfair, and we often wish our leaders would be more circumspect in the use of our money, but whatever our political and economic sentiments, living the Jesus way requires us to pay our taxes honestly. Following Jesus includes being subject to Rome, as it were, and paying our taxes. By so doing we affirm our loyalty to him and set an example to others.

To think about

- Why was Jesus on the hot seat on the tax issue?
- What civic responsibilities enable you to show others that you follow Jesus? How has this worked in your life?

Thank you, God, for my citizenship in heaven. But while I am here, help me to be an honest citizen. I want to reflect Jesus in every area of my life.

Jesus, Living Water

John 4:1–10; 7:37–39

Bottled water crowds supermarket shelves and fills millions of vending machines. Nothing like it existed when Jesus and his disciples tramped the Judean hills. In many parts of the world today, people trudge with their vessels to draw water from solitary wells and single community pipes, much like the woman whom Jesus met at the well.

We cannot live without water, yet no company has the temerity to suggest that its bottles contain living water. Florida's Fountain of Youth attracts thousands of visitors, but its water is not alive.

Jesus said that if we drink the water he offers, we will never thirst again. The thirsty Samaritan woman at the well soon figured out that Jesus was not talking about the literal water she was drawing from the well. He addressed her heart and soul not her physical thirst. Jesus exposed a gaping moral hole in her life. He wanted to pour his living water into her moral depravity.

Later on, Jesus dramatically offered himself to the nation as the source of water that turns people's lives into vibrant, refreshing, gushing springs. In a desert environment his graphic spiritual analogy must have seemed like a promise to give everyone a private, verdant oasis of plenty.

We know that physical death awaits anyone cut off from water. However, it is not so obvious that we die spiritually if we do not accept Jesus's invitation to come to him and drink. People die of spiritual thirst because they do not believe it is essential to drink of Jesus.

Our lives can be pictured either as a dry, barren, death-dealing desert or as a bubbling spring full of life and vitality.

Jesus makes the difference. To find life in him, all that is required is a drink of his living water.

Jesus described this life-giving drink as believing in him. Eventually the Samaritan woman believed in him and received living water. To believe in Jesus means to believe the record about him and to count him as a trustworthy object of our faith. The New Testament record declares that Jesus died for our sins and rose again.

When we believe in Jesus, we establish a personal relationship with him. "Come to me," he shouted to the crowd. When we drink a glass of water, the water becomes part of us. When we believe in Jesus, he comes to live in us. He quenches our spiritual thirst by giving us new life.

Back at the Samaritan well, all the woman had to do was ask Jesus for a drink of his water, just as he had asked her for a drink from her well. His offer did not make sense to her until she realized who he was. By exposing ourselves to the power of his words, and admitting that our sins keep us from satisfaction and fulfillment in life, we are driven to Jesus. Something magnetic about Jesus draws us to him. Deep down, we confess that we need him because he alone can satisfy our spiritual thirst. We accept his offer of a drink and we keep on drinking of him, because our circumstances keep pushing us back to him.

To think about

- What is the value of comparing physical thirst to spiritual thirst?
- What discipline is required if we are to develop the habit of drinking deeply of Jesus?

Thank you, Lord Jesus, for your generous offer of living water. I confess my thirst. I need streams of life-giving water for myself and to share with others.

Jesus, Healer of the Blind

John 9

In the days of Jesus, blind people were especially vulnerable to the vagaries of society. There were no institutes for the blind where they could be trained for useful occupations. They were tossed away like so much useless garbage and reduced to begging for their survival.

The Gospel writers describe the lowly place of the blind. In one case, the blind sat by the side of the road, and when Jesus passed by, they cried out for mercy, only to be told to shut up. However, their condition aroused Jesus's compassion. Never one to accept the heavy burdens his peers put on people, Jesus relieved the men of their terrible handicap and healed them. Because of Jesus, they could see (Matt. 20:29–34).

At another time, when one of the blind men whom Jesus had healed was asked to explain what happened, a satisfactory answer eluded him. He knew one thing for sure: he had been blind, and Jesus gave him his sight (John 9:25).

Blindness carried a religious stigma. Common belief, as expressed by Jesus's disciples, held that someone in the family, or even in a prior incarnation, had committed some terrible sin that brought blindness as a punishment from God (v. 2).

Jesus smashed the false idea that someone was to be blamed for blindness. Then he put himself forward as the answer to both physical and spiritual blindness.

Jesus's healing of the blind was intended to show that he could also bring the light of forgiveness and salvation to anyone who believed. Throughout Scripture darkness stands for the spiritual condition caused by rejecting God's light. The prophets, Jesus, and the apostle Paul used blindness as a metaphor for spiritual darkness and rejection of God (vv. 39–41; 12:37–41; Rom. 11:25 KJV, NEB; 2 Cor. 4:4). Light, on the other hand, stands for the domain of those who have received God's salvation in Christ.

When Jesus healed the man born blind, such a terrible brouhaha erupted that John devoted an entire chapter to the incident. Here was another powerful example of the great controversy between Jesus and the chief priests and the Pharisees that began at the Feast of Tabernacles in Jerusalem. When he said he brought living water, they tried to arrest him (John 7:37–44). When Jesus said he was the light of the world and then later said "Before Abraham was born, I am!" they said he was demon possessed and tried to stone him (8:12, 58–59). When he healed the blind man, they said he was a sinner (9:1–16).

Jesus wanted his disciples to focus on God's power and glory when he healed the blind man. He gave them an object lesson as well: they must work while it is still daylight, because darkness is coming.

After the healed man had been expelled from the synagogue, Jesus led him to confess his faith. Then Jesus rebuked the Pharisees for their self-righteous spiritual blindness. In this story Jesus stands as both the compassionate healer and the accurate, uncompromising judge of unbelief.

Whenever we review the evidence of his miracles, we are required to look at our own condition. Do we confess our blindness and our need of Christ's light, or do we think we have 20/20 vision and no need of healing?

To think about

- Why were the chief priests and Pharisees so hostile to Jesus?

- How do you explain to those who cannot see the miracle of your own "sight" and healing?

Thank you, Lord Jesus, for healing my spiritual blindness. Show me how to work for you while it is still daylight.

Jesus, the Great "I Am"

John 8:33–59

Does it really make any difference where Jesus came from? Jesus's contemporaries thought so, because if he came from God, they had to listen to him and change their ways. But if he did not, they could disregard him.

Truth as Jesus presented it has a cutting edge. His truth carries a moral sword, described by the writer of Hebrews as so sharp that it judges our thoughts and attitudes (Heb. 4:12). The chief priests and Pharisees fought Jesus for much more than their doctrines and traditions. They fought for their right to keep on living as self-righteous hypocrites who fooled ordinary people and led them astray.

Therefore, if they could use Jesus's words to discount his claim to have come from God, they would be home free. Jesus struck their jugular. He told them he knew where he had come from and where he was going. Because he belongs to heaven, not earth, he is the way to knowing the Father. Again and again he declared that he spoke what his Father told him to speak. He always pleased his Father by speaking his truth.

His opponents kept asserting the priority of their truth because they could trace their ancestry and their religion to Abraham. How could anyone be so bold as to claim supremacy over Abraham? Jesus upended their pride of pedigree by asserting that he existed before Abraham. Enraged by his effrontery, they tried to stone him.

Jesus made his startling claim in such a striking way that the chief priests and Pharisees did not miss its implications. Jesus did not say, "I was before Abraham," but, "Before Abraham was born, I am" (John 8:58). Clearly, they took this to mean that he had always existed with God and that God had sent him to earth.

They knew that "I AM" was the name for God. When Moses wanted to know who was talking to him on the mountain, God answered, "I AM WHO I AM" (Exod. 3:13–14). Therefore, by saying "I am," Jesus claimed to be God. During the Feast of Tabernacles, the priests quoted Isaiah's prophecy, "I am he" (Isa. 43:10, 13). Perhaps this was fresh in their minds when they challenged Jesus.

"I am" authenticates Jesus's truth claims. As God incarnate, he alone has the right to shape our minds, hearts, and wills. What we believe about Jesus is important for our Christian creeds. The world needs to know where we stand.

"I am" also validates Jesus's right to determine my faith commitments and my conduct. Because he is God and came from God, he irrevocably changes my intellect, will, and emotions. He calls for my trustful obedience because he is my truth King. As my Lord, he tells me how to think and behave. I cannot profess to believe in him without determining to follow his moral and spiritual standards. If I choose not to do so, in effect I stone him.

To think about

- In contemporary terms, how would you describe the raging debate over Jesus's origin?
- In what ways has "I am" shaped your beliefs, values, and conduct?

O Lord, help me to see clearly the implications of your "I am" claim. I confess that often I have rejected your lordship in my life. I want to obey. Overwhelm my lack of trust in you.

Jesus, Friend of Sinners

Luke 7:31–50

Jesus grew up in a highly segregated Jewish community. Because of their inherited traditions, and the strictures of the self-righteous Pharisees, most people refused to associate with Gentiles and "sinners." Because of their fear of religious contamination, they justified their separation on moral grounds.

You could be an outsider because of your race, disease, handicap, poverty, or your disreputable past. Of course the tax collectors came in for special ostracism because of their collaboration with the Romans. When Jesus called Matthew to join his team, he signaled that the kingdom of heaven was open to anyone. To prove it, Matthew gathered an assembly of bad characters for dinner at his house and Jesus sat down with them (Matt. 9:9–13).

Consequently Jesus's reputation took a hit. Public opinion scorned him because he had become known as the friend of unsavory characters. He could not possibly be a prophet of God because his behavior violated their preconceived notions of Messiah. In the face of such criticism, Jesus clearly set the terms of his mission. He announced that he had not come to invite good people but sinners to follow him.

One day Jesus seized the opportunity to prove his point. For some unexplained reason Simon the Pharisee invited him to dinner. He had not invited a local prostitute, but somehow she made her way into the house to Jesus. As she bowed before him, she wept so profusely that her tears wet Jesus's feet and she dried them with her hair. The woman also kissed his feet and anointed them with myrrh (Luke 7:37–38).

It's understandable that Simon took offense. He did not utter a word, but Jesus knew he was thinking that what had happened was outrageous and totally unbecoming a prophet. In the end, Jesus taught him a powerful lesson about love and forgiveness. Despite the loose woman's many sins, she went home forgiven by Jesus. Her demonstration of affection and worship—what Jesus called her great love—validated her confession.

It does not matter who we are or what we have done, everyone who comes to Jesus hears his words, "Your faith has saved you; go in peace" (v. 50). Jesus welcomes social outcasts and people marginalized for many reasons. Breaking the rules of sterile religion, he brings us forgiveness, hope, and peace.

By declaring that sinners were the very ones he came to save, Jesus revolutionized his day and ours. Sinners would have a place in God's future kingdom. People who rejected them and crossed the street to avoid passing close to them would not enter the kingdom. The first would be last and the last first.

Courageously Jesus confronted the status quo to show that there is wideness in God's mercy that the clean, the well, the smug, and the self-righteous refuse to accept. When I admit the enormity of my sins, Jesus becomes my only hope of forgiveness and righteousness. Clinging to him because he is the friend of sinners gains me freedom from condemnation and makes me a new, better person.

To think about

- What kind of religious and social pressures conspired to keep Jesus from welcoming sinners?
- Are you more like Simon or Jesus in your attitudes toward sinners? Why?

O God, forgive me for judging who is fit for your kingdom and who is not. I confess a standoffish attitude. Give me grace, love, and power to welcome all people graciously.

Jesus, the Good Shepherd

John 10:1–21

Even though many people who heard Jesus were spiritually blind, he kept on shining as the light of the world into the dark recesses of their hearts and minds. His mission required faithful endurance, love, patience, and wisdom. Perhaps his remarkable authority and clarity would penetrate the darkness of their souls.

He used two simple metaphors to portray his mission: he identified himself as the gate to the sheepfold (John 10:7) and as the shepherd of the sheep (v. 11). As the gate, he is the entrance to fulfilling life. As the shepherd, he not only guides and cares for his sheep, he sacrifices his life for them.

Jesus described the shepherd-sheep relationship in the most intimate terms. They know and trust each other so completely that the shepherd knows the name of each sheep and each of them recognizes his voice. The shepherd sets the pace, and they follow him because his voice projects guidance, protection, and sustenance.

Surely this description of the believer and Jesus far surpasses anything offered by the world's "thieves and robbers" (v. 8). Here we plunge the depths of what it means to belong to Jesus. We travel far beyond just knowing the Jesus story to walking with him in loving companionship and obedience.

For people unfamiliar with sheep and shepherds, we can use a different metaphor. The relationship is akin to that of a father and his little boy while the child explores the neighborhood or a park. Potential hazards loom, but the boy runs ahead because his father is there to protect and guide him and even to feed him when necessary. His father's voice gives the "stop-and-go" signals. When some danger or crisis arises, perhaps a threat from a stranger, the father reacts immediately and risks his life for the safety of his little boy.

Jesus said he would die for his sheep. Here we peer into God's heart and discover that he sent Jesus as our Good Shepherd to die for us.

In his picture of Messiah's mission, Isaiah the prophet compared us to wayward sheep and said, "the LORD has laid on him [Jesus] the iniquity of us all" (Isa. 53:6). Christ's death on the cross was according to God's purposes. It was not a mistake, an accident, or a miscarriage of justice.

Lostness, the condition of the sheep, is a terrible predicament. The good shepherd must die for his sheep if they are to be saved. Willingly Jesus assumed this role. Because he died and rose again, we live to discover the abundant life he promised.

Such a proposition confounded many in Jesus's audience, who decided he was mad. Why would anyone risk death to save some sheep? Only the Son of God in the flesh, consumed with passion to save the lost, would make such a sacrifice. We find our way out of darkness and judgment only by following the Good Shepherd who died for us.

Tranquility and satisfaction overflow in abundance in those who follow the Good Shepherd. Jesus's sheep share the same kind of intimacy with him that he enjoys with his Father.

To think about

- Why did Jesus use the shepherd-sheep figure of speech? Why did some hearers fail to get the point?
- What metaphors would you use to describe your relationship with Jesus? For example, complete this sentence: My relationship with Jesus is like that of . . . and . . .

Heavenly Father, how grateful I am to know Jesus as my Good Shepherd. Thank you, Jesus, for loving me and searching for me even when I go astray. Help me to trust you more fully.

Jesus, Provider of Abundant Life

John 10:7–13

Every politician running for office, every dictator seeking to cement his rule—all of them promise abundant living. They know that people respond to peace and prosperity platforms. Never mind that no one has ever been able to provide universal peace and prosperity. Generally, while millions wallow in poverty and destruction, relatively few are prosperous.

What did Jesus have in mind? What did he promise to provide? He made his promises while explaining his story about sheep, shepherds, robbers, thieves, hirelings, and wolves. Sheep could either be well cared for or savaged and lost. In that context, Jesus promised guidance, safety, and pasturage.

Here we see our world in microcosm. The world looks like a fearful battleground. Thieves, robbers, hirelings, and wolves thrive everywhere. They pose constant threats to life and limb. Despite society's best efforts, these bad guys turn up again and again with ever more devious plots and devastating weapons. No one is safe.

Paradoxically, on the other hand, Jesus declared that in the midst of all this it is possible not just to be safe, but to experience life in all its fullness. Regardless of living among those who steal, kill, and destroy, people who belong to Jesus enjoy the abundant life, because Jesus is more than sufficient to meet all of their needs.

Jesus is more than sufficient to meet our needs for good guidance. When we pay attention to his voice, we hear exactly where we are to go and what we are to do. As we follow his instructions, we learn wisdom and sound judgment; we are filled "with the knowledge of his will through all spiritual wisdom and understanding" (Col. 1:9).

Jesus is more than sufficient for our soul's nourishment. As the bread of life, the water of life, and the light of life, Jesus establishes all the values of a healthy spiritual diet. Whatever pasturage means for sheep, Jesus makes sure we have it. In Christ, "Total" means more than the contents of a cereal box. That's why we eat and drink Jesus.

Jesus is more than sufficient for whatever life brings. His promise of safety does not carry an insurance policy against suffering. In Jesus, safety means that he cares for us during our sickness, pain, sorrow, and loss. He offers relief and comfort. Because he lives in us, he joins us in our sufferings, feeling every pain and emotion that we do. He is totally adequate and trustworthy when we need him most. We are safe with him!

Enjoying life in all its fullness includes heaven, and Jesus is more than sufficient to get us there. Jesus's promise of abundant life extends to eternity when we will know what abundance really means. He gives us a foretaste now, but his love and what he has in store for us surpasses our present understanding.

Knowing the resources we own in Christ, we face the world's thieves, robbers, wolves, and hirelings without discouragement, worry, and fear. We have Jesus. He is more than enough. Because Jesus gave his life for us, God will forgive us and accept us, unfit as we are. Those who have received God's abundant provision of grace reign in life through Jesus Christ.

To think about

- Thinking about Jesus's description of the shepherd and the sheep, how would you describe abundant living?
- In what life issues do you need to tap the wealth of Jesus? How can you do this?

Lord Jesus, I confess my lack of faith. I confess trying to find answers to my needs apart from you. Thank you that you are more than sufficient to care for me.

Jesus, Friend of the Family

John 11:1–44

Jesus was born and raised in a family. He lived, worked, and worshiped with his family for thirty years until he embarked on his mission. Soon thereafter his family showed concern about his welfare, thinking he had crossed the bounds of what might be considered normality (Mark 3:31–32). Later his brothers rejected his claims of being God's Son (John 7:5). The Gospel writers do not reveal how his mother, Mary, expressed her faith in him until the end of his life.

So for about three years, Jesus enjoyed the friendship of what might be called his surrogate family: Mary, Martha, and Lazarus. In the comfort of their home, he found both physical and emotional rest. In short, they were his friends and he loved them. Their home and their friendship provided a much needed respite for Jesus from his daily spiritual warfare. At Bethany he found an oasis of faith in a desert of unbelief.

Jesus loved this family in spite of their human imperfections. He intervened when Mary and Martha squabbled (Luke 10:38–42). He put up with their complaints about his late arrival after Lazarus had died and he wept with them. Even the onlookers marveled at how much Jesus loved Lazarus. He overcame the sisters' unbelief that he could raise Lazarus and patiently led them in their commitment to him, offering them hope of life beyond the grave.

Jesus needed this family, and they needed him. This is the essence of true friendship. Ultimately, one might argue, Jesus didn't need anybody, since he came from heaven. But in the mystery of the incarnation, we see how deeply committed Jesus was to the friendship of his Bethany family.

Mary, Martha, and Lazarus looked to Jesus as the fulfillment of their messianic hopes and dreams. Among the crowds of the curious and the coterie of critics, they stood out as sincere believers in Jesus. So they offered him the best they could, not just casual hospitality but costly and risky friendship that touched Jesus's heart.

Imagine how relaxing it must have been for Jesus to settle down with them for short periods! The Gospels reveal that Jesus was under relentless pressure. Often he went away alone to pray but he also appreciated and needed the values of human families and friendship. With Mary, Martha, and Lazarus he found rest of soul and peace of mind.

True, his disciples comprised a circle of companionship for Jesus, but they were a source of constant strain. Jesus had no wife to come home to each evening for encouragement and consolation. His hometown had rejected him, so he found no refuge in Nazareth. In all of this God provided the family he needed.

Physical refreshment and emotional security are components of satisfying Christian experience. Purposeful relaxation gives us time to rest, pray, and recover. Jesus pours out his love on all of our family relationships, so that our human love for one another can help us reach the deepest levels of our spiritual needs as well.

To think about

- Why did Jesus need Mary, Martha, and Lazarus?
- In what dimensions of your family life do you need the blessings of Jesus? Why?

Thank you, heavenly Father, for the solace and comfort of family. Make me a patient, loving listener as Jesus was. May I be a minister of his grace and show his love to all of my family members.

Jesus, the Resurrection and the Life

John 11:1–27

Of all the claims that Jesus made for himself, possibly this is the most magnificent, that he is the resurrection and the life. Of course there is no reason to compare the relative merits of his claims but, nevertheless, to meet someone who says he is resurrection and life is doubtless the most stunning encounter one could have.

As the old saying goes, there is nothing more certain than death and taxes. But can there be any certainty about being raised to new life? Obviously not, if you listen to various voices from the world's religions and philosophies.

Something of the same climate of opinion prevailed in Jesus's day. For instance, the Greeks thought the whole idea of resurrection was ridiculous. Among the Jews, the Pharisees believed in a resurrection (as did Martha), but the Sadducees denied it. The Old Testament lacked clear teaching on this point, although Daniel 12:2 refers to awakening to everlasting life.

So when Lazarus died, doom rather than hope came over his sisters and friends. That's when Jesus electrified everyone by saying that he himself was resurrection and life. Jesus promised life in the face of death, hope in the face of fear and grief.

His words have consoled countless believers since he first spoke them to Mary and Martha. His promise is the staple of Christian funerals and memorial services. Because of Jesus and his resurrection, Christians know that life does not end with physical death. On the contrary, death opens the door to eternal life.

Jesus's promise of eternal life is backed by his power and his person. Because he conquered death, those who follow him are assured of resurrection and eternal life. After Christ's resurrection, Christians boldly told the world that his resurrection is the heart of Christian faith. The Greeks scoffed at the apostle Paul for declaring the resurrection. He told his judge that he was in chains because of his faith in the resurrection (Acts 23:6). Later Paul wrote that without the resurrection, our faith is worthless (1 Cor. 15:18–19). His lifelong desire was to know Christ and the power of his resurrection (Phil. 3:10).

When we meet Jesus, we meet someone who is capable of transforming death because he has life in himself. He said, "I was dead, and behold I am alive for ever and ever" (Rev. 1:18). Therefore, he will raise all his own at the last day (John 6:39–40). Jesus explained, "For just as the Father raises the dead and gives them life, even so the Son gives life to whom he is pleased to give it" (5:21).

Only in Christ do we gain such certified hope. Those who dwell in him, and in whom he dwells, possess eternal life now. Death will not separate them from their Savior. In the last day the dead in Christ will rise and enjoy heaven with him forever (1 Thess. 4:13–18).

Out of this glorious prospect arises hope, the hope that comforts and sustains us in our grief and loss.

To think about

- How did Jesus transform the gloom and despair that Mary and Martha felt because of Lazarus's death?
- In what circumstances have you found Christ's promise that he is the resurrection and the life to be most significant? Why?

Lord Jesus, you are resurrection and life. I honor, praise, and thank you for bringing me life and hope. May that hope shine through me and touch others in their grief and loss.

Jesus, Worthy of Worship

John 12: 1–19

Against the backdrop of repeated criticism and opposition, Jesus received worship at a private dinner party and on the streets of Jerusalem. We know how his story ended. To put it colloquially, the bad guys won, at least temporarily. They throttled Jesus and put an end to the worship of the upstart Galilean Prophet. But knowing this should not cloud our minds to the worship given to Jesus before his crucifixion. Although the recorded examples are few, they stand to remind us that at least some people recognized him as sent from God and therefore worthy of their worship.

We can look back doctrinally, as it were, and list all of Jesus's divine attributes, so we do not question that Jesus is fully qualified and eminently deserving of our worship. But in the days of his flesh and blood, this was not a foregone conclusion.

Curious onlookers heard many reasons for scoffing at Jesus rather than worshiping him. They knew the experts detested him and called him a blasphemer, lunatic, lawbreaker, and drunkard. On the other hand, thousands had experienced firsthand the power of his divine love as he fed them, healed them, drove out their demons, and even raised the dead. In fact a large crowd was attracted to Bethany because there Jesus had raised Lazarus from the dead.

In view of the plots on his life (11:53), the dinner party given in his honor at Bethany surely struck many as a courageous gesture. Even more astounding was Mary's dramatic, sacrificial act of worship. By crossing social and religious boundaries, she demonstrated that Jesus merited her worship. The cost of her worship was not limited to her expensive perfume. Married women simply did not uncover their heads and expose their hair to men. Of course, she may have been single, but even so she

154

performed an audacious deed of faith, courage, and worship. True worship of Jesus requires all that Mary gave to him.

Mary's lonely act stands in sharp contrast to the multitudes Jesus encountered at what we call his triumphal entry into Jerusalem. Crowds of cheering people welcomed him, hoping that he was the harbinger of peace and freedom for the Jews. While the people celebrated Jesus, the chief priests plotted how to kill him and Lazarus too, because many Jews were turning to Jesus when they heard that he had raised Lazarus from the dead.

People were praising Jesus to such an extent that the Pharisees decided the whole world was following him. When the throng joyfully praised God, the Pharisees demanded that Jesus silence them, but Jesus said if he did, the stones would cry out (Luke 19:40). The chief priests choked when the children shouted praise to Jesus in the temple, but Jesus rebuked their unbelief by reminding them that the children's cries fulfilled Psalm 8:2 (Matt. 21:15–16).

Privately and publicly, the Lord Jesus Christ fully merits our worship. Mary's open, unabashed worship at his feet is a model for our worship of Jesus, as is the cheering of the crowds in the streets. We join with heaven's throng singing, "Worthy is the Lamb, who was slain, to receive power and wealth and wisdom and strength and honor and glory and praise!" (Rev. 5:12).

To think about

- What inspired Mary's worship of Jesus? What inspired the crowd to worship him?
- What moves you to worship Jesus?

Lord Jesus, I worship you as my Lord and Savior, as my Prophet, Priest, and King. You alone are worthy. Deliver me from the praise of false gods. May I worship you in spirit and in truth.

Jesus, the Grain of Wheat

John 12:20–29

At times it seems that Jesus discouraged people deliberately from following him. When an entourage of Greeks came seeking an interview with him, he did not welcome them with traditional Middle Eastern hospitality. Of course he had no home to which to invite them, but his response to their inquiry via his disciples still appears rude.

To speculate about the reason for their request to see him is pointless, but apparently the news about Jesus's miracles had reached them. Jerusalem buzzed with hosannas when Jesus arrived, and perhaps these Greeks were among those who threw palm branches before him. Some Greeks had converted to Judaism and this group was among them, because they had come to Jerusalem to keep the Passover.

We cannot be sure about how widely the reports of Jesus's miracles, claims, and teachings had spread. Whatever their reasons, the Greeks certainly were not prepared to be rebuffed by an agricultural object lesson. Often Jesus used everyday knowledge to assert profound spiritual truths. To hear that a grain of wheat had to fall into the ground and die before it could bear fruit would probably draw a "So what else is new?" response.

But immediately Jesus threw that axiom against an entirely different background. When he said he was about to be glorified, he announced that his death was imminent. When he confessed a troubled heart, he admitted to his listeners that his cross was beckoning him. When he said that the key to eternal life was losing one's life here and now, he focused not on his immediate acceptance by the Greeks and the accolades of the crowds but on Golgotha. Therefore, in effect, Jesus said, "I am the kernel of wheat that is going to die, because if I do not die, no harvest will follow. My death is necessary for the production of a bountiful crop." To prove that Jesus was on the right track, and to authenticate his atoning death, God spoke from heaven and said that this dying grain of wheat would glorify his name.

"We would like to see Jesus," the Greeks requested. See Jesus? Look at that dying kernel of wheat. Look at this man telling you to lose your life. Look at this man agonizing over his imminent crucifixion.

We'll never know what the Greeks thought of this, but we cannot miss the implications for ourselves. "Whoever serves me must follow me" (John 12:26) means we must be like that grain of wheat and lose our lives for Jesus's sake. That is the only route to spiritual fruitfulness and eternal life.

In Jesus's response to the Greeks, we learn the profound lesson of Christian discipleship. Only death to self leads to life everlasting. Only death to self links us inextricably with Jesus and his mission.

Everything we see and hear urges us to protect our lives, to pamper and indulge ourselves, to clamor for the best things in life. To protect his followers from the lusts of the world and the pride of life, Jesus points us to his agricultural object lesson. Your flower and vegetable seeds will reveal the key to real success and prosperity, here, now, and forever.

To think about

- Why do you think Jesus treated the Greeks the way he did?
- What will it cost you to fall into the ground and die? Why are you willing to pay the cost?

Lord Jesus, thank you that you did not pander to the Greeks' curiosity and try to win them with smooth words. Your hard words strike at the heart of my own soul. Make me brave enough to be planted like a kernel of wheat.

157

Jesus, Conqueror of the World

John 16:29–33; Ephesians 1:18–21

Jesus Christ came to save the world, but the world was about to crucify him. In spite of this he told his disciples to cheer up because he had conquered the world. Did his declaration make any sense to them? Does it make any sense to us? Probably his disciples didn't understand this any more than his promise that they would find peace in the midst of violent disruptions in their lives.

For three years Jesus kept pounding into his disciples the fact that he was the world's Savior. He was giving his life for the world, even though the world hated him. He would drive out the prince of this world, the devil, and overcome the world. But now as Jesus's crucifixion was imminent, all of his spectacular promises seemed to dissolve like a melting ice-cream cone. Defeat not victory was at hand. Jesus told his disciples he was leaving and returning to his Father and that they, his believing flock, would scatter.

How could they not worry? To believe that Jesus would conquer the world sounded like pure fantasy. It still does, because on the surface the world wins and Jesus loses. To say that he is the conqueror sounds like misguided wishful thinking. Nevertheless, ever since his resurrection, believers in Jesus have staked their lives on him because he is the world's conqueror.

The apostle Paul's glorious summation of Christ's exaltation and victory energizes our faith. Jesus is Victor because God raised him from the dead and seated him at his right hand. He exerts supreme authority over all other rulers, powers, dominions, and authorities (Eph. 1:20–21). Therefore we anticipate the day when every knee will bow before Jesus the conqueror and every tongue will confess him as Lord (Phil.

2:10–11). In his revelation to the apostle John, Jesus foresees the day when he gains possession of all the world's kingdoms (Rev. 11:15).

Our faith in Jesus's ultimate victory allows us to stare down and rebuff any claims the world has on us. We are not helpless victims of blind fate. We do not suffer bad luck. We accept hard times and suffering as Jesus did, dwelling in his peace, joy, and triumph. The world tests our faith and attacks us from many angles, but we resist by building our faith and saturating ourselves with Jesus and his truths and promises. Because he has conquered the world, so will we.

As John later wrote, we overcome the world as Jesus did through our faith (1 John 5:4). We believe in Jesus, the Son of God, the One who died to save us from our sins and to deliver us from whatever the world throws at us. Everything depends on who Jesus is. By faith we say that he is strong, wise, and loving and will keep us safe.

Walking with Jesus empowers us to march boldly into the world's cauldron without fear because in Christ we are "more than conquerors" (Rom. 8:37). One day Jesus will rule the nations. "On his robe and on his thigh he has this name written: KING OF KINGS AND LORD OF LORDS" (Rev. 19:16).

To think about

- Imagine how you would have felt as one of Jesus's disciples when he told them that, even though they would be scattered, they should not worry.
- When fear and worry arise from your battles in the world's arena, how does your faith help you to overcome?

Heavenly Father, I confess my shaky faith. Sometimes I wonder if Jesus is with me. Help me to grow stronger so that I can conquer the world as he did.

Jesus, Our Commander in Chief

John 14:21–23; 15:7–10

In his last teaching session with his disciples before his crucifixion, Jesus assured them that he was the certified way to heaven and to knowledge of his Father. The disciples could not understand this, so their questions tumbled out. "How can we know the way?" Thomas asked (John 14:5). "Show us the Father," Philip demanded (v. 8).

In response, Jesus emphasized the essential nature of their walk with him. To love him was to obey him. Their loving obedience would bring them the love of the Father and the Son (v. 21).

Something about this troubled Judas (not the traitor). How would Jesus reveal himself to the world? Was Jesus abandoning his world mission for the sake of the chosen few? Jesus repeated his earlier dictum: love and obey me and my Father and I will live in you (v. 23). In other words, the unbelieving world would see Jesus in his loving, obedient followers. Therefore it is imperative that we follow our commander-in-chief's orders. If we fail here, we miss his presence, and the world does not see him living in us.

Then Jesus compared his disciples to the branches of his vine. You will bear abundant fruit, he explained, if you dwell in my love and do what I say (15:7–10). Follow my example, he said, and see how I have heeded my Father's commands and live in his love. Again, when our commander-in-chief speaks, we are compelled to obey, if we want to be prosperous fruit bearers for him.

Of course the disciples had heard their commander's words for three years, but that did not guarantee they would remember them. Therefore, Jesus promised them that the Holy Spirit would transmit his commands to them (14:26; 16:12–15).

Things work out in similar fashion for us. Christ's commands were written down and preserved for us, so that we have daily access to them. Our ignorance of his commands is inexcusable. Likewise, the Holy Spirit is our reminder and teacher. He knows our needs and he knows how to apply Christ's words to us most effectively.

Almost miraculously, it seems, the Holy Spirit takes Jesus's words and lights up our heart, soul, and mind. However, for this to happen we need disciplined exposure to his words. Once-a-week listening fails the test. Hearing good sermons helps, of course, but substantial growth in love and obedience to our commander-in-chief depends to a great extent on how much time and effort we put into small-group and personal Bible study.

Seeing Jesus as our commander-in-chief nudges us into paying careful attention to him. He is, after all, "our only Sovereign and Lord" (Jude 4). Convinced that his orders are the very best for us, we pay heed to them. The more we heed them, the more we sense his presence in us. Obedience keys our relationship with Jesus. That's the most important issue of all.

To think about

- Why were the disciples confused? How did Jesus help them understand?
- Someone has said that when you know Jesus, you know more than you know you know. How can you extend the frontiers of your knowledge of Jesus?

Heavenly Father, I confess my failure to love and obey Jesus as I should. My commitment sometimes wavers. Implant in my heart and will the supreme desire to obey you.

Jesus, Giver of a New Command

John 13:31–35; 15:11–17

From his forceful repetition of his command to love one another, we assume that Jesus prescribed this potent medicine to meet a critical need among his disciples (and his followers today). In a nutshell, for three years Jesus had loved his men, but on the eve of his cross, they were still a scrappy, fractious bunch. In the upper room they argued about who was the greatest (Luke 22:24).

At the same time, Jesus looked far down the road beyond the upper room dispute. He saw love as the critical element in the future relationships of the disciples and of all believers to come. In the absence of love, Christ's mission would have floundered from the outset. Without love, they could not achieve the unity that would speak to the world about Jesus (John 17:20–23).

The early Christians loved one another, emotionally and practically. They shared love feasts and possessions. They prayed and worshiped together. They injected into the callousness of Greece and Rome the tenderness and sacrifice that immediately stamped them as different people.

The word *love* overpowers us in Scripture, because it includes so many dimensions: God's love, Christ's love, our love for God and his Son, our love for one another, and our love for our neighbors and our enemies. Mutual love in the body of Christ includes friendship, but it also transcends friendship. Jesus laid down the model for us to follow: "Love each other as I have loved you" (15:12). To appreciate his example, we must allow our minds and hearts unencumbered range in the Prophets, Gospels, and Epistles. We must be fueled by a high-calorie diet of stories about Jesus if we are to obey his command.

Supremely, of course, his sacrificial love in dying for our sins on the cross satisfies our souls. When we love others reluctantly and with limits, the utter totality of Christ's love rebukes us immediately. In other words, if we love as Jesus does, we will not limit whom we love and how much we love.

When Jesus commands us to love, he does not mean mere human affection; he called for a radically new kind of love by which his followers respect, trust, sacrifice for, and empower one another. That's the reason his command is so much a part of the rest of the New Testament. "Love" sticks out all over the place. The apostles knew that without love everything else was a sham (1 Corinthians 13).

In his Epistle, John established love as the test by which Christians validate their faith (1 John 3:14; 4:7–8). Paul summarized the Ten Commandments and said love fulfills all of them (Rom. 13:8–10). "Live a life of love," he said, "just as Christ loved us and gave himself up for us" (Eph. 5:2).

To think about

- In light of all the parting commands Jesus might have given his disciples, why did he highlight the command to love one another?
- What are the chief obstacles to your obedience to this command? How do you deal with them?

    Lord Jesus, I confess I do not love others as you love me. I confess that some fellow believers are hard to love. Help me to love them and find ways to show them my love.

Jesus, the Way, the Truth, and the Life

John 14:1–6

In his disciples' darkest hour, Jesus pointed them to himself as the way to God, the truth about God, and the life of God. Apologists for the Christian faith have long insisted that his concise statement solidified Jesus's claim to divine uniqueness. He alone offers humanity the way to knowing God.

Since Jesus's dogmatic statement of exclusiveness, Christians have been accused of intolerance, bigotry, narrowness, obscurantism, and arrogance. How can Christians be so audacious as to insist that salvation comes through Jesus and no one else? There are two good reasons: Jesus said there is no other way to the Father (John 14:6), and the apostle Peter said the same thing (Acts 4:10–12).

However, sometimes our necessary insistence on Jesus as the only way to God has clouded our understanding of the context and application of his statement to his disciples (see John 13). In the upper room they sat stunned while Jesus washed their feet and the traitor Judas was exposed. Self-confident Peter insisted that even though everyone else might betray Jesus, he would never do such a thing. He was prepared to die for his Lord. Jesus drove a stake into Peter's heart by telling him that he would deny his Lord before the rooster crowed next morning. But wisely and lovingly Jesus lifted up Peter and pointed him to heaven.

The disciples had to learn (and so must we) that there's much more to life than the here and now. Life has an eternal dimension. Our destiny rests with the Father's house in heaven. Take your losses, if you will, but remember the best is yet to come.

Of course, such a prospect seemed highly improbable to his disillusioned, fearful disciples, so Jesus spelled out how they might attain a permanent home with him in heaven. The answer to their troubled hearts could be found in their friend Jesus. He covered all the bases in his magnificent summary of who he is. His description encompassed everything his disciples needed to know, and we too learn from him all we need to know about who he is, his mission, and our destiny.

Following Jesus, we meet God. Believing Jesus, we learn truth. Trusting him, we gain life. When we consider our poverty-stricken condition, we marvel at Christ's total competence and sufficiency. We stand under God's judgment, but Jesus takes us to God.

We need truth because we are constantly bombarded by the world's lies. We follow falsehoods, which originate with Satan, the Father of lies. All truth comes from Jesus. When we know him by faith, he dispels our spiritual ignorance and blindness. Jesus brings light to our heart, mind, and will.

We need life because we are dead in our sins. Jesus gives us life everlasting, a life of eternal abundance and wholesomeness. No longer do we suffer under the shadow of death, because Jesus conquered death and rose again.

While insisting that Jesus is the only way, we do so with humility and love so that others might see Jesus in us. They will not be won over by hard-nosed doctrine but by truth spoken in love.

To think about

- What comfort did Jesus's claim of being the only way to the Father bring to his disciples? Why?
- How has Christ's total sufficiency changed your life? In what settings do you need to be reminded of his claim?

Thank you, Lord Jesus, for bringing an end to my spiritual ignorance, death, and darkness. When my faith wavers, remind me to find all I need in you. Give me love and compassion for those who do not acknowledge your exclusive claims.

Jesus, Preexistent One

John 17:1–5, 14–26

In the upper room, just prior to his crucifixion, Jesus promised his disciples that he would prepare a place where they could be with him. Later in his prayer he revealed that he wanted his men to discover the incomparable and virtually inexpressible joy of his glory with his Father. Thoughts of his return to his preexistent glory comforted and consoled Jesus in those terrible days and hours leading up to his atoning death for our sins. How he longed for his total participation in the glories of the Godhead!

Words fail us when we try to understand something that far surpasses our intellectual competence. This is true when we think of the glory that Jesus knew before he became a human being. We find hints of this glory in Jesus's final revelation to John, after all his enemies are destroyed. In his prayer on the way to Gethsemane, Jesus simply longed not just for his return to glory, but for his faithful friends to discover glory and experience it for themselves.

The New Testament makes clear that Jesus lived before he became Jesus of Nazareth. Although he entered our world physically via human birth, this was not his beginning. Before time began he was with God. He was the Godhead's agent of creation. Jesus was fully, completely, totally, and absolutely God from eternity past. He is the Alpha and the Omega, the beginning and the consummation of all time and history.

The apostle Paul aptly summarized the staggering fact that Jesus willingly, and for our sakes, relinquished his preexistent glory and became a human person. Not only so, but Jesus took the role of a humble, obedient slave and died—not an ordinary death, but death on a cross (Phil. 2:5–11).

The gulf between preexistent glory and ignominious death on a cross is beyond human understanding. Therefore, even though we lack a rational explanation, we know that our response must be praise, honor, and worship in light of Jesus's power and dominion. Anything less betrays our insolent, overweening pride.

Bible scholars find in various Old Testament stories evidence of Jesus's work before his incarnation, primarily as "the angel of God" and "the angel of the Lord." We see him as the one who spoke to Hagar in her distress (Gen. 16:7–12), as Abraham's visitor (Genesis 18) and the one who stopped Abraham from killing Isaac (22:11–12), and as the one who saved the men from Nebuchadnezzar's fiery furnace (Dan. 3:24–28). All of these stories reveal the Lord as compatible with the character of Jesus in the four Gospels. They also fit the image of Jesus interceding for his own after his return to glory. While we contemplate the glory he shared, shares now, and will share forever, we gain some insight into our own personal destiny as well.

The relationship we begin with Jesus when we confess him as Lord and Savior continues forever. How humbling to think that Jesus, knowing us as he does, wants us to be with him to share his glory!

To think about

- What does Jesus's prayer in John 17 tell you about his relationship with his disciples?
- How can you increase your anticipation of eternal glory with Jesus?

O God, how limited is my understanding of eternal truth! How amazing that Jesus left you to come here to save me! Grant me new insights into the glory of my Savior and build my security in him.

Jesus, Protector of His Own

John 17:6–19

On the way to Gethsemane, Jesus talked to his Father about his fearful, disillusioned disciples. He asked God to protect them from division, defection, and the devil. In his prayer we learn what was uppermost in his mind as he prepared to leave them. Jesus knew that his men had to be protected if his mission was to succeed. God alone could do this for the team he had given to Jesus. During his time on earth, Jesus had kept them, except for Judas, and now it was up to his Father to do the rest.

"Protect them," Jesus prayed, "so that they may be one as we are one" (John 17:11). He asked for protection from division and disunity, which had already ruptured his team. Fighting over the chief places, they were hardly "one." Their unity, in fact, would be the key to their witness to the world (v. 21). Jesus wanted his team to live in the same kind of intimate fellowship that he enjoyed with his Father. If they did, multitudes would be convinced that Jesus had come from heaven.

Jesus had told his disciples that their love for one another was crucial. Unity was so important that the apostle Paul fiercely challenged the malcontents who were splitting the church at Corinth. It was so critical in the early church that God struck down Ananias and Sapphira for lying and jeopardizing unity and trust.

We learn much from Jesus by considering what he did not ask from God. For example, he did not pray for his disciples' protection from persecution; he told them to expect it. He did not pray for their safety, good health, prosperity, and long life. Rather, he asked God to protect them from defection and desertion (vv. 11–12). Spiritual safety, not physical safety, was foremost in his mind. They could not forget the treachery of

168

Judas. Jesus knew that desertion under fire would become a serious problem. Therefore, above everything else, his followers must stand true, no matter what.

Disunity and betrayal have always caused disruption and weakness in the body of believers. During his ministry, the apostle Paul suffered because of defectors.

Long ago, when some nine thousand missionaries fled the Communists in China, Christians rallied to pray for their safety. One of the mission's leaders reminded them that the missionaries' physical survival was not the key issue. Rather, it was their spiritual survival and well-being that was crucial.

Jesus asked his Father to protect his men from the devil, the source of disunity and defection (v. 15). Satan loves to sidetrack the church into fighting the wrong battles. He attacks with lies, innuendoes, gossip, and slander. If the evil one cannot subvert our faith, he will attempt to disrupt our churches with partisan conflicts, urging us to believe gossip, suspect each other's motives, and believe the worst about fellow Christians.

The perils of division, discouragement, dissension, and defection loomed before the disciples. God protects us as we pray for each other in the same way that Jesus prayed for his own.

To think about

- If you had been walking with Jesus to the Garden of Gethsemane, what prayer requests would you have made of him?

- How do your prayers match those of Jesus when you petition God for friends, family, missionaries, and Christians worldwide?

  God, I confess that selfish prayers predominate in my mind. Health and safety are really big issues. Help me to give priority to my spiritual welfare and that of others.

Jesus, Affirmer of Marriage

Matthew 5:31–32; 19:1–12; John 2:1–11

Jesus never married; however, he grew up in a family that held to the highest standards of married life. He observed Mary and Joseph for a long time and knew how Joseph had preserved Mary's reputation. Their love, caring, and fidelity to their marriage vows were stamped on Jesus's mind as a boy, a youth, and a young man.

Also Jesus carried into his life and ministry a profound knowledge of and respect for God's ancient laws regarding marriage. He involved himself freely in the social customs of his day and rejoiced when friends and loved ones entered marriage. Distinguished guests and prominent teachers were invited to join the marriage festivities that lasted a week.

Jesus happened to be at a wedding when disaster struck. The hosts ran out of wine. He saved the day by turning gallons of water into wine. What striking evidence not only of his power but also of his care for a hapless couple and the host family!

Later on, his critics assaulted him on the issue of divorce, another matter of contentious debate. In this setting, Jesus reaffirmed God's will that the marriage relationship should be kept inviolate. Marriage vows were made to be kept, not broken. God instituted marriage for the blessing and happiness of the human race. Breaking God's intention courts disaster.

Divorce has become commonplace in Western culture, even among Christians. Scholars debate the Jesus teaching about marriage. Did he allow divorce under any circumstances?

Generally, it is safe to say, the pendulum has swung from strict adherence to the Jesus way toward a much more relaxed attitude. If we are serious about walking as Jesus walked, we will not casually divorce our marriage partner for our own lusts or convenience. Anyone contemplating divorce must be fully persuaded that God's Holy Spirit permits such action. The Jesus way demands that we do everything possible to protect our marriage. Living as Jesus lived does not permit us to exchange marriage partners just because it's legal to do so. Our children, and our Lord, deserve better.

To think about

- Why did Jesus insist on the sanctity of the marriage relationship?
- If your marriage has been stressful to the breaking point, what can you do to restore it to a Jesus-honoring relationship? If your marriage is not under stress, what can you do to make your relationship even stronger?

O God, I need your blessing on my marriage.
Forgive my selfishness and crankiness. Keep sin
from spoiling our relationship. My marriage is
supposed to be a picture of Christ and his church.
Show me what that requires of me.

Jesus, Comforter of the Bereaved

Luke 7:11–17; John 11:17–44

Death stings, hurts, separates loved ones, and smashes hopes. Empty places at the table represent gaping holes in our lives that are hard to fill. Never to be restored is the companionship of many years, broken by death. Grief attacks us in waves that seem as though they will never subside.

We don't know how often Jesus confronted death, grief, and loss during his thirty years of community life. In his day, however, average life expectancy was short. Reading between the lines of his story, we assume that his father, Joseph, died fairly early, perhaps when Jesus was a teenager. That hurt Jesus. Without specific details, we accept Isaiah's prophetic picture of Jesus—a man acquainted with grief and sorrow (Isa. 53:3).

Often Jesus healed people with chronic diseases, and he raised the dead. One day he was so touched by the sight of a grieving mother on the way to bury her only son that he interrupted her and the crowd of mourners. Jesus did not know these people. He could have allowed the funeral procession to pass by, which is what would have been expected. Instead, he stopped the grieving mother and told her to stop crying. Then, with his disciples and the mourners watching in utter amazement, Jesus did the unthinkable. He touched the coffin and spoke to the corpse. The young man got up, and Jesus gave him to his mother.

With thoughtful, loving action and words, Jesus brought new life, hope, and comfort to the forlorn widow. Had she remained childless, she was doomed to poverty and despair.

Later on, Jesus's dear friend Lazarus died, and Jesus cried in sorrow. The surviving sisters, Mary and Martha, knew that Jesus could have prevented their tragedy. Overcome with grief,

172

they gently chided him, whereupon Jesus comforted them by affirming that he is resurrection and life. Those who believe in him will never die. Then he brought Lazarus back to life.

When we grieve the loss of loved ones, we turn to Jesus and find that he comes to us just as he did to the widow of Nain and to Mary and Martha. He conquered death and he lives to revive our depressed, sorrowful hearts and spirits. His heart is open to our cries. We must not fear bringing our tears and losses to him.

As we follow Jesus and observe how he comforted people in distress, we are careful to attend to the needs of those who mourn. We may feel awkward or shy, not knowing what to say, but our presence speaks volumes. Mourners who know that we love and care, and that we pray for them, receive strength. We must not forget their tears but minister to them in their daily battle with their sorrow. Bringing comfort can be as simple and as profound as standing by, holding someone's hand, and saying a prayer. The main thing is to be there. We can be Jesus to those who grieve, reminding them that Jesus is our resurrection and life. He is the ultimate comforter of those who mourn.

To think about

- Why did Jesus break custom and religious rules to comfort a widow he did not know?
- What personal inhibitions do you have to rise above to comfort someone you know who grieves?

Thank you, Jesus, for caring for the widow and weeping for Lazarus. Show me how to be a comforter like you were and are. Help me to point mourners to you.

Jesus, Liberator from the Perils of Wealth

Matthew 6:19–21; Luke 9:58; 12:13–21; 18:18–25; 21:1–4

Money was a common subject of Jesus's teaching. Many people think that money is a dangerous trap for the rich, and it is, but we may forget that the poor are also hungry for money. Money can become an idol for poor and rich alike. That's the reason Jesus talked so much about it.

In a money-hungry world, it's hard to talk about the perils of wealth. Instead, our culture entices us with the attractiveness of wealth. Our culture promises that wealth brings success, happiness, prominence, power, and freedom from worry about where our next meal comes from. Money can buy anything and anyone, so get all the money you can and relax and enjoy it.

No longer are millionaires a rare species in the United States, but in ancient Palestine, where Jesus lived, poverty, not wealth, was the rule of the day. So Jesus lived and taught in a society that closely resembles poverty-stricken people in most of our contemporary world. Sure, there were a few rich people, like the man who wanted to follow Jesus but was not willing to sell all that he had. Jesus told a story about a stupid, wealthy farmer who kept on building bigger and bigger barns, without a thought for his own mortality.

Jesus surrendered a reasonably comfortable life after thirty years and became an itinerant evangelist, living off the land, not in sumptuous hotels. He shunned all the accoutrements of wealth, confessing that even the animals had a more secure existence than he had. He told his disciples to live a Spartan life and not to bother packing many provisions when they went on mission trips.

Above all, Jesus said, we waste our time if we worry about money and about the basics money provides. Why should we worry about money when God takes care of sparrows?

Such statements shocked his contemporaries, who thought the righteous should be rich. Didn't God tell the Israelites he would bless them if they obeyed him? Such was the Old Testament economy, but Jesus turned it upside down when he said the poor are blessed. He praised a poor widow who gave her last penny to the temple.

To the poor caught in a hopeless economic noose, Jesus offered a better way. Stop striving to be rich in money. Instead, be rich in faith and hope in the living God who knows all your needs. Jesus demands that we stop grasping for more money and that we live modestly and give generously. Liberating us from the perils of wealth is one of the best things Jesus does for us. As we follow in his steps, not only will we talk biblically about money, we will live as Jesus did.

To think about

- Summarize Jesus's teachings about wealth and money.
- Is his teaching realistic for your life? Why or why not?

Heavenly Father, you give me all I need, yet I confess to wanting more. I want to be comfortable, living safely above the poverty line. Help me to keep my eyes on Jesus, not on my bank accounts, so I can give generously and sacrificially.

Jesus, Our Model of Patience

Matthew 20:20–28; Mark 9:14–19; Luke 19:41–44; John 21:15–23

Everyone concedes that patience is a virtue, yet we all succumb to impatience virtually every day. Simple things, like standing in the supermarket checkout line or waiting for a freight train to pass, test our patience. Worse, we get impatient with our best friends, spouse, and children.

Of course nothing good comes from impatience. In fact it's very destructive. Israel's ancient King Saul lost his throne because he could not wait for the prophet Samuel to arrive to make the offering. Disciples and friends of Jesus were impatient with him because he refused to play the role of king and liberator that they expected.

Probably as Jesus grew up, he lived with impatient siblings. His patience no doubt was tried many times when he was making a chair and could not get the rungs to fit properly. However, he never lost his cool. He needed the tests of family life and carpentry to prepare him for tests of his patience later on.

If he had been impatient with his heavenly Father's plan, he could have succumbed to Satan's offer of ruling the world's kingdoms without following the road of suffering on the cross. He could have been impatient when the crowds followed him for the miracles without accepting his message. He could have lost his temper when his disciples failed to heal a sick boy. He could have exploded when his disciples argued about who was the chief among them.

Instead, Jesus took the high road. He never quit on his disciples and friends, in spite of their limited understanding. He took charge of his last Passover feast in the upper room and patiently explained the keys to his disciples' future success (John 14–16). After his resurrection, Jesus patiently brought Peter back to his life's calling and agreed to Thomas's demand to see the nail prints in his hands and the spear wound in his body.

Whatever the test, Jesus met it with equanimity. Yes, he got angry with the money changers in the temple. Sin really upset him and he let his critics know they were headed for certain doom unless they repented. But Jesus patiently plodded up and down the hillsides of Galilee, teaching the people, despite their limited response. Even under the injustice and provocations of his accusers, patiently Jesus refused to call down God's wrath on them. Life's irritations and interruptions that cause us to explode pale into insignificance in light of what Jesus endured without protest.

Patient faith is our calling as it was for Jesus. Injunctions to be patient pack the letters of Paul, James, Peter, and the book of Hebrews.

Walking obediently with Jesus, we grow stronger in patience, and it is not an easy road. It comes through tribulation. Looking to Jesus, we find the right and best way to handle irritations large and small with grace and patience.

To think about

- If you had to face what Jesus did, what would upset you the most? Why?
- Think of recent examples when you have lost your patience. What could you have done differently?

Lord Jesus, I confess I fall short in patience. Little things bother me. Temper is a problem. Help me to relax and trust you. May you conquer my impatience.

Jesus the Vine

John 15:1–9

One sturdy grapevine produces an abundant harvest. When Jesus compared himself to a vine, he used an adjective that would never have occurred to a vinedresser. By saying he was the "true" vine, he touched a sensitive issue. God chose ancient Israel to be his fruitful vine (Isa. 5:1–7), but his people turned out to be a false vine worthy of judgment because it "yielded only bad fruit" (v. 2).

Jesus intends for his followers to produce much fruit because they are linked to the true source of spiritual success. As branches, their vital union with Jesus guarantees fruitfulness. For Christ's vineyard to succeed in his purposes, God, the divine vinedresser, prunes the vine's branches. He accomplishes this by the power of his Word.

In this passage in John, Jesus asserts seven times that the key to spiritual productivity is remaining in him. He also stated the obvious: failure to abide in him leads to barrenness.

What does *remain* mean? Synonyms such as *dwell* and *abide* seem too passive. Actively, Jesus calls us to remain united with him. That means I must keep on growing in him.

Of course, after hearing their Lord's command to remain in him, the disciples did not do so but abandoned Jesus to his crucifixion. Not until they were empowered by the Holy Spirit after his resurrection did they continue their walk with him.

Our choices may not be as agonizing as theirs, but we must choose to remain in Jesus and to keep on growing as his fruit-bearing branches. To remain in the true vine brings risks as well as rewards. The unbelieving world makes clinging to the true vine an uncomfortable business. Perhaps that's the reason Jesus repeated his promise seven times.

Jesus fingered the primary issue. To what, or to whom, do we choose to give ourselves—to Jesus or something else? "Remain in me," he said, implying that we have other choices. Saying yes to Jesus, the true vine, means saying no to false vines that yield only bitter fruit. We make our basic choice to follow Jesus as Lord and Savior; then we work out the implications of our commitment in determining our ambitions, loves, and dreams.

"Stay with me," Jesus says, in effect, "and I promise you will not be shortchanged, because I will stay with you." Each time he commanded his disciples to remain in him, he promised to remain in them. That is the heart of the matter: the resurrected Jesus living in us. His presence guarantees the fruitful life we desire.

The sustaining life of Jesus, the true vine, courses through his branches. We receive spiritual nourishment from him. We grow strong from his words, our prayers, our worship, and our fellowship with other branches. To remain in him requires energy, discipline, courage, and faith. Keep on growing in Jesus and you will glorify him with your abundant harvest—the fruit of godly character produced by the Holy Spirit (Gal. 5:22–23).

To think about

- Why was it helpful for Jesus to compare himself to a vine?
- What have been your most productive steps to fruitfulness for Jesus?

Thank you, Lord Jesus, for giving me the privilege of an intimate relationship with you. I want to be your fruitful branch. Thank you for living in me all my days, the good ones and the bad ones.

Jesus, Our Model of Humility

John 5:41; 8:50; 13:1–17; Philippians 2:5–11

For most people, humility ranks last in the list of worth-while aspirations. It's assumed that to be humble means taking the lowest position and doing the most menial tasks, being willing to be stepped on so someone else can get ahead.

But when we read the Jesus stories, we are struck with a shocking paradox. The most powerful person of all time was the most humble. Jesus healed the sick, fed the hungry, freed demon-possessed people, and calmed vicious storms. He raised the dead. He had legions of angels at his disposal. But at every success we never see his head swelling.

Satan appealed to pride when he offered Jesus the world's kingdoms and when he asked him to use his power to turn stones to bread, but Jesus humbly refused. He never let the accolades of the crowds go to his head. He never bowed to popular sentiment. Humbly he accepted whatever people gave to him and his disciples.

Not only did Jesus teach that humility is the way to bless-ing, he also demonstrated it supremely when he took the towel and basin and washed his disciples' feet (John 13:1–17). This was the most demeaning role he could take. At that last meal he warned his disciples about the perils of pride.

Following that, he faced his critics at his trials and he steadfastly refused to use his divine powers against them. We see Jesus accepting with humility the lies of false witnesses. We see him humbly taking the scourging and mockery, the taunts of his accusers, and the jeers of the crowd. For this he was prepared when he left heaven's glory and became a servant until death.

180

Nothing offends God as much as human pride. The Tower of Babel was a monument to human pride and God destroyed it. Ancient kings paid dearly for taking credit for their achievements. Failure to acknowledge God as God brought certain disaster. When Pharaoh of Egypt refused to take orders from God, his country suffered grievously and his army perished in the Red Sea.

These lessons of history fail to make a dent in the thinking of our popular culture. We seem obsessed with being the best. Parents force children to follow rigid training, hoping the children will rise to the top athletically or academically and satisfy their pride. To become number one in business, sports, politics, medicine, or any other field is something of a national mania.

When we decide to follow Jesus, we repress our pride and take the low road, however difficult it may be. We make a strong faith statement that in the end humility is far better for us. Walking the Jesus walk means standing up to our culture and refusing to seek privileges and positions. We will not tramp on people so we can be number one. We will not be like the Pharisees, seeking the "most important seats in the synagogues" (Matt. 23:6). We will not try to impress others with our acts of devotion (Luke 18:9–14).

To think about

- What stands out in your mind as the supreme example of Jesus's humility? Why does this impress you?
- When pride assails you, how can you take the low road with Jesus?

Lord Jesus, I confess my insufferable pride. Teach me what it means to be humble as you were. Help me to take the lowest place graciously, with thanksgiving.

Jesus, Our Source of Peace

John 14:1, 27; 16:31–33

Evidence for the elusiveness of personal peace abounds. Fear, anxiety, illness, and disappointment gnaw at our souls like so many rats in the corncrib. Panaceas for our lack of peace pervade our culture as well. Selling peace is big business because of the huge toll that stress exacts.

When we turn to Jesus as our source of peace, a paradox confronts us immediately. He offered peace to his disciples, but the scene at the Last Supper smacked more of fear than peace. He exposed Judas and told Peter that he also would deny him (John 13:25–38). Nothing was left for them to cling to, except Jesus. In spite of the darkness, Jesus told them to set their troubled hearts at rest and banish their fears, because his parting gift to them was peace (14:1, 27).

His men, in spite of what they had seen and heard of Jesus, still looked for peace in worldly, temporal terms. Peace for them meant release from Rome and the establishment of Messiah's kingdom. Jesus disabused them of this notion and explained that his peace was unlike anything their world had to offer. His stark delineation of two sources of peace—his and the world's—makes our choice unambiguous.

His disciples had more than Jesus's words to live by. They had witnessed peace in Jesus in a multitude of peace-robbing circumstances. Jesus was at peace with himself because he knew where he came from, what his mission was, and where he was going. His powerful self-image paved the way for his peace in the midst of criticism by religious authorities, terrible accusations, character assassinations, his family's misunderstanding, attacks by the devil, and the daily grind of preaching and reaching out to the hopeless rejects of society. Daily he replenished his peace at the wells of meditation and prayer with his heavenly Father. All of this could not have escaped the notice of his disciples.

Finally, in the upper room Jesus washed their feet with equanimity and then calmly walked to Gethsemane toward betrayal, arrest, trial, and crucifixion. Peace radiated from Jesus, and he offered this kind of peace to his men and to all who trust him.

It's no wonder, then, that the New Testament writers seized the peace of Christ as the centerpiece of their greetings and benedictions. Christ's peace distinguished the early Christians from the crowd. His peace saturated their souls when persecution came and scattered them. His peace prevailed when they were imprisoned and condemned to the stake. They found what we too can discover, that Jesus living in us conquers our troubles.

Also peace was the cornerstone of their theology. Peace with God comes only through his forgiveness, which is attainable because Jesus died for us. Our assurance of forgiveness through Christ opens the door to peace. This peace is not a product to be bottled and sold. Peace is a person, our living Lord and Savior Jesus Christ.

To think about

- What did Jesus mean when he offered his peace to his disciples?
- Under what circumstances do you find Jesus's peace to be your significant resource?

Thank you, Father, that you sent Jesus to be my peace. When I am troubled and distressed, make Jesus strong to me. May my life show his peace to others as well.

Jesus, Gentle Servant

Matthew 12:14–23

It's curious that when Matthew chose an Old Testament prophecy to portray the essence of Jesus's character and his style of work, he selected Isaiah's prophecy concerning the Persian ruler Cyrus (Isa. 42:1–4; 45:1). Isaiah made clear that Cyrus was God's servant. As ancient conquerors go, he was not cruel and vindictive.

Matthew's choice of context is also instructive. If there was a time when Jesus could have blown his top, it was when the Pharisees attacked him for eating and healing on the Sabbath, thus boldly violating their standards of righteousness. Consequently, they plotted to kill him.

Jesus simply withdrew from the conflict and kept on healing the sick, while admonishing them not to talk about what he had done. Jesus's response to attacks and murderous plots perfectly fit Isaiah's prophetic picture of him. He was God's gentle Servant, refusing to retaliate and crush his enemies.

God chose Jesus to be his Servant, not a prideful overlord. Even though Jesus came from heaven with all the necessary credentials of deity, he humbly assumed the role and character of a servant.

Once here, Jesus received God's highest affirmation—"my beloved"—at his baptism and transfiguration. On those occasions the Holy Spirit came on him and completely empowered his life and ministry. In the end, he offered himself on the cross by the Holy Spirit and he was raised from the dead by the Holy Spirit.

Having authenticated Jesus's deity, Matthew via Isaiah went on to describe how Jesus carried out his mission. He taught justice as the heart of God's nature and his desire for the nations. At the same time, he did not strive and shout in the streets like a demagogue. The word Matthew used for "cry out" also was used to describe, variously, barking dogs, cawing crows, obstreperous drunks, and rowdy theater audiences. Jesus simply turned away from such antics and refused to scream and shout and demand his own way.

The prophet chose two other vivid metaphors—the crushed reed and the smoking flax or wick—to illustrate Christ's gentle spirit. The reed might barely stand and the wick may be giving its last flickers of light, but Jesus did not and does not and will not stomp on the reed or pinch the wick. The reed and the wick represent people who need Christ's encouragement, joy, peace, satisfaction, and purpose in life.

Contrary to other rulers, Jesus did not treat the weak with contempt. Rather, he helps and restores them to vitality and wholeness. His gentleness replaced despair with hope.

Isaiah looked far down the road of history and saw God's servant bringing justice, peace, and hope to the nations. In due course, Jesus will accomplish this. He will return and establish his glorious reign of righteousness.

How distinctive was the way Jesus conducted himself! The Creator, Sustainer, and Savior of the world took the gentle road, not the ruthless road, to establish his kingdom. He wins our hearts because he is gentle. His followers must emulate him, gently touching the bruised reeds and flickering wicks of this world.

To think about

- Why is Isaiah's prophecy of Jesus's acts so countercultural?
- What steps can you take to be a gentle servant in your family, workplace, church, and community?

Thank you, Lord Jesus, for being the great encourager and bringing hope to those who are on the verge of quitting. Make me an instrument of your peace and hope to those who need to know you.

Jesus, Savior of the Fallen

Luke 7:36–50; John 4:1–26

It surprises us that the stories of Jesus include his encounters with fallen women. They were despised in his day just as they are in ours. With all the people whom Jesus helped, why did he take the time and trouble to interact with loose women and treat them with respect?

Obviously, he wanted to say something to his disciples, the self-righteous Pharisees, and to us. Simon the Pharisee was dumbfounded when a loose woman anointed Jesus. His disciples were shocked when they saw him conversing with a fallen woman by a well. They squirmed because custom and religion demanded that they avoid such people. But Jesus turned their world upside down.

Challenging the prevailing attitudes and behaviors, Jesus brought life and hope and forgiveness to those who languished in their sins. When the outraged Simon berated Jesus for allowing a local whore to touch him, Jesus rebuked him, taught him a lesson about forgiveness, and promptly forgave the woman's sins.

The woman at the well was astonished by Jesus's claims and thought he was a free ticket to water. Patiently he led her into a self-revelation of her background and showed her what the real issue was in her life. The fallen woman ran off to town and announced that the man at the well knew her past. Hearing her testimony, the Samaritans invited him to stay and many believed. The fallen woman was the key to salvation in her village.

Nathaniel Hawthorn's novel *The Scarlet Letter* shocked many people when it was published in 1850 because his plot concerned an unmarried woman who had become pregnant and refused to identify her lover. As a result, she was condemned to wear the red letter *A* the rest of her life.

Stories of women becoming pregnant outside of marriage are commonplace now, not just in fiction but in life. There is no shock value in revealing that a single woman is going to have a baby or that women and men divorce and remarry regularly. Our culture simply accepts this, unlike the nineteenth-century folks in Salem, Massachusetts.

When Jesus offered to lift the yoke of heavy burdens—including scandalous behaviors—he showed what he meant by standing up to the self-righteous and giving his hand to the fallen. His critics pointed to such associations to smear his name. Certainly no true prophet of God would go near a fallen woman.

Jesus confounded his critics and showed us what it means to love the unlovely. He refused to bow to those who rejected the fallen as unworthy of anyone's time or attention. If we profess to walk as he walked, we must radically change how we think about and treat the fallen of our time and culture: prostitutes, addicts, AIDS patients, prisoners, and the homeless and exploited here and around the world. Many Christian agencies would welcome our participation—not just our money but also our time and our skills.

To think about

- Why did Jesus associate with disreputable people?
- What makes you uncomfortable about helping people generally despised by society?

God, forgive me for not caring about the fallen and for thinking that they might somehow contaminate me. Stir my concern for them, so they can see Jesus and his love in me.

Jesus, Seeker of the Lost

Luke 15; 19:1–10

When news reports tell us that a lost hiker in a remote mountain wilderness has been found, we rejoice. Fear grips us when our children disappear for just a few minutes in a crowded shopping mall. The ubiquitous "child missing" posters testify to one of the most depressing aspects of our culture. Regularly Amber alerts summon law enforcement officials into action.

Probably very few children got lost when Jesus was growing up. His parents lost him in Jerusalem one day and they panicked as any parent would. They found him and rebuked him, not knowing that even as a twelve-year-old he sensed a higher calling from God. But this was a rare exception in their day. People knew where their children were in uncrowded Palestine.

Of course, when the Prodigal Son ran off, he was lost to his father for a time (Luke 15:11–32). Jesus told this story so we would always keep the door open and never lose hope when people turn away from us. Also he told it to illustrate his own mission of seeking and saving the lost.

Being lost was a big deal to Jesus because he was consumed by compassion for people whose spiritual shepherds had betrayed them. He compared Israel to a wandering flock of sheep with no one to care for them. To Jesus, being lost meant more than a temporary absence from home. In his terms, being lost carried eternal consequences.

People were lost because they had strayed from God's good and perfect will. They had disobeyed their Creator and botched their lives. Being lost meant having no purpose now and no hope for the future. Jesus warned of being lost eternally in hell, cut off from God's love.

188

Being lost means being separated from loved ones. It also means trying to live independently of our supreme Lover in heaven. Jesus pointed the way back to God through repentance and faith. He actually cared for and sought lost people. He knew the stakes were high, so he condensed his mission to seeking, finding, and saving the lost.

The word *lost* in this spiritual sense has disappeared from some of our religious vocabulary. We must regain the powerful imagery behind what it means to be lost. The consequences of judgment and condemnation must seize our hearts, attitudes, and actions.

Just as Jesus sent his disciples to seek and to save the lost, so he commissions his followers today to do the same. Our hearts must bleed for the lost as his did.

To think about

- Why did Jesus tell three stories, recorded in Luke 15, about being lost and found?
- What demands and what hope do you find in these stories?

Lord Jesus, I confess my lack of compassion for the lost. Fill me with your zeal and love to seek the lost and bring them to you.

Jesus, Hope for the Hopeless

Matthew 15:21–28; Luke 4:18–19; 8:43–48; John 5:1–15

Hopeless, helpless people of all stripes populate the earth's landscapes, though they may fall out of sight behind the gleaming skyscrapers of our metropolises or disappear in the teeming villages of Africa, Asia, and Latin America. Their stories, however, have been recorded on pages and pages of newsprint and reels and reels of videotape.

We get so used to their plight that we carry on, blissfully absorbed in our interests, jobs, families, investments, homes, careers, vacations, and health clubs. On our occasional forays into our cities, we encounter panhandlers with disdain. When they knock on our church doors, we struggle with how to respond. Our governments and social agencies talk about providing safety nets for the hopeless, and, indeed we are blessed by multitudes of welfare services and Christian missions.

When Jesus was growing up, nobody cared for hopeless outcasts, lepers, cripples, widows, and everyone else rejected as "sinners." Jesus enjoyed a certain measure of security as a carpenter, but he could not escape noticing the sufferings of hopeless people who had no one to care for them.

When he began to preach, he announced that he was God's fulfillment of Isaiah's prophecy to bring Good News to the poor and the prisoners. As his prophetic mission exploded throughout the towns and villages, hopeless, helpless sufferers flocked to hear him. They hung on his words and his touch because he offered them hope and a chance to join God's new kingdom and be liberated from sin and oppression.

Jesus did not attack the causes of their stark conditions. Rather, he said that in him they would find relief and salvation.

190

He offered people a distinctive yoke, not another yoke of oppression but the yoke of freedom in a faith relationship with him. He replaced their despair with hope. Time and again he walked and talked with them, bringing healing and encouragement to those who had no other available remedies.

Jesus touched the untouchables of his day. He loved the unlovable. If we are to walk the Jesus way, we must find ways to give the helpless both material and spiritual aid, comfort, and hope. Often helpless people confront us: panhandlers, people needing food and rent money, those requiring good medical care, legal assistance, tutoring, and decent jobs. Single parents may come to us seeking care for their children as well as prayer and spiritual guidance.

As we listen to Jesus, we may grow increasingly uncomfortable with our comfortable situation. We must become generous in our giving and get used to taking risks in relationships with the hopeless. If necessary, we'll get tired and dirty too. Being Jesus to the helpless and hopeless will be costly in terms of pride, money, and energy, but it is the example he set for us.

To think about

- What risks did Jesus take to reach out to hopeless, helpless people?
- Why is it scary and costly to move out of our comfort zone for the sake of hopeless, helpless people?

Lord, touch me with the love and compassion that you had for the hopeless. Show me what it means to bring them hope and healing in you.

Jesus, the Example of Self-Denial

John 12:23–26; Philippians 2:5–11

Self-denial is basic to the character of Jesus. No one ever accused him of seeking his own needs before anyone else's. His coming to earth in human form and yielding himself as a crucified servant was the epitome of self-denial. He gave up heaven's glory for agony on the cross.

We have no stories of Jesus's self-denial as a youth and young man. However, for eighteen of his thirty years, he denied himself access to heaven's privileges. From age twelve Jesus was aware that he was about his Father's business, yet he never bragged about his superiority and he accepted willingly the role of a carpenter.

When the time was ripe, Jesus began to teach and heal without any show of pomposity. He denied himself the normal channels of power and influence. Rather, he told the religious leaders, whose authority and recognition were ordinarily deemed necessary for acceptance, that they needed to repent.

Jesus denied himself anything close to first-class accommodations when he traveled. He lived a simple, hand-to-mouth existence. No power lunches for him, no prime-time media exposure. Nothing in the record indicates that he ever vaunted his power or used it to benefit himself.

Repeatedly Jesus made clear that self-denial was the heart of his mission. How incredible it must have seemed to his disciples when he told them that he must go to Jerusalem to die! Even harder was the idea that they, too, had to deny themselves and take up their crosses. Family relationships had to take second place, if necessary, as they served the Lord

At the crucial moment when he arrived in Jerusalem, Jesus did not ride through the gates on a stallion; he rode on a donkey. Thus the King of Kings showed that those who enter his kingdom must likewise take the low road of self-denial. Pride and the desire to be honored and pampered must yield to sacrifice and pain.

Of course self-denial has never been the popular road to triumphal success. After the cheering crowds welcomed him to Jerusalem, they turned on Jesus at his trial and screamed for his blood. In a supreme expression of self-denial, Jesus allowed himself to be crucified. For Jesus, self-denial was painfully more than a nice sermon. He walked the talk. Denying self, Jesus suffered humiliation, scourgings, spitting, nails, and a spear.

If we propose to grow in our love for Jesus, we cannot dodge the bullet of self-denial. This might mean refusing to take a higher paying job if the job requires some ethical shortcuts. It might mean spending less for a vacation to help support a missionary. It might mean losing face for the sake of saying a prayer before one's co-workers. Whatever the case, there is no other way to follow Jesus and to enter his kingdom.

To think about

- In how many different ways did Jesus exemplify self-denial?
- How can you squelch our culture's pressure to focus on self?

Thank you, Lord Jesus, for showing me what self-denial means. When I want to satisfy my selfish desires, speak to me about the cost of following you, no matter what that may be.

Jesus, Antidote to Unholy Separatism

Mark 2:13–20

The Jewish community of Jesus's day understood clearly Moses's instructions about how to treat outsiders (aliens) fairly. Their rights were protected by Mosaic law. The Israelites were to take aliens in and offer them favorable living conditions if they decided to stay. This was truly a novel idea in the world at large, where it was popularly accepted that the majority ruled. Nothing compelled the surrounding nations to extend charity and justice to impoverished victims of another race, religion, or nationality.

For many reasons, by the time Jesus arrived on the scene, the people had gradually tightened the noose around Gentile outsiders. This was not done through economics or politics but through religion by building higher and higher walls of separation between themselves and ungodly Gentiles. Any person who transgressed the restrictions was viewed as contaminated and therefore cut off from God.

Into this muddy mess came Jesus with such shocking behavior that he was thought to be unclean and unfit to claim to be God's Son. Whenever he stepped over the line and rubbed shoulders with outsiders, he was roundly condemned. He could not possibly be a prophet. Holy men did not do such things.

Even more revolutionary was his statement that outsiders were the very ones he came to save. They would have a place in God's future kingdom (Matt. 21:31). People who rejected them and crossed the street to avoid passing close to them would not enter the kingdom. The first would be last and the last first.

The rigid caste system, based on race and religion, had to be smashed. Courageously Jesus confronted the perpetrators

194

to show that there is a wideness in God's mercy that the clean, the healthy, the smug, and the self-righteous refuse to accept.

The word in vogue today for outsiders is *marginalized* people. While this word may be perfectly suitable academic jargon, it lacks the punch of "outsiders." Every country and community decides who the outsiders are—the people who don't fit their race, religion, or national origin.

Those who love Jesus refuse to accept prevailing social barriers against outsiders. They will have dinner with them, as Jesus did, and not expect them to conform to their preconceived notions of what's acceptable. The Good News of Jesus, in its purity and power, is the best antidote to unholy separatism.

To think about

- How did Jesus cross social barriers to love outsiders?
- What built-in prejudices keep you from loving all people as Jesus did?

Lord Jesus, forgive me for judging someone on the basis of race, religion, nationality, and appearance. I confess a standoffish attitude. Give me grace and power to welcome all people into my circle.

Jesus, the Epitome of Perseverance

2 Thessalonians 3:5; Hebrews 12:3

Perseverance scares us. If we think we might be called on to persevere, we believe we will face tough times and somehow struggle to get through them. Inspirational stories abound about heroes and heroines who have endured incredible hardships or overcome huge obstacles and setbacks. Say *perseverance* and you recall examples like Helen Keller, Thomas Edison, Abraham Lincoln, and Charles Lindbergh.

How does Jesus fit into this group? A quick scan of the Gospels shows how he kept going in the face of opposition and misunderstanding. Satan tempted him after forty days of fasting. Jesus endured not only the physical hardship but also Satan's powerful and very alluring propositions.

Jesus never quit preaching, although most of the miracle-hungry crowd turned away from his discipleship demands. He endured the crafty traps set by his religious enemies. He endured the demons' taunts. Jesus persisted despite his followers' abysmal ignorance of the Scriptures and the power and love of God. He remained steadfast when people refused to repent. He kept on preaching about the inner sickness of the soul and the blessings and power of God's kingdom.

When John the Baptist was arrested and beheaded, Jesus persevered (Matt. 14:1–13). Though saddened by that tragic event, he did not go back to carpentry. When his own family urged him to give up his ministry, suggesting he had lost his mind, Jesus stayed the course (Mark 3:20–35). He did not flinch when his hometown citizens tried to kill him (Luke 4:28–30).

Critics accused him of being a drunkard (Matt. 11:19). They said he made friends with "sinners" and performed

196

miracles in league with Satan (12:24). They said he broke their traditions. But Jesus marched on.

Jesus endured the failures of his own team. In spite of his teachings and his miracles, by the time Jesus came to the end, his disciples argued about who was the greatest among them (Luke 22:24). In the upper room Philip demanded, "Lord, show us the Father and that will be enough for us" (John 14:8). This after Jesus had told them, "I am the way and the truth and the life" (v. 6).

It's amazing that Jesus persevered in spite of what he knew was coming. He told his disciples, "We are going up to Jerusalem, and the Son of Man will be betrayed to the chief priests and the teachers of the law. They will condemn him to death" (Matt. 20:18).

Of course Jesus exhibited the epitome of endurance when he was betrayed and arrested and during his trial, condemnation, humiliation, scourging, and crucifixion. His perseverance in his divine mission took him to the cross.

Therefore, the writer of Hebrews says, in effect, when things get tough, look at Jesus and what he endured (12:3). You haven't suffered anything like that, so keep going. Don't quit. Don't give up your faith. Don't complain. Hang on. Persevere. Endure. Be steadfast. Pray that God will direct your heart to his love and Christ's perseverance.

To think about

- Why do you think Jesus had to endure so much?
- What things in our culture pressure us to escape tests so that we do not have to endure in our faith?

Thank you, Lord Jesus, that you persevered in spite of the worst your enemies did to you. I confess I am not that strong. Help me to find encouragement in your example, and through your Spirit, fill me with the strength I need.

Jesus, Lover of Children

Matthew 18:1–9; Luke 18:15–17

When we read of how Jesus valued and treated children, we cannot help but be reminded of the horribly wretched way some people abuse, cripple, torture, sell, and kill children today. Probably nothing sickens us as much as the almost weekly diet of such stories in our news media.

Usually when such a story hits the press, reporters inquire of psychologists: "Why do parents murder their own children?" Their answers vary but rarely satisfy. Many factors are involved. Regardless of what they may be, the long and short of it is that some people do not value their children the way Jesus did.

Jesus had to put aside the conventional thinking of his contemporaries—including his disciples—to show how valuable children are. He said what seems incredible and impossible to us: "Whoever welcomes a little child like this in my name welcomes me" (Matt. 18:5). How then can we abuse and mistreat a child? How can we refuse to give a child the spiritual nurture that leads him or her to faith? Jesus issued stern threats of eternal doom to those who lead children astray (v. 6).

By taking children in his arms, Jesus showed unmistakably that they are worth all we can invest in them. He loved them, he healed them, he brought them back to life, and he told us that each one has a guardian angel. His disciples thought the children were a big pain and interruption to more important business (Luke 18:15). Not so, said Jesus. In fact, if you do not become like a little child, you cannot enter God's kingdom (v. 17).

This is stern stuff that speaks not only to those who abuse their children verbally and physically, but also to those who indulge their children, giving them so much stuff that their rooms look like Noah's ark and they have anything they desire in the way of sports, music, parties, and travel. Some even try to make their children fit their own educational and career molds. Rarely do they encourage their children to serve the church and the world.

Parents who are following Jesus must invest primarily in their children's spiritual welfare. It means we love them, provide for them, and discipline them as needed. It means we will never violate them physically or emotionally.

Of course the values Jesus taught and practiced apply to all adults, not just to parents. Relatives, family, and friends can care for children, too, and invest time in their emotional, physical, and spiritual growth and welfare. Even neighbors can be Jesus to little children, as can our extended church family, Sunday school teachers, and youth leaders.

To think about

- What do you learn from Jesus about the value of children?
- What does it mean to become like a little child? In what settings have you found it hard to do this? Why?

Lord Jesus, help me to respect and value my children and grandchildren—and all children—as you do. May I see you in each one of them and treat them accordingly.

Jesus, Threat to Entrenched Religion

Luke 11:14–32; 20:45–47; John 8:12–32; 12:37–50

Religion permeated the life of Jesus as a boy and as a working man. Every aspect of society was influenced by religious traditions and values. People prayed, gave charitable gifts, made sacrifices, attended synagogues, and went to Jerusalem to the temple according to the prescribed rules of Moses, plus thousands of added traditions. Theirs was not a godless, irreligious society.

The stories about how Jesus tore into entrenched religion are astonishing. His opposition made him powerful enemies and ultimately cost him his life. Why was he so unabashed in his opposition to the religious setup of his day? Because the values, traditions, and practices—assumed to be things handed down by God—constituted insurmountable roadblocks to eternal life. Jesus knocked down the religious externals so that the water of life could plunge through the valleys and villages of Palestine. Anything that stood in the way of the water of forgiveness, hope, and eternal life had to be smashed. This was a life-and-death issue that was so crucial Jesus risked everything to fix it.

Traditions and externals so deeply embedded in contemporary culture did not yield without a fight. The enemies of Jesus attacked him unmercifully when he exposed the rottenness that lay beneath the surface. When he established the satanic paternity of the religious hierarchy, Jesus made clear for all time that religion often can be God's most powerful enemy.

To challenge lifeless, entrenched religion requires the utmost sincerity, love, caution, and grace, but if we claim to follow Jesus, we must do it, however risky it may be. We cannot fall into the trap of accepting anyone's religion as valid for the sake of tolerance. In such cases, our silence is not golden; it is plain yellow.

Like a clear, flowing mountain stream clogged by a beaver dam, religion often gets in the way of true spiritual life. Religion is a universal social and psychological phenomenon. As such, it is fair game for scholars, pundits, and charlatans. Study the world's religions and find an amazing kaleidoscope of beliefs and practices. In many cases, people have to discard the accretions of religious tradition before they can find what Jesus called life. Consequently the most fundamental question of all is not whether people have religion; it's whether they have eternal life with the living Jesus.

Part of following Jesus in this huge responsibility and opportunity includes our gaining significant knowledge about other religions from books and then building personal relationships with people who may be religious but not committed to Jesus. If we befriend people because of our genuine love for them, this love will shine through us, and then it is more likely that our message about Jesus and the life he offers will be given a hearing.

To think about

- Why was Jesus so hard on established religion?
- How can you be gracious and understanding with friends, who are religious but who are not following Jesus, and still maintain the claims of Jesus?

God, keep me from feeling superior in my attitude toward people who follow other religions. May my love for them be so obvious that they will accept my efforts to help them find life in Jesus.

Jesus, Respecter of Secular Authority

Luke 20:19–26

Secular authorities have been both a bane and a blessing to humanity. Too often the story of human governments has been the story of tyranny, repression, suffering, and mass killings. On the other hand, when governments have striven for justice and equality, their people have been blessed with peace, stability, freedom, and prosperity. The truth is, authorities suffer the same strengths and weaknesses that ordinary citizens do.

The stories about Jesus make it clear that secular authorities played a prominent role in his life and ministry. His story is firmly anchored in the prevailing political structure. The heavy hand of Roman emperors cast a dark shadow over the life and times of Jesus. He was born in Bethlehem because Caesar Augustus in Rome decreed a census for his empire, which included Palestine, so Mary and Joseph had to travel to Bethlehem.

Did Jesus have any encounters with the authorities while he made furniture in Nazareth? Certainly he and his fellow subjects of Rome were keenly aware of garrisons of Roman soldiers, because rebels and rebellions festered almost around the clock in those days. Palestine seethed, not only because of Roman oppression, but also because of centuries-old prophecies and hopes of a restored kingdom free of Gentile overlords.

Then there were the hated taxes and turncoat tax collectors who worked for Rome. But perhaps most galling of all were the puppet rulers the Romans had established. These men came down hard on the people. One of them, Herod, massacred all the male babies two years and younger after Jesus was born. Another one imprisoned and then beheaded

John the Baptist. The Herods lived lavishly at the expenses of ordinary people.

When Jesus became a public figure, tensions and expectations ran high. He appeared to be on a collision course with Rome. But Jesus did not play the role of a rebel. He never encouraged rebellion, even though his miracles caused people to try to make him king. Rather, he respected secular authority and fully obeyed the laws.

Face-to-face with Pilate, the Roman governor, Jesus explained that his kingdom was not like Rome's. The astonished man, who held the power of life and death over Jesus, failed to grasp the significance of what Jesus said. How can someone be a king and not have a throne and subjects, he wondered?

When we follow Jesus, we confess our allegiance to two kingdoms—the earthly and the heavenly. When there is freedom to do so, we participate in the political realm as responsible citizens. But we are not naive enough to think that any secular authority can solve all our problems and meet all our needs. As we work and pray for peace and justice, we study the issues and join with others to make our voices heard in small and large public forums. But when we must make a choice, we put our Lord's kingdom first and obey him, no matter what.

To think about

- What was so brilliant about Jesus's answer to his critics' question in Luke 20:22–25?
- In what settings is it hard for you to decide what is Caesar's and what is God's? Why?

Help me, Lord, to be like Jesus in my attitude toward secular authority. May I be faithful to him as I try to work for the values he taught in my own spheres of influence.

Jesus, Empowered by the Holy Spirit

Matthew 3:13–16; 4:1; Luke 4:14–18; 10:21; John 14:16–17; Acts 10:38; 1 Peter 3:18

Mysteries about the Holy Spirit can be solved by looking at Jesus. The stories clearly show that, regardless of his eternal deity, power, and glory, he lived under the Holy Spirit's control. Thus, when the apostles tell us to walk by the Spirit, we need to consider the life and teachings of Jesus.

We first meet the Holy Spirit in the stories about Jesus's virgin birth. His conception came about, not by normal human means, but by the instrumentality of the Holy Spirit. As a young man, during his long years of carpentry work, Jesus no doubt knew the fellowship of the Spirit as he grew in understanding of his life's calling.

God sent John the Baptist to prepare the way for Jesus. He gave a powerful preview of what Jesus would do. Jesus would not baptize with water, but with the Holy Spirit and fire. Later on, after Jesus's resurrection and ascension into heaven, tongues of flame fell on the early Christians on the day of Pentecost as a sign that the Holy Spirit had possessed them.

At his baptism the Holy Spirit fell on Jesus in the form of a dove. Thus empowered and endorsed by God Almighty, Jesus followed the Holy Spirit, not into preaching but into temptation. After his successful encounter with Satan, Jesus embarked on his mission. From that time forward he loved, served, suffered, died, and rose from the grave in the power of the Holy Spirit.

Thus the disciples could learn what it meant to be Spirit-led and empowered. Jesus said they might receive the Holy Spirit through prayer (Luke 11:13). But he saved his most extensive teaching about the Holy Spirit until they had hit bottom. In the upper room the disciples were clutched by fear because it finally dawned on them that their kingdom hopes had been dashed. Jesus brightened their gloom by telling them he was sending the Holy Spirit to be their counselor and guide—another one just like himself. He was not leaving them like helpless orphans. They could know the Spirit's peace and power (John 14:16–17).

True to his word, Jesus sent the Holy Spirit and the defeated, despairing disciples were transformed into courageous evangelists (see Acts 2). They found that the secret of spiritual power was not a mystery after all. Because they loved and obeyed Jesus, their spiritual thirst was satisfied and they rose above persecution to spread the gospel and establish the church.

Jesus shows us that he and the Holy Spirit are inseparable. As we grow in our knowledge of Jesus, the indwelling Spirit empowers us to do what Jesus expects of us.

As we are fully occupied with Jesus, the Holy Spirit will do his gracious work. Following Jesus means obeying the Holy Spirit as he did and enjoying the fullness of the Spirit's holiness and power. Because he is the Spirit of truth, we can trust him to guide us in becoming fully pleasing to God.

To think about

- Why did Jesus need the Holy Spirit's power for his life and ministry?
- How has the Holy Spirit ministered to your needs? What can you do to increase your dependence on him?

Heavenly Father, thank you that I received the Holy Spirit when I received Jesus. Keep me under his control as I love and obey you.

Jesus, Our Great High Priest

Hebrews 2:16–3:2; 4:14–16; 5:5–10; 7:23–28;
9:11–15; 10:19–25

When he received God's call to begin his mission, Jesus did not come through the ranks of the Jewish priesthood. He came from the ranks of the common people without any religious trappings, power, or prestige. Humility, love, and wisdom marked his character.

In the crowds, astounded by his teachings and his miracles, some people declared that a new prophet had arisen in Israel. Jesus did not assume the mantle of a prophet. He accepted the title of rabbi or teacher. He always respected the authority of the chief priests, while demanding that they repent of their self-righteous hypocrisy.

On the other hand, Jesus met fully all the Old Testament requirements of prophet, priest, and king. Not until after he had ascended into heaven did his followers recognize these foundational facts about Jesus. Then they began to explore the depths of what his life, death, and resurrection had accomplished for them.

The Epistle to the Hebrews vividly and practically expanded the horizons of Christ's priesthood. For all practical purposes, the writer asserted that the old priesthood was finished, superseded by Christ's far superior priesthood, which was rooted in the mysterious Melchizedek (Heb. 5:6, 10).

The writer returned again and again to this critical truth about Jesus, relating it to central issues of faith and conduct. He executed a perfect welding of theology and practice. Christ's priesthood is the rock of our doctrine of salvation and the pattern for our worship and obedience.

The writer of Hebrews focused on the high priesthood of Jesus because his readers were sorely tempted to revert to Judaism. He argued that whatever their needs, Jesus was eminently qualified to meet them, whether for forgiveness and salvation or for divine help in difficult circumstances.

Because Jesus is faithful and merciful, he responds to our cries for help. He was made human precisely for that reason; he was made like us so he would know what we face. By suffering he learned obedience (2:17–18). Somehow, he met and passed every test without sinning, so we can go to him boldly with our requests for help (4:14–16).

To make his point more emphatically, the writer of Hebrews declared that because Jesus lives (he is not a dead priest like all the others), he is absolutely and unequivocally able to save and keep all those who come to God through him. The power and supremacy of Christ's blood validates this liberating claim. We should not allow one shred of doubt to keep us from living this truth (7:23–25; 9:11–15).

Among other things, knowing Jesus as our great High Priest frees us to approach God with unshakable confidence, to be firm and unswerving in our faith, to stir up others to love and active goodness, and to maintain faithful worship with fellow believers. Such is our guaranteed formula for spiritual prosperity (4:16; 10:19–25).

To think about

- How does our understanding of Jesus grow through Old Testament imagery and New Testament history?
- How can you grow more confident in approaching God through Jesus for the fulfillment of all your spiritual needs?

Thank you, Lord Jesus, that you are my fully qualified and completely understanding High Priest living in heaven for me. Forgive me for not drawing on you with abandon. Help me to overcome my reluctance to know your love more deeply.

Jesus, Lord of the Sabbath

Luke 6:1–11

Jesus grew up knowing all the rules about Sabbath keeping. For thirty years he observed them scrupulously. But early in his public ministry, in the eyes of the Pharisees, he broke their laws by healing on the Sabbath. Thus he incurred their anger and inspired their desire to get rid of him.

They collided on the Sabbath issue at least six times. On the surface it might appear that, for someone trying to establish his claim as Israel's Messiah, such action on Jesus's part would be a colossal blunder. He certainly knew that healing on the Sabbath would antagonize the country's religious authorities.

Before looking at why Jesus did it, we need to ask why the Jews so jealously guarded those laws. Why were they so enraged when Jesus healed on the Sabbath?

Jesus's Jewish contemporaries lived with the haunting memory of Israel's past failures to keep the Sabbath. Perhaps Ezekiel's searing words about Israel's pollution of the Sabbath were ringing in their ears (Ezek. 20:12–24). Israel's failure to keep the Sabbath, God had said, justified his judgment. For this transgression, and for others, the Israelites served seventy years in Babylonian exile.

Indelibly etched in the Jewish psyche, the Babylonian captivity taught the Jews never again to fail to keep the Sabbath. They established strict performance codes that spelled out what was needed for compliance. Their codes placed huge legalistic, nit-picking burdens on the people. Guilt and fear motivated compliance, rather than love for God.

Consequently, for the Pharisees, Sabbath keeping, rather than centering on God's intention to set aside a special day

208

for rest for families, servants, and their animals, became a feeding tube for self-righteousness and legalism.

By healing on the Sabbath, Jesus seized the moment to break with burdensome traditions and to liberate the Jews from unyielding, external requirements and observances. Jesus set in motion the later apostolic dictum that we receive righteousness from God as a gift, not by keeping the works of the law.

Jesus also reversed the common perceptions about the Sabbath when he taught that the Sabbath was given for our benefit. God did not create us simply to be Sabbath keepers (Mark 2:27).

In the end, Jesus's challenging behavior made the most important point of all: he is Lord of the Sabbath. Such a claim, of course, put him on a par with God. Being Lord of the Sabbath, he established that "works" of mercy—such as his healings—were absolutely legitimate and were allowed in Old Testament times. Not only did Jesus fulfill the letter of the law, he far exceeded the spirit of the law. Our faith in him delivers us from legalism's clutches and sets us free to worship our God.

The early Christians soon realized that, in light of Christ's resurrection on the first day of the week, Sunday should be set aside in the spirit of the fourth commandment for rest, worship, and deeds of mercy. It is the Lord's Day. Jesus owns it and we must invite him to control how we use it.

To think about

- Why did Jesus heal on the Sabbath?
- What binds you to obedience to Jesus in regard to what you do on Sundays? How can you keep from arguing with others about what is permissible on Sundays and what isn't?

Thank you, Lord Jesus, for setting me free from legalistic Sabbath keeping. I want you to be Lord of every part of my life. May I be an example to others of joyful worship and service.

Jesus, Our Sin Bearer

Hebrews 9:23–28; 10:1–18; 1 Peter 2:21–25; 3:18

The sufferings and death of Jesus Christ tower like Everest over the New Testament stories about him. The apostles penetrated the unbelieving armor of Jerusalem's Jews by preaching his death and resurrection. Jesus's crucifixion focused the mind and heart of the apostle Paul when he trumpeted Jesus to the Greeks.

Painters through the ages have taken Jesus on the cross as their theme. The crucifix hangs in humble churches and mighty cathedrals and it dangles from millions of necklaces.

But the meaning of the cross far exceeds the sobering fact that Jesus hung and died there. Pondering the crucifix forces us to ask, "What is going on here? What's the meaning of all this?"

John the Baptist recognized the full impact of Christ's death before it occurred. Seeing Jesus approaching him, he declared that he was God's Lamb, destined to take away the world's sins (John 1:29). The cross lacks meaning unless we connect it with our sins. Our sins nailed him there.

We cannot escape our personal complicity in Christ's death. Jesus is God's appointed sin bearer. Our sins are so grievous and our guilt is so damning that we must look to someone else to take the judgment from God that we deserve. Our sin bearer must be spotlessly pure, without any blemishes. Only Jesus meets this qualification. Perfectly holy, nevertheless he took our sins on himself. He became God's sacrificial Lamb, offering himself in our place.

The significance of Christ's suffering as our sin bearer surpasses his physical pain. As the sinless Son of God, he carried our sins to the cross so that God's holiness and justice might be satisfied. Every violation of God's laws means that someone has to pay the consequences. On the cross we see Jesus taking our place in God's judgment hall. This is what theologians call Christ's substitutionary atonement.

The constant visible reminders of Calvary tell us what happened there but not the reason it happened. Therefore, we grasp for ourselves and for others the apostle Paul's succinct explanation: "Christ died for our sins" (1 Cor. 15:3). As we make this confession, we step beyond what seems like a miscarriage of justice, in which Jesus was executed though innocent, and plunge to the depths of our personal sins, guilt, and condemnation before a holy God.

In a concise explanation, Jesus captured the essence of his role as our sin bearer, explaining that he had to suffer so that repentance and remission of sins might be announced to the world (Luke 24:46–47).

To claim anything less than this for the cross constitutes a cowardly refusal to accept what Jesus and his apostles so boldly preached. The specter of sin darkened Golgotha and cut the Son off from his Father. That's what it cost Jesus to be our sin bearer. Therefore our love, obedience, praise, and glory rightly belong to our Savior.

To think about

- In simple words that anyone can understand, explain why Jesus died on the cross.
- What worthy responses can you make to Jesus because he bore your sins on the cross?

Lord Jesus, your death on the cross for my sins is so big I can't get my mind around it. But I know that because you died for me, God has forgiven my sins and has granted me eternal life. Thank you, Lord Jesus.

Jesus, the Revelation of God

John 12:44–50; 14:7–14, 24; Hebrews 1:1–3

Driving Germany's autobahn for the first time, I missed a crucial sign and crunched to a stop in a village looking like it had just been bombed. Every street was torn up for new sewer lines. The other drivers had seen and obeyed the detour signs that I had ignored because I could not read German.

The Gospel writers packed their biographies of Jesus with stories about the important signs he gave to the people: raising the dead, healing the sick, casting out demons, changing outcasts to decent people, and controlling nature. These miracles are called signs because Jesus intended them to point to his supernatural power and his divine origin.

He wanted to show people that he had come from God and that he was strong enough to overcome their problems. Jesus conquered every kind of human need, both physical and emotional. His signs clearly showed that he was strong, loving, and worthy of their trust.

His signs also proved that he was the promised Messiah because he fulfilled the ancient Jewish prophecies. He did what Messiah was supposed to do. When John the Baptizer developed doubts about Jesus, Jesus reminded him of his signs (Matt. 11:2–5).

However, in spite of plentiful signs done before many people in a host of different circumstances, people generally did not believe that he was the promised Messiah. Jesus's signs were designed to inspire belief, faith, and trust in him. Their unbelief was not due to lack of evidence.

John quoted two passages from Isaiah to show that the Old Testament predicted the public's unbelief (John 12:38–41). However, some did believe Jesus, including some Jewish authorities. Not until after Pentecost and Peter's preaching do

212

we see large numbers of people confessing their sins and believing in Jesus.

During his final week, controversies surrounded Jesus. The chief priests, scribes, and elders challenged his authority. The Pharisees and Herodians argued with him about paying taxes. The Sadducees questioned the resurrection. The lawyer debated the commandments. But Jesus never lost his cool. He maintained his focus on his oneness with his Father, his speaking with the Father's authority, and his bringing light to the world.

Constantly Jesus emphasized that he was a "sent one." His mission was not his own but his Father's. When it comes to personal faith, we cannot separate Jesus from his Father. Seeing Jesus equals seeing the Father. Jesus declared that when a person "looks at me, he sees the one who sent me" (John 12:45). Unmistakably, he revealed the Father. Who could make such a monumental claim unless he was either mad or really God in the flesh?

As God's revelation, Jesus was the complete picture of God and he spoke with God's authority. The Father sent him and the Father told him what to say. Both Jesus's signs and his words give us more than sufficient evidence for placing our faith and trust in him. He is fully trustworthy to provide total care for all who welcome him into their lives.

To think about

- Why did some people refuse to accept the signs Jesus gave?
- What can you do to stretch the horizons of your faith in Jesus so that you do not miss the full impact of what he wants to do for you?

O God, forgive me for spiritually going the wrong way on one-way streets so many times. I want to reach out for the height and breadth and depth and length of Jesus's love for me.

Jesus, Beacon of Blessing

Luke 6:20–49

At first glance the Jesus way of blessing in Luke 6:20–23 seems as alien as Mars invaders. On reading his words, our first response could very well be, "Ridiculous!" Very clearly, his beacon of blessing revolutionizes our usual understanding of how to be blessed.

Ask a man if he is blessed, and he will say yes, if he has few troubles and enjoys good health, a good job, ample resources, and a wife and children who are reasonably satisfied. Such concepts of blessing completely miss how Jesus defined it. Spend a few minutes with him as he teaches the multitudes and you discover that Jesus is on an entirely different wavelength. In fact it would not be difficult to find people who think Jesus was out of touch with reality when he defined blessedness as he did.

Jesus demolished popular conceptions in his day. His beacon of blessing banishes the darkness that lies just beneath the surface of contemporary happiness. Calling his sources of blessing radical fails to convey adequately what he taught. Basically, he turned blessing upside down. He taught us to look at blessing from a completely different perspective.

Even a cursory look at Jesus reveals a blessed, contented person, although he possessed none of the elements of happiness as the world defines it. He was blessed because he knew who he was. He knew his purpose and mission. He knew where he came from and where he was going. Endowed with everything he needed, Jesus exuded incomparable richness.

Blessing tumbled out of him. His inner being flowed with rivers of living water. His words and deeds dripped with sweetness. In prayer, worship, and the fellowship of the Holy Spirit, Jesus lived what he taught. Poverty of spirit and

214

humility exalted him. He was hated and insulted. Often he was hungry. He claimed no home for himself. As far as the culture's priorities were concerned, he was last, but in God's economy he was first.

When we allow the brilliant beacon of Jesus to focus on us, we find our soul satisfaction and happiness. Simultaneously, his way of blessing both fortifies our soul and protects us from danger. Without demagoguery, Jesus's beacon of blessing also shines as a beacon of warning. Just as the lighthouse warns of rocky shoals, so Jesus's beacon exposes the dangers of wealth, popularity, and prosperity. If our happiness grows from a full belly and a good laugh, we are in serious trouble. Our lives may crash on the "rocks" of material abundance (Luke 6:24–26).

Jesus's beacon of blessing not only directs his followers to different measures of happiness but also lights the way to generous, forgiving behaviors toward those who abuse us and take advantage of us.

To gain maximum benefit from Jesus's blessings, we spend time with him and allow his principles to saturate and satisfy our soul. Bountifully his blessings provide our peace, strength, and stability, no matter what waves batter our lives (vv. 46–49).

To think about

- Define happiness according to Jesus's standards.
- Why is it so hard to think of blessing the way Jesus defined it? What steps forward can you take to live by his standards?

Lord Jesus, I confess my failure to live up to the standards of your blessings. So often my outlook is colored by my circumstances. Help me to find my blessedness in you and your riches.

Jesus, the Storyteller

Matthew 13

Jesus was a storyteller par excellence—he told more stories than he preached sermons. His stories, or parables, gripped people because he talked about familiar things, and his audiences were able to identify with the characters and plots he created.

Jesus told stories to illustrate spiritual truths, presenting common experiences—planting on the farm, cleaning the house—and turning them into vivid, easily remembered lessons about God and his kingdom. Usually his parables taught one main point that Jesus wanted his listeners to grasp. They were not puzzles to be solved by trying to find some lesson in every detail.

Often he closed his stories with unexpected twists. Jesus used this method to stimulate his listeners to look at a subject from an entirely fresh viewpoint. Whatever they thought the kingdom of heaven was like, Jesus told a story to teach what it really *is* like.

For example, Jesus's simple story about a farmer sowing his crops presented something his disciples had never understood and they questioned him about it. Their curiosity opened the door to further teaching.

Jesus felt the powerful undertow of animosity and hatred that had been building against him in the crowds. He called these people a "brood of vipers" and "a wicked and adulterous generation" (Matt. 12:34, 39). With people sharply divided about him, he resorted to stories to bring truth to those who would follow him. At the same time, truth would be hidden from those who had rejected him or were indifferent.

Today we can sit and ponder Jesus's stories for as long as we like, but the people who heard Jesus could only react to his spoken words. He stabbed them with one big point, a major blow directed to their spiritual hardness and inertia. He gave them more than ample food for thought.

Jesus the storyteller used wisdom, grace, and irony in his stories. On some occasions those to whom he directed his stories recognized themselves in them and reacted furiously. He gave his disciples enough teaching to whet their appetites for more and to be alert for those who were moving toward accepting Jesus as Lord and Savior.

Our joy of knowing and serving Jesus increases as we ask him to remove the spiritual blinders from our eyes. When we read about people who were close to him and still missed the point of who he was and what he came to do, we ask him to open our heart, mind, and will so that we will not miss something important about him.

His stories rebuke, correct, and encourage us. Jesus loves and nourishes his family of believers. He knows our blind spots and those things we love that hinder our spiritual growth. Reading his stories, we ask Jesus to teach us.

We can also appreciate the value of stories for teaching our children and our friends about Jesus. When he teaches us, and intersects our lives in special ways, we must become his storytellers.

To think about

- Why did Jesus tell so many stories?
- Which of his stories has taught you an important spiritual truth? What did you learn?

Lord Jesus, I want to learn more about you and your kingdom. Help me to grow in wisdom and understanding. Teach me how to tell stories that will draw people to you.

Jesus, the One Who Refuses Deals

Matthew 12:38–42

God, I'll serve you, if . . ."
"Jesus, I'll trust you, if . . ."
"[God,] give me a sign that it is really you talking to me"
(Gideon in Judges 6:17).

"Teacher, we want to see a miraculous sign from you"
(Pharisees and teachers of the law in Matt. 12:38).

Ancients and moderns alike make conditional offers of
faith. Risk takers they are not. Before they leap, they want to
be sure a safety net is in place to catch them. How does Jesus
handle people who make conditional offers of faith? He is
unflappable and unrelenting. He is confrontational. He refuses
to make deals. It's all or nothing. He reminds such deal makers
that they have more than sufficient reasons to trust him and
believe who he is—God's Son and the world's Savior.

Justifiably, Jesus could have retorted when the lawyers and
Pharisees questioned him: "What? Where have you guys been?
Haven't you seen the signs I have already performed?" But
he didn't do that. Instead, he taught them a spiritual history
lesson that showcased repentance and faith.

So where were the lawyers and Pharisees when Jesus performed signs to prove his messianic credentials? Their stubborn refusal to see in Jesus God's incarnate Son clogged
their spiritual arteries. They had prejudged him and decided,
among other things, that he was in cahoots with the devil.

Jesus had warned them against blaspheming the Holy Spirit
(vv. 31–32). In no mood to confess their sins, they requested a
miracle, perhaps having in mind something spectacular like
the fire from heaven that fell on Mount Carmel after Elijah's
prayer (see 1 Kings 18).

Whatever their motive, Jesus bluntly refused. Their demand
for another sign proved they were "a wicked and adulterous

generation" (v. 39). Their religious orthodoxy and zealotry could not save them. Their spiritual ears were plugged and their spiritual eyes were blind.

With spiritual electricity crackling around them, Jesus recalled the Jonah story and said it was a sign of his impending death and resurrection (the most powerful sign of all time). Of course they weren't looking for any signs from Jonah. What did he have to teach them?

Jesus did not dwell on his rejection but calmly addressed the critical issues for the deal makers: repentance and faith. Nineveh repented before Jonah's preaching. Since Jesus far surpassed Jonah, it was logical that the lawyers and Pharisees should repent. Jesus reminded them of the Queen of Sheba, who sought King Solomon's counsel. She would condemn them as well, because Jesus is superior to Solomon. They should be seeking wisdom from him instead of demanding a sign as the price for their faith. At their trial before God, the doctors of the law and the Pharisees would be condemned by Nineveh's repentance and the ancient queen's quest.

Jesus speaks to moderns: "Don't make deals with me. You have more than enough evidence to trust me. Look to my death and resurrection. They prove my incomparable power and my overwhelming love for you."

To think about

- Why were the Pharisees and lawyers blind to the signs Jesus had already given?
- What has Jesus done for you that you have not fully appreciated and allowed to change your values and ambitions?

*God, I confess that I have often asked for signs
to believe you. Help me to grow so attached to
Jesus that I will never doubt that you are with me,
always doing what is best for me.*

Jesus Responds to Faith and Grief

Luke 7:1–17

Following Jesus on a day when he heals a critically ill person without seeing him and raises a grieving widow's son when she did not beg him to do so is a formidable assignment. His healing of the centurion's servant and raising of the widow's son would have shocked us on a number of counts.

Jesus was in Capernaum, his home since being thrown out of Nazareth, perhaps trying to catch his breath after some exhausting teaching. The knock at the door brought in some Jewish elders. Were some of them trying to get rid of Jesus, as is implied in Luke 6:11? If they were, why did he let them in?

This delegation brought a request from the local Roman army captain, whose job it was to keep peace and order among the unruly, rebellious Jews. The elders liked the captain because he had favored them with a synagogue. So they carried his appeal to Jesus to come and save his slave's life.

How long did Jesus ponder the captain's plea? Why should he respond to a Roman army officer's appeal for help? He decided to go, but on the way the captain's friends intercepted him and told him not to bother. Walking along with Jesus, we are astonished to hear them report that the captain had said that he wasn't worthy of a visit from Jesus. All Jesus had to do was say the word and his servant would be healed.

We wonder how this Gentile army man gained such respect for Jesus. Probably by giving thoughtful consideration to widespread stories about Jesus's miracles and teachings. While the Jewish leaders were plotting to kill Jesus, this Roman had learned of his love and power. Jesus's credentials were so authentic for him that he confessed his unworthiness and his faith.

"Just say the word" from the lips of a Roman exposed the stubborn unbelief of the Jews. Nowhere in Israel had Jesus found such faith (7:9). If a Roman soldier's faith had been found greater than our own, how would such a devastating analysis have affected us? How would we have reacted when we learned that the servant had been healed at that very moment?

Meanwhile, down the road at Nain we encounter a funeral procession. Nain's mourners tell us the grief-stricken mother is a widow and the dead person is her only son. Well, we're sorry to hear that but we have other things to do on the road with Jesus.

Whatever Jesus had on his mind was not what we were thinking. His heart broke for the woman. Disregarding all the rules, he spoke to her and told her to stop weeping. Then he touched the coffin and told the corpse to get up. He gave the young man back to his mother.

We are awestruck. God cares for his people, whether a Gentile Roman army man or an insignificant grieving widow who did not even cry out for help. Jesus's compassion wins every time. He could have refused the centurion's case. He could have allowed the widow's funeral to go by, but he didn't.

Hurting people require the same compassion from us. We must be willing to see people through Jesus's eyes and be willing to be inconvenienced so that we can help them. This is what he has called us to do.

To think about

- Why did Jesus intervene in these cases?
- What obstacles stand in the way of your helping people? How can you overcome them?

Lord Jesus, I praise you for your compassion. I am totally unworthy of your love. Thank you for loving me when I hurt. Increase my faith.

Jesus Forgives Much

Luke 7:36–50

Simon the Pharisee threw a dinner party for Jesus and inadvertently set the table for a feast of forgiveness. That's because a disreputable woman somehow crashed his party and astonished him with a lavish outpouring of love and faith for Jesus.

Generally the Pharisees hated Jesus. They had refused John's baptism and continually found fault with Jesus, some of them even plotting to kill him. But evidently Simon wanted to check out Jesus for himself, so he arranged the meal.

As it turned out, offering Jesus a meal was as far as he was willing to go. He did not offer Jesus the customary respect and treatment accorded dinner guests. But the uninvited woman did.

When Simon saw what the woman had done for Jesus, he drew the religiously correct but spiritually wrong conclusion: no self-respecting prophet in Israel would permit such atrocious behavior and be ritually contaminated in the process. So he got what he was looking for. Now it was obvious to him that Jesus of Nazareth was not from God.

However, Jesus turned the tables on the self-righteous Simon, who was oblivious to his own paramount need for forgiveness. Simon gave the right answer to Jesus. He knew that the man who had been forgiven the greater debt obviously would love the more. His correct answer betrayed him. The sinful woman's faith had inspired her sacrificial worship of Jesus: wetting his feet with her tears, drying them with her hair, kissing his feet, and anointing them with expensive perfume. What Simon thought an atrocious breech of etiquette really was the outpouring of faith and love for Jesus— something totally absent from the Pharisee's heart.

222

Her tears, her kisses, and her perfume proved the depths of her sin and the depths of her faith in and love for Jesus. She knew she had much for which to be forgiven. Jesus forgave much in her case and sent her away in peace.

Our bottom line is this: Jesus is faithful and just to forgive us (1 John 1:9). All of us have much for which we need forgiveness. But do we recognize and confess the wretchedness of our sins? Not everyone sinks as low as some others do, but we do not stand before God on a sliding scale of goodness, hoping that he will forgive us because we have not been as bad as we might have been.

Until we confess much, and are forgiven much, we will not love Jesus much. One way or another, we must fall on our knees before him, shed our tears, and, as it were, wipe his feet and anoint them with expensive oil. Such faith brings Christ's forgiveness. To be forgiven: that's the biggest and best thing of all.

To think about

- Describe Simon's inner thoughts. Why did he feel this way?
- Regarding Simon's thoughts, are you in his camp or the woman's? How do you know?

Lord Jesus, help me to face up honestly to my own sinfulness. I am ashamed that I have never approached you as this woman did. My simple prayer is, "More love to you, more love, O Christ, to you."

Jesus Answers the Big Question

Matthew 11:1–19

One day John the Baptizer's men approached Jesus with the big question: "Are you the Messiah we're looking for, or shall we wait for someone else?" Languishing in prison, John had lost his focus and his faith certainty. Doubt overwhelmed him. He knew the big question, but he was no longer sure of the answer.

In the flush of his highly successful revival, John had unequivocally pointed to Jesus as Israel's Messiah, the one who would baptize with the Holy Spirit, the one who would burn Israel's chaff (Matt. 3:11–12). More than that, he declared that Jesus was God's sin-bearing, sacrificial Lamb (John 1:29–34). But somehow the devil got to John and assaulted him with the big question: Was Jesus really God's promised Messiah? In the dark night of his soul, John no longer possessed absolute assurance about who Jesus was.

Jesus allayed his doubts and fears by reminding John's messengers of all that he had done and said to establish his messianic credentials. Turning to the crowd, Jesus said there had never been a better man than John (Matt. 11:11).

Again and again, John's big question rises up from the New Testament pages like Mount Everest. It's always there, demanding an answer. Jesus challenged his disciples with the big question. Pilate threw it up to Jesus. The apostles confronted the world with it. Boiling everything down to its essence, John the apostle explained that the only thing that really matters is whether or not Jesus Christ is God in the flesh.

How we answer the big question settles our fate. In his revelation to John, Jesus dramatically illustrated the eternal destiny of those who reject him as King of Kings and Lord of Lords. The closure of all things brings heartrending terror (Rev. 20:7–15).

To find the correct answer to the big question is not difficult. Follow Jesus, look at him, examine him from every angle, read his story again and again, reflect on his deeds and words, and ask him to ratify the right answer by giving you the inner witness in your heart. Jesus promised that if we're serious about knowing the answer, he will show it to us.

As John found out, saying yes to Jesus is not a onetime thing. The devil attacks our confident confession every chance he gets. In the darkness of depression and fear, our faith candle may flicker and go out. To rekindle our flame, we go back to Jesus and ask him to reinforce our heart and mind with his truth one more time. "Yes," he says, "I am God in the flesh, his eternal Son, given to die for your sins. Look to my deeds and words one more time, especially to my death on the cross for you."

To think about

- How do you account for John's doubts?
- Explain Jesus's answer in your own words. How do you think this answer helped John?

Lord Jesus, I confess times of doubt. Keep me always looking to you. Refresh my soul and strengthen my faith, for your glory and my good.

Jesus Living in Us

John 14:15–23; 15:4–10

Jesus confronted his men with deepest mystery when he told them he was leaving them but he would still be with them and in them. Nothing in their experience or religious tradition had prepared them for this. Like us, these men depended on sensory experiences for truth.

Of course Jesus's promise was conditional. They had to love and obey him after he was gone, but how do you love and obey a memory?

Enter the Holy Spirit. He would be for Jesus's disciples everything Jesus was for them in person. Another member of the Holy Trinity was coming to teach and guide them in the ways of Jesus. He is the Spirit of truth. He is all-knowing and all-powerful. Therefore they would know what Jesus wanted them to do. They would know what it meant to love and obey Jesus. The Holy Spirit would confirm to their hearts and minds the presence of Jesus himself.

Sinners as we are, we are likewise unprepared to be the dwelling place of Father, Son, and Holy Spirit. Like Isaiah, Peter, and Paul, we count ourselves unworthy of God's presence in our lives. Nothing in our pedigree or religious heritage says we can count on Jesus living in us. Besides, God just doesn't live in human beings.

Faced with such an enormous conundrum, we listen to Jesus: "My Father will love him, and we will come to him and make our home with him. . . . Remain in me, and I will remain in you" (John 14:23; 15:4). The next step is up to us. Jesus's words will be true in our experience in the same measure as we love and obey him.

There is no scientific explanation for this spiritual phenomenon. It just happens when we trust and obey Jesus.

That means we must spend time in his presence so we develop a keen sensitivity to what he says. We hear his words from Scripture and from the inner voice of the Holy Spirit witnessing to our spirit.

His disciples went on to validate what Jesus promised. In the Acts of the Apostles are stories about how God spoke and they listened. Jesus was with them in their trials and their triumphs. The love, wisdom, grace, and power of Jesus energized and sustained them. Paul's testimony perhaps summed it up the best: "We are more than conquerors through him who loved us" (Rom. 8:37).

This intense desire to love and obey Jesus drove the early Christians to penetrate their world with the gospel. Since then, Christians have been encouraged and strengthened by many stories of hope and faith generated by Jesus's living presence.

Is this all a mystery? Yes. But it is not unsolvable. Jesus keeps his word. We know we are his dwelling place when we walk in obedient fellowship with him in prayer, worship, witness, and service.

To think about

- Did Jesus give an adequate explanation to his disciples of the coming Holy Spirit? What more would you have wanted to know had you been there?
- How have you experienced Jesus's presence in your life?

Lord Jesus, thank you for your indwelling presence. Thank you for never leaving me. May I keep on growing in my relationship with you.

Following Jesus on a Typical Day

Luke 8:22–56

How'd it go today, honey?" my wife kindly asks me as I wearily trudge through the door.

"Not bad," I said. "Just the usual stuff."

Imagine Jesus in a similar setting. "How'd it go today, Teacher?" his hosts in Capernaum inquire when he returns for the night. Would he reply, "Just the usual stuff"? Let's follow him and see what a typical day was like for him.

In Luke 8:22 the first thing he encounters is a nasty storm on Lake Galilee that terrifies his disciples. He rebukes the violent wind and waves as if they are old pals. Suddenly everything falls still. Now fear overwhelms his men for another reason: they can't figure out someone who gives orders to the elements. Despite their lack of understanding of who Jesus is, Jesus takes it with magnificent poise.

Next, he steps onshore and a wild, naked madman charges him, screaming his name and imploring him to let him alone. Not repulsed by his appearance or his reputation, Jesus looks him straight in the eye and commands the unclean spirit to come out of him. Legion (the many demons inhabiting the man) flees for a nearby herd of pigs.

That's enough fright for one day, but the day isn't over. The crowds can't wait to get at him. A well-dressed, quite normal, upstanding synagogue president accosts him. Jairus throws himself at Jesus's feet and begs him to heal his twelve-year-old daughter who is dying.

Perhaps Jesus would rather go home and rest, thinking that the need of this poor fellow could wait until tomorrow. But Jesus decides to go with Jairus, and the crowd almost suffocates him.

Somehow or other, a very sick, bleeding woman manages to squeeze through the throng and lunges desperately for his cloak. When she touches it, her bleeding stops. Jesus, sensing what happened, asks who touched him. Everyone denies the deed, and Peter says it's impossible to find out in such a crowd. Just then the healed woman steps forward, confesses, and testifies to her healing. Fearing the worst, she is relieved to hear Jesus say, "Your faith has healed you. Go in peace" (v. 48).

So far, Jesus has saved people from three impossible conditions. The fourth—death—awaits him at Jairus's home. Someone dispatches word that the girl has died. "Don't bother Jesus," they say to Jairus. But Jesus interrupts and tells the father not to be afraid but to have faith and his daughter will live.

When Jesus says she's not dead, the people laugh because it's so obvious the child is gone. But Jesus takes her by the hand, and she gets up. "Give her something to eat," he says. "Don't tell anyone what I've done."

Is Jesus big enough, wise enough, strong enough, loving enough for us? Does his typical day convince us that he is totally, absolutely, undoubtedly sufficient for us? To be sure, to be reminded of who Jesus really is, we must join him on a typical day again and again.

To think about

- Had you been there, how would you have felt at the end of this day in Jesus's life? Why?
- What keeps you from entrusting everything to Jesus?

Lord Jesus, all I can do is sing, "How great you are!" Magnify your greatness in my heart and soul. Be glorified in me.

Jesus Provokes the Big Question—Again

Luke 9:7–22

Doubts flooded John the Baptist, so he sent emissaries to ask Jesus the big question. Herod demanded that his flunkies answer the big question and told them to arrange an interview with Jesus for him. Jesus probed his disciples to tell him how John Q. Public answered the big question. Then he asked them to answer it.

Jesus kept on provoking people to ask, "Who are you?" because we all need the answer to this most important question. Everything hinges on who Jesus is. Our eternal destiny depends on how we answer. The value and meaning of our lives depend on our answer. When people ask us, "Who is Jesus?" what do we say? Do we substantiate our answer or are we too tongue-tied even to try?

Herod tried to fit Jesus into his religious and political box. He had heard enough about what Jesus was doing to pique his curiosity. Would this Galilean miracle worker draw enough people to pose a threat to Rome and thus to himself?

Herod heard reports that perhaps Jesus was the reincarnation of Elijah or one of Israel's old prophets. Some even said he was John, whom Herod had just beheaded. If that were true, he certainly was in trouble. Apparently nothing came of Herod's proposed interview, but he later let it be known that he might kill Jesus (Luke 13:31). To Herod, Jesus was a potential rival.

Jesus tested his disciples to clarify their thinking. They had witnessed his words and deeds. Every day they confronted crowds of sick people wanting to be healed. Who did these people think Jesus was? The disciples confirmed what Herod had heard. The popular feeling was that God had raised one of their heroes from the dead.

Why the popular mood had progressed no further seems a bit perplexing to us. Of course people appreciated Jesus's miracles, but moving from there to being convinced he was Israel's promised Messiah required a huge step of faith. Further, both John and Jesus connected the Good News of the kingdom with personal repentance and confession of sin. Such personal turnarounds are costly.

Peter, however, was convinced. Jesus was God's Messiah (9:20). Did the others share Peter's conviction? Perhaps not as confidently. Making such a confession brought considerable risks, and Jesus heightened the risk factor by explaining he was going to be killed by the religious authorities. Although he added that he would be raised, were they still willing to confess him as God's anointed Son come in the flesh?

"Who do you say I am?" The question will not go away. God calls us to consider carefully before we answer. Spend time with Jesus. Get to know him well. Then prepare your answer.

To think about

- Why is the answer to Jesus's question so critical?
- How did you arrive at your conclusions about Jesus? What difference do your conclusions make in your life?

Lord Jesus, I pray for family and friends who are still undecided about you. Keep them restless until they decide. May they look at your deeds and words honestly and commit themselves to you.

231

With Jesus on the Mountain

Mark 9:2–32

Today's hike with Jesus takes us up the mountain with Peter, James, and John, the inner circle of the Twelve. Let's assume we're trekking along a narrow, rocky path absorbing warm sunshine. We chat cordially among ourselves, trying to mask our uncertainties about what Jesus has in mind. At least we can breathe a little easier, freed from the oppressive throngs of sick people.

But disturbing doubts gnaw at us. What could possibly be on Jesus's mind? It's been a week, but we can't expunge from our heads his strange talk about his coming in the glory of his Father with his holy angels and that some of us won't die until we see the kingdom of God (Mark 8:38–9:1).

Peter's embarrassment stands out all over him. Jesus called him Satan for rebuking him (8:33). We can't exactly blame Peter, because all his followers were deeply saddened when Jesus said the chief priests and scribes were going to kill him.

Talk about being terrified! Suddenly the mountain explodes in brilliant light and Jesus disappears. It all happens so fast we don't have time to think or react. It's as though God himself has landed on the summit, but in an instant there stands Jesus, or is it Jesus?

The dazzling light transforms his cloak into material so white we cannot describe it. Just as our eyes adjust to this incredible brightness, two other figures appear. Stunned beyond belief, we sense by God's Spirit that they are Moses and Elijah.

In this incomprehensible scene we see them talking with Jesus. As we try to absorb everything, speech fails us. We are too frightened to say anything. But then an idea seizes Peter.

He speaks to Jesus and proposes erecting tents for each of them.

Peter's impetuousness betrays him again. Quickly a cloud blots out everything and God's voice booms from heaven, telling us that Jesus is his beloved Son and we should listen to him (9:7).

Just like that it is all over. Moses and Elijah disappear as quickly as they came. Jesus looks like himself again. He warns us not to tell anyone what we have witnessed, that is, not until he has been raised from the dead. Well, we don't talk about it, but we have no idea what he means by rising from the dead.

Looking back, we appreciate the magnificence and the importance of what the scene told us about Jesus. God knew how much we needed to hear his affirmation of his Son. We just weren't ready to believe what Jesus was telling us about himself. We didn't want him to die. But that voice: we never forgot it. It was a spine-tingling moment, but hearing God's authoritative voice supporting Jesus—that's what stayed with us after he was gone. We really did see God's kingdom, didn't we?

To think about

- Why did Jesus allow Peter, James, and John to witness his transfiguration?
- How is your confidence in Jesus boosted by this scene?

Heavenly Father, there's much about this event I can't explain. But you know how much I need to see Jesus in his glory. I'm so easily distracted by the mundane. Help me to spend more time on the mountain with Jesus.

Jesus, the Key to Answered Prayer

John 14:12–14; 15:7–8; 16:23–24

Jesus taught and modeled prayer. Often his disciples watched him go off alone to pray. He sketched an outline prayer for them that has since guided and refreshed millions of Christians. As he was about to leave them, he told them to pray boldly with faith in his name (John 14:14).

Obviously, huge obstacles awaited the disciples as they gathered with Jesus in the upper room. They feared for their lives. If they somehow survived the authorities, what would they do? How would they do it?

Jesus did not sketch on the tablecloth a master plan for them. He spoke in broad, powerful generalities. Rather than a plan, he laid out principles. The Holy Spirit would come and guide them. As they followed and obeyed the Spirit, they would know exactly what to do. Whatever happened, prayer would sustain them. Prayer would be their conduit to heaven and to the Father. Through prayer they would receive knowledge, wisdom, insight, courage, and power. Jesus told them to abide in him. They had to learn to talk to him in prayer.

Learning to sail in uncharted waters, the disciples would call on their Chief Navigator in heaven for everything they needed. They had to believe his promise that he would respond to their prayers. Christ's promise tested their faith, obedience, and commitment. In the end, no other resources were available. They were shut up to prayer.

Jesus guarded his promise to answer their prayers with the qualifier, "in my name." He also explained his purpose: "so that the Son may bring glory to the Father" (v. 13). Prayer enabled them to "bear much fruit" and thus glorify God (15:7–8).

Fruit bearing depended on their abiding in Christ with trust in his Word and living in conformity to his will. Asking in Jesus's name kept them from asking from pure selfishness. The disciples could pray in Jesus's name because, having lived with him and observed him, they knew what would be consistent with his holy, sacrificial life.

We follow both the encouragements and the boundaries of praying in Jesus's name, to bear fruit and glorify our Father. Our basic calling is to please Jesus and live according to God's will. We do not live to please ourselves but to please him who died for us and rose again.

As we pray, we confess our sins and ask the Holy Spirit to cleanse us of greedy, selfish prayers that would dishonor Jesus's name. As we desire to be like Jesus, and to be conformed to his likeness, we find our prayer requests purified of selfishness.

Each day God loves to hear and answer our prayers, not just our petitions for our needs, but also our confessions, praise, and intercession for others. Jesus opened the way for us to come boldly to God's throne of grace. Happy and blessed are we if we follow him to it.

To think about

- How did Jesus's teaching about prayer help his disciples?
- How can your prayer life play a more significant part in your getting to know Jesus better?

Heavenly Father, thank you that I can talk to you at any time, in any and all circumstances. Lord, increase my faith and my understanding of your will so that I can pray in Jesus's name in obedience to what you want.

Jesus, Builder of His Church

Matthew 16:13–19; Ephesians 5:25–29

Jesus did not organize his team. There were no organizational charts or company seminars to improve the productivity of his workers. Tersely, he declared he would build his church, but he did not say how. He said it would be constructed on Peter, the rock, and his confession that Jesus is the Son of the living God. He predicted that hell would assail his church, but would not conquer it.

Some church traditions insist that Peter himself was the church's foundation, while others insist that the church's foundation was his confession of Christ's deity. My conviction is that Jesus himself is the church's foundation, as Paul and Peter testify (1 Cor. 3:11; 1 Peter 2:4–8).

Be that as it may, we would have no church at all apart from the confession of Peter and the apostles and the early Christians that Jesus Christ is Lord. Those who made this confession constituted the original "church," a word that simply means "called out ones." The early believers took an ordinary word for any assembly or gathering and applied it to themselves. Later the apostle Paul expanded the concept and called believers the body of Christ and God's temple. New Testament "church" means God's people, Christ's family, his body—not a building or an organization.

The apostle Paul aptly pictured Jesus as loving his church, giving himself up for it, making it holy, spotless, and without blemish. Believers are living parts of his body. He provides and cares for us, protecting us against all the devil's attacks. He is the head of the body. The church is a vital, living extension of Jesus himself.

Jesus has so skillfully built his church that each member belongs not only to him but also to every other member.

Our joint membership transcends all denominational, racial, national, ethnic, and gender differences. We are all one in Christ Jesus (1 Cor. 12:12–13).

In astounding ways using human instruments, Jesus builds his church. He builds through our worship, witness, and service as we care for one another and take his Good News to people not yet members of his one, universal church.

We are his hands, arms, and feet. In a wonderful way, we are both Christ's workmanship and his workers. As we grow together in the grace and knowledge of Jesus our Lord, his church grows corporately as well. No single believer can remain isolated from other believers. Jesus has made us so that we need and appreciate one another.

The apostle Paul wanted to be sure he was building things that lasted. Whatever time, energy, prayer, and money we invest in Christ's body will stand the test of time and bear eternal fruit for his glory. Loving Jesus calls us to love and build up all those who name him Lord and Savior.

To think about

- Why is "body" an apt metaphor for Christ's church?
- How have you been edified by other members of Christ's body? How can you build up a fellow believer?

Lord Jesus, what an astounding privilege to belong to your body! Thank you for caring for me. Help me to take your care of other members of your body.

The Magnanimous Jesus

Luke 9:46–56

Occasionally Jesus applied the brakes to his overzealous disciples. They throttled an exorcist because he was not one of them. James and John, the Sons of Thunder, wanted to call down fire from heaven on the unbelieving Samaritans. Such actions violated totally the principle of childlike humility that Jesus had just taught them.

We can look at these incidents as examples of how *not* to follow Jesus. We can blame the disciples for protecting their turf and trying to display their power before people who refused to recognize their Master. Such tactics are unbecoming to Christ's followers. But in these meditations we want to see Jesus, not his headstrong disciples. What is there about him in these episodes that gives us a desire to be like him? Is there something in his attitudes that we can emulate?

First, we learn that Jesus shunned gaining and protecting a private corner on ministry. His superlative modesty and humility allowed him to grant others the right to do what they wanted to do. Not all workers had to work his way.

Because Jesus possessed a remarkably positive self-image, he could open the door to anyone casting out demons in his name. He did not need to feed his own ego by putting down players who didn't play on his team. God's kingdom loomed so huge in his vision that there was no room for selfish kingdom building. His philosophy of live and let live allowed him to have such an attitude. Besides, the exorcist was casting out demons in his name. A generous spirit and big heart constituted the DNA of Jesus's life and work.

Second, Jesus refused to use his power to get rid of those who chose not to receive him. He could have called down the fire suggested by James and John, but he refused to do so and rebuked them for such a fleshly, worldly proposal. The idea was utterly foreign to the temperament of Jesus (Luke 9:54–56).

Jesus came to serve, to give, to love, to witness, and to encourage faith. He did not come to destroy but to build. Of course he warned of the terrible judgment awaiting unbelievers, but fiery judgment was not appropriate when Jesus was ministering on earth.

Jesus exhibited gracious patience. He demonstrated the values of his own Beatitudes. He was love in action. By refusing to destroy the Samaritans, he took the high ground and fulfilled the demands of love according to 1 Corinthians 13.

Pride and revenge played no part in Jesus. Humility, open-handedness, long-suffering, and patience were his attributes, and they should be those of all who profess to follow him.

To think about

- Compare the attitudes of the disciples and Jesus in these incidents. What differences stand out?
- On what occasions have you faced similar tests? How did you handle them? Why?

Lord Jesus, I admire your humility and patience. I confess I have often failed to be like you. May your grace and love empower me to do better.

Jesus Sharpens Priorities

Luke 9:57–62; 10:17–20, 38–42

Following Jesus demands that we sharpen our priorities. Jesus's announcement of the Good News of God's kingdom cut to the heart of what people were doing with their lives. They had to learn to focus on what was most essential.

For Jesus, sharpening priorities meant going beyond what was good and acceptable behavior. It meant choosing the best for your life in terms of your relation to Jesus. Very simply, Jesus is far and away our top priority.

When some potential disciples came to Jesus, he advised them to count the cost of following him. Obedience to him outranked even the comfort of having a bed. When he invited some others to become his followers, they gave priority to some ordinary but necessary activities. They refused to put their commitment to Jesus on the fast track as Peter, James, John, and Matthew had done when he called them.

Seventy followers of Jesus returned with glowing reports of successful ministries, including victories over the devil. Jesus rejoiced with them but sharpened their priorities by saying it was more important to have their names written in heaven.

How often have we ranked earthly success, even in spiritual warfare, above heaven itself? Perhaps this is the reason for the apostle Paul's command that we focus our hearts and minds on things above and give priority to where Jesus is (Col. 3:1–4).

Even in the circle of Jesus's closest friends, he chose a family spat to sharpen Martha's priorities. Martha's immersion in household affairs was a good thing but not the best thing.

Mary's lingering at the feet of Jesus to soak up his words revealed where her priorities were.

"But only one thing is needed" (Luke 10:42) stands as our clearest, sharpest guide for setting our priorities. "Only one thing" cuts away all extraneous, even worthwhile, activities. Jesus is it. If he outranks everything else in our lives, then we have discovered that one necessary thing.

God's Word "penetrates even to dividing soul and spirit . . . ; it judges the thoughts and attitudes of the heart" (Heb. 4:12). When our desire to know, love, and obey Jesus surpasses everything else, it is the effect of God's Word on our heart. We learn by the Holy Spirit's counsel what we must throw overboard to put Jesus first.

When Jesus comes to live in us, he wants to own everything. He does not want to stand on the periphery of our life, accepting leftovers. Because he is the incomparable Lord of glory, he winnows and burns the chaff in us that keeps us from making the best choices.

Only one thing is necessary, to sit at the feet of Jesus and to enjoy him forever.

To think about

- Why did Jesus find it necessary to sharpen people's priorities?
- How do you decide what comes first in your life? How do you listen to what Jesus has to say?

Lord Jesus, you know how I go back and forth, trying to put you first but sometimes allowing other things to get in the way. Keep sharpening my priorities, I pray, so that you will stand above everything else in my life.

Jesus, Antidote for Troubled Hearts

Mark 13:5–11

I t's no sin to have a troubled heart. Consider, for example, the cries of David, Jeremiah, Jesus, his disciples, and Paul.

> David: "Be merciful to me, O LORD, for I am in distress" (Ps. 31:9).
>
> Jeremiah: "Why is my pain unending and my wound grievous and incurable?" (Jer. 15:18).
>
> Jesus: "Now my heart is troubled" (John 12:27).
>
> Jesus: "He began to be deeply distressed and troubled" (Mark 14:33).
>
> Jesus to his disciples: "Do not let your hearts be troubled" (John 14:1).
>
> Paul: "We are . . . perplexed, but not in despair" (2 Cor. 4:8).

If we're honest, we will add our own name to the list.

What exactly is a troubled heart and how can Jesus fix it? When Jesus described for his disciples the terrible days ahead, he cited enough vivid calamities to cause worry and fear. Yet, he said, do not let tumultuous days bring tumultuous hearts. Do not be intimidated by what's coming.

When we invite Jesus to calm our hearts, he directs us to look for the causes of our disquiet. We go off by ourselves in some quiet place and talk to ourselves. What exactly has happened to cause my distress? Is this a major event or a minor irritation?

Then Jesus tells us to talk to ourselves about God. Is he still God? Has he changed? Is he still in control? Has my situation caught him by surprise?

Next, we talk to Jesus. Has he abandoned us? Does he still care? Has his love for us expired? Is he still powerfully alive in heaven, interceding for us?

Jesus is not playing games with us when he tells us not to be distressed and fearful. Every unsettling circumstance drives us to our knees. Troubled hearts travel to God's Word for solace and relief. We simply ask Jesus to be for us everything he said he would be.

Stressful times cause troubled hearts. That's part and parcel of our humanity. But we do not have to carry a troubled heart to the point of breaking. Jesus himself is our antidote. As we deepen our knowledge of the height, breadth, length, and depth of his love, he will radically relieve our turmoil and distress.

In Christ we are liberated from bondage to anxiety. We release everything to him. We pray and ask others to pray, to help us carry our troubles. In the strong name of Jesus, we prevail.

To think about

- Why did people like David, Jesus, and Paul suffer troubled hearts?
- Rehearse in your mind the steps you need to take when troubles overwhelm you.

Thank you, Lord Jesus, that you are there when I need you most. Thank you for lifting me up when I am down. Help me to carry the troubles of my friends.

Jesus, More Powerful than Satan

Luke 11:14–22; Hebrews 2:14–15; Revelation 1:18

Jesus thwarted the devil's attacks immediately after he was baptized, but those temptations marked just the opening salvo of a continuous assault by his mortal enemy.

It's strange, from our perspective at least, that Jesus's human enemies also sought to subvert his mission by accusing him of working with the prince of demons. Jesus exposed their stupid logic. How could he possibly be working with Satan to destroy Satan's own emissaries?

Then he drove home his punch line with a commonsense story about a burglar who disarmed the homeowner in his own house. Jesus said, in effect, "By casting out demons, I have disarmed Satan in his own fortress. I am stronger than Satan" (see Luke 11:17–22).

Ultimately, when Jesus suffered on the cross for our sins and rose from his grave, he overpowered Satan. This is the reason the apostles declared victory in the name of Jesus. Death was Satan's stranglehold on people until Jesus came, but Jesus defeated death and freed his children from the fear of death.

In a paroxysm of triumph to John, Jesus pronounced victory over Satan: "I am the Living One; I was dead, and behold I am alive for ever and ever! I hold the keys of death and Hades" (Rev. 1:18). Jesus has smashed Satan's domain forever. As a result, Christians prosper gloriously, free of Satan's power.

The apostles made clear that believers are not free of Satan's attacks, however. Sometimes he attacks like a roaring lion (1 Peter 5:8), sometimes disguised as an angel of light (2 Cor. 11:14). As the father of lies, he deceives as well as threatens (John 8:44). Jesus asked God to protect his disciples from the evil one (17:15).

As Jesus's story made clear, he is stronger than Satan. Jesus is our protector and our defender. He alone enables us to stand. The Holy Spirit equips us with Jesus's spiritual armor to resist Satan.

We draw on Jesus's power through prayer and spiritual meditation on his words. We fortify our mind, heart, and soul with the words of Jesus. Because he lives in us, he is able to provide abundant soul food to keep us alert to Satan's devices and to give us patience, perseverance, and long-suffering in the face of his frontal assaults.

Sometimes Satan lulls us to sleep, encouraging us to think we are safe in some kind of spiritual bomb shelter. Often he attacks us where we think we are strong and have nothing to worry about, but we are most vulnerable when we assume we are least vulnerable. Pride goes before a fall.

Therefore, our key to Jesus's victory over Satan in us is our spiritual preparation and alertness. Because we know that Jesus is stronger than Satan, we trust him to fight and win our battles for us. As Martin Luther wrote in "A Mighty Fortress Is Our God," one little word of faith defeats our enemy.

To think about

- What did Jesus's enemies hope to achieve by aligning him with Satan?
- What have you found to be your best protection against Satan's attacks? Why is it effective?

Thank you, Lord Jesus, for being stronger than Satan. Thank you that, because you defeated him, I do not have to listen to him. Fill my mind, heart, and will with your strength when Satan attacks me.

Jesus, Smasher of Traditions

Mark 7:1–23

Leaving the hospital room of a friend, I am favorably impressed by numerous postings to wash my hands. Dispensers of antiseptic cleansers sprout from the walls like so many mushrooms. I've even read newspaper articles that advise hospital patients to remind their doctors to wash their hands.

I feel as though I've been transported back some two thousand years in time to the days of Jesus and the Pharisees. In those days it was a command for Jews to wash their hands, but the command was not for the purpose of avoiding infections. It was the means of escaping something far worse: God's punishment.

No quick scrub would do. With hands pointed skyward, water had to dribble down over your hands to your wrists. Then you had to do it again in the opposite direction. Finally, you had to rub your hands together.

Zealously the Pharisees guarded a voluminous repository of accumulated wisdom called the traditions of the elders. Although it held no direct support from Scripture, the Pharisees exalted the command to wash before meals to the level of the Ten Commandments. Therefore they assailed Jesus when his disciples broke a tradition that carried the weight of a divine command. By not washing according to the rules, his disciples provoked a head-on collision between Jesus and the religious leaders over the value of outward religious observances.

Jesus addressed the fundamental spiritual issue behind hand washing and religious washing of all the kitchen utensils. Essentially, he charged that the people's religious traditions fed their hypocrisy and were useless as ways to clean one's heart. In reality, by keeping their traditions, they had rejected

God's commands. For example, they had found ways around his command to honor father and mother.

Further, one's hands and dishes might be spotlessly pure by traditional standards, but one's heart could be totally corrupt at the same time. Hypocrisy and sins of all kinds originate in our heart, not in our dirty hands and dirty dishes. Under these conditions, Jesus declared totally useless their scrupulous worship. "They worship me in vain" is one of the scariest verses in the Bible (Mark 7:7).

As we center our attention on Jesus, he not only smashes our traditions and our vain worship, but opens our eyes to see the true source of our defilement. Jesus liberates us from bondage to useless ceremonies. He redeems us to worship with a clean heart in spirit and in truth.

Somehow, traditions try to sneak back into our spiritual repertoire. We must be alert and trap them before they entangle us and strip our walk with Jesus of vitality, power, and love.

> Stand fast therefore in the liberty wherewith Christ hath made us free, and be not entangled again with the yoke of bondage.
>
> Galatians 5:1 KJV

To think about

- Why did the Pharisees challenge Jesus on the issue of hand washing?
- What traditions do you suspect of fostering hypocrisy? How can you keep them from gaining a foothold in your life?

Heavenly Father, I confess it is easier to follow rules than to follow Jesus. Give me a clean heart, Lord Jesus. I want to be free to worship you authentically from my heart and not be bound by human traditions.

Jesus, the Confronter

Luke 11:37–54

From the standpoint of our Western manners, Jesus wasn't very nice to some very important people. In fact we might say he was rude. He told the Pharisees they were fools who didn't care about justice and God's love. He charged them with pomp and pride because they loved the seats of honor in the synagogue and relished the greetings they received in the market. They were like unmarked graves that people fell into.

The lawyers heard this and accurately understood that Jesus had insulted not just the Pharisees but the lawyers as well. Nevertheless, Jesus did not apologize for hurting their feelings. Instead, he poured gasoline on the fire by blaming the lawyers for loading people with intolerable burdens and not lifting a single finger to help them.

Further, they had built tombs for the prophets their forefathers had murdered and, therefore, were also guilty, and the blood of the prophets was on their hands. They would also be judged for barring people from gaining knowledge. They would have to answer for these crimes.

Jesus's denunciation of their sins produced neither repentance nor faith. Instead, the Pharisees and lawyers assailed Jesus and tried to trap him with his own words. Was his confrontation therefore a mistake?

First, we have to ask if there are any ways in which we fit Jesus's description of the Pharisees and lawyers. By confronting them, Jesus gave us a specific checklist particularly suited for those who practice strict religious conformity. We can perform required Christian services and still fall miserably short of a genuine love affair with Jesus. So we need to thank Jesus for digging into the hearts of the religious leaders and experts. What he found there was indeed messy and insulting, but until our rotten hearts are exposed and our sins confessed, we will never enjoy God's grace and forgiveness.

Second, we need to look again at Jesus in this testy scene. Yes, he did confront. That was essential if these people were to come to repentance and enter his kingdom. But notice also that Jesus was bold, courageous, wise, loving, and instructive. With his wisdom and love he drove unerringly to the heart of the issue. He taught courageously in the face of certain opposition. By insulting the Pharisees and lawyers, Jesus taught them that faith was the only true path to God and his righteousness.

To deal with heart issues lying beneath the veneer of holiness requires unusual grace and confidence in God's Word. To walk with Jesus means we allow him to scour our souls of pride and self-righteousness. We also ask him to deliver us from self-imposed rules and make us his instruments of true righteousness and peace.

To think about

- Why did Jesus insult the Pharisees and lawyers?
- What parts of your life does Jesus need to confront? Why?

O God, forgive my self-righteous pride. Make me humble, bold, wise, and loving as I try to help people see the difference between religious rules and true life in Christ.

Jesus, Our Ransom

Mark 10:35–45; I Timothy 2:5–6; Titus 2:11–14; I Peter 1:18–19

The kidnapping of the Charles Lindbergh baby, and some others of prominent families, scared me when I was a youngster. Often I lay awake at night, wondering if someone would climb in my bedroom window and snatch me. Of course it never occurred to me that my parents were so poor that no self-respecting kidnapper would take me for money. "Besides," my mother tried to console me, "who would want you?" Be that as it may, the word *ransom* figured prominently in everyone's vocabulary in those days.

Later on, I discovered the word in the Bible, but it didn't exactly fit my early impressions. When kidnappers demanded a ransom, they wanted a huge sum of money in return for the child. But Jesus said he ransomed me with his life—not with a million dollars. Now that was a new angle. I also discovered that the ransom Jesus paid with his life secured my redemption from sin. Ransom/redemption/sin are inseparable. When Jesus gave his life for me, he redeemed me from slavery to sin and its terrible consequences.

Here we enter the mystery of divine justice. My sin is no mystery. I have broken God's laws and violated his holiness innumerable times. Neither is judgment a mystery. Nothing makes sense in this world without justice and judgment. Because I sinned, I deserve God's judgment. There is a warrant out for my arrest, so to speak, because I am a lawbreaker. God, my righteous Judge, delivers the penalty. Sin brings death and eternal separation from him.

God is holy, righteous, and just, but I am dead in my transgressions and sins and am utterly incapable of satisfying God's justice. Someone must rescue me. Enter the Lord Jesus Christ.

When Jesus died on the cross and rose again, he paid the ransom that held me in bondage to sin, guilt, judgment, and death. I was ransomed at incalculable cost and set free to love and serve him. The apostles used the verb "to purchase" to describe what Jesus did for me through his shed blood. It was the same word used for the redemption of slaves.

Jesus, our ransom, is our model. When his disciples sought preferred positions, Jesus rebuked them and said he was a servant who would ransom sinners by giving his life; they were to follow his example. Jesus, our ransom, redeemed us to make us humble servants of others. He gave his life for us, not only to satisfy God's justice, but also to inspire us to give our lives for him and for those he died to save.

To think about

- What does the word *ransom* bring to your mind? Why did Jesus use it to describe his mission?
- What is the connection between your awareness of your sins and your appreciation of Jesus as your saving ransom?

Thank you, Lord Jesus, for giving your life to ransom me. I belong to you. Use me, I pray. Use my life and witness to serve others.

Jesus, Our Secure Home

John 14:1–7

As I write this, thousands of people are losing their homes because they can't pay their mortgages. Peter, James, John, and the others had staked their homes and businesses on Jesus. "We have left everything to follow you!" Peter had said (Matt. 19:27). But now in the upper room, they learned that Jesus was not going to take them with him on the next leg of his journey.

"Where I am going, you cannot follow now," Jesus said (John 13:36). To his disciples this amounted to a default on his promises of land, houses, and thrones, and they would be left holding worthless mortgages, so to speak (Mark 10:29–30; Luke 22:30). But then Jesus issued an astounding promise, incomparable to anything they had heard before. "I am going [to my Father's house]," he said, "to prepare a place for you" (14:2). He would give them a secure home after all.

Probably Jesus's disciples wondered what kind of a home it would be, just as we do. Imagining what heaven will be like often crosses our mind and heart. Jesus gave no details. He did say God's house has ample space for everyone. But most important, he revealed the primary purpose of heaven—to be with him—and he told them how to get there. In effect, he said, "You know the way to heaven because you know me."

Thomas, saying what they may have all been thinking, confessed their ignorance (v. 5). Then Jesus pronounced a singularly clarifying explanation: "No one comes to the Father except through me" (v. 6). In other words, the Father is the destination and Jesus is the only way for anyone to make it to heaven.

Our eternal security rests solely on Jesus and his acceptance by our Father in heaven. After his death and resurrection for our sins, Jesus ascended into heaven. Among other things, he prepares a secure dwelling for every single one of his followers. Heaven is where we meet Jesus. He is ready for us. Are we ready for him?

Because Jesus is God's only Son, because Jesus left his glory and came to earth, because Jesus is our Creator and Redeemer, because he took our sins on himself and satisfied God's justice and holiness, because Jesus defeated sin, death, and the grave, because he both lives in us and lives in heaven, our eternal home is secure.

Nothing will ever cut us off from the supreme love and power of the Lord Jesus Christ. Nothing will ever rob us of our investment in heaven. No one will ever foreclose on our property, because Jesus holds the title deed to it. No creditors will assail us for our past debts. We are safe forever because Jesus is safe forever. Our destinies are linked with his, and he will never forsake us. We are fit for heaven only because Jesus is fit for heaven. We gain heaven by his righteousness not ours.

To think about

- Why did the disciples not understand that Jesus was going to heaven?
- What difference does it make to you now that your home in heaven is secure?

Thank you, Lord Jesus, for my deed to a place in heaven. You paid the debt I owe. I am free and clear of all liens and mortgages. May praise, honor, glory, majesty, and power all be yours.

Jesus, Superior to Angels

Hebrews 1:1-4

To say Jesus is superior to angels may not impress us. But then we don't know much about angels and don't pay much attention to them anyway. But angels rank right up there at the top, next to God himself, in the divine order of things. The Bible sparkles with angelic activity, and the original Bible readers among the Jews took angels a lot more seriously than we do.

Therefore, to convince those early readers that Jesus was indeed worth following, the writer of Hebrews fired his opening salvo in their direction. And what an explosive salvo it was!

Are angels really so great? Well, look at this:

God chose Jesus as his spokesman. He supersedes the prophets.

God appointed Jesus to be the heir of all things.

God made the universe through Jesus.

Jesus is the radiance of God's glory.

Jesus is the exact representation of God's being.

Jesus sustains all things by his powerful word.

Jesus provided purification for our sins.

Jesus sits at God's right hand in heaven.

Jesus's name is superior to angels' names.

Therefore, Jesus far surpasses the angels in his being and works, so we don't worship angels; we worship Jesus. He is fully qualified to receive our faith, trust, love, and obedience. All the old ways of God's speaking have been fulfilled and superseded by Jesus. Keep on following him.

Regardless of what we think about angels, the Spirit of God takes the arguments of Hebrews 1 and uses them to reinforce our faith and to keep us growing in Jesus. Our mind, heart, and will tend to stray and become indifferent to him. We forget his supremacy. We forget the key facts that verified his credentials to be our Lord and Savior in the first place.

So Hebrews 1 not only provides food for our souls, but sorts out ideas and angles that tend to diminish the superiority of Jesus over anything else out there in the world. If it isn't angels, something else comes along and tries to force Jesus to the sidelines.

When my life seems to spin out of control, there's Jesus who sustains everything. When sin, guilt, and judgment slam me, there's Jesus who made purification for my sins. I do not need to feel guilty and defeated because I have sinned. Jesus tells Satan, my accuser, to shut up. I am clothed in Christ's righteousness.

When other "words" muddle my thinking, there's Jesus, God's last Word. When the world seems to be going crazy, there's Jesus, the Heir of all things. He will reign and make all things right. His righteousness and peace will prevail.

To think about

- Why was it important to compare Jesus with the angels in the New Testament?
- What ideas threaten to crowd out Jesus in your life? Why? What can you do?

Heavenly Father, I praise and thank you for the total adequacy of Jesus for all my needs. Keep the power, love, and majesty of Jesus foremost in my thinking. May no rivals for his supremacy lurk in my heart.

Jesus Walked His Talk

Luke 12:1–31

Finding teachers who fail to walk their talk is not difficult. Those who do live up to what they teach and preach sparkle like diamonds in a crush of rocks. Jesus was one of those sparklers. Flawlessly, he did what he told his followers to do.

"Don't worry about people who can kill you," Jesus admonished (see Luke 12:4–5). Ha, easier said than done! How did Jesus do? Did he worry about the religious authorities who could accuse him of blasphemy, a capital offense? Did he worry about Pilate and his soldiers who could kill him? Never. Was this because Jesus was unusually brave? Not really. Many brave men have gone to their deaths valiantly and proudly. Jesus did not worry about those who held life-and-death power over him because their powers were physical and temporal not spiritual and eternal.

Jesus said eternity is the big issue. Being cast into hell—now that's something to worry about. Jesus did not fear those who could kill his body because they were totally powerless to send him to hell. Jesus didn't worry because he knew his heavenly Father would never overlook him and his physical needs. God knows when a sparrow falls; God knows when a hair disappears from our head. Don't be afraid, because God values you much more than sparrows (vv. 6–7). Jesus was not afraid because he knew God and his limitless power and love.

"Don't worry when they bring you to trial," Jesus taught (see vv. 11–12). Now there's a sweaty issue. What was Jesus's record? Did he worry at his trial? Not one iota, because the Holy Spirit lived in him. The Holy Spirit instructed and empowered him. His wisdom and his self-control came from the Holy Spirit.

"Don't be greedy for more money," Jesus commanded (see v. 15). That's tough medicine. What about Jesus? Did he fall into the lifestyle of itinerant teachers who demanded exorbitant fees? Absolutely not. Not one shred of evidence points to greed in Jesus. In fact his life was just the opposite; he was totally generous, sacrificial, and self-giving. Whatever he had acquired as a carpenter, he probably left with his mother, Mary, and his siblings. The Son of Man was not known as a sharp-dealing, acquisitive tradesman.

"Don't worry about your necessities," Jesus taught (see vv. 22–23). This is another extremely tall order. Jesus walked his talk in this regard by living like a pauper: no home, no wardrobe, no stocked pantry, no bed, no money. How did he do this? Rationally, he knew that worry never lengthened anyone's life span. If you can't do that, why worry about the rest? Besides, Jesus looked at the ravens and lilies and built trust in God from what he observed. Spiritually, he knew his heavenly Father so intimately that he trusted him for everything. He had set his mind on God and his kingdom and thus was liberated from anxiety about his necessities. Jesus walked his talk.

To think about

- How do you suppose Jesus's disciples reacted when they heard his radical teaching? How do you react to his teaching?
- What resources have you found to enable you to walk your talk?

Thank you, Lord Jesus, that you set an extremely high standard and kept it. I confess your demands are tough. May I grow in my knowledge and use of all you have to offer me, to be your obedient disciple.

Jesus, Our Supreme Passion

Philippians 3:1–14

Jesus's disciples hoped and suffered with him. The apostle Paul persecuted him, but it was Paul, the tormentor of Christians, who declared that Jesus was his supreme passion. Jesus had become his passion because he had met the living Christ on the Damascus Road.

Paul never got over his encounter with Jesus. Again and again he testified what a totally life-changing event it was. When he met Christ, his life did a one-eighty, and Jesus showed him and all succeeding generations of Christians what a radical thing conversion to Christ is. The passionate, zealous Pharisee became the passionate, zealous evangelist, missionary, church planter, and author of a big chunk of our New Testament.

Quite apart from what Paul did for Jesus was his intense love for Jesus. Paul recounted what his love affair with Jesus cost him. For Jesus to become his supreme passion, he surrendered his religious pedigree, standing in the Jewish community, reputation, self-righteousness, and his zeal for God. Not only did he discard such eminently worthwhile attributes, he figured they were garbage compared to his knowing Jesus. Knowing Jesus was worth far more because Jesus gave him righteousness, or right standing before God.

Paul's theology also took a one-eighty, away from legalism and trying to please God by religious zeal and toward righteousness through faith. His supreme passion for Jesus exploded when the truth of salvation by grace through faith gripped his heart, mind, and soul. Thereafter, all Paul cared about was knowing Jesus. By knowing Jesus, Paul gained access to his resurrection power. He also became a partner in Christ's sufferings. Through Jesus and by faith alone, Paul knew for sure that he would be raised from the dead.

Paul's supreme passion motivated him to full obedience. Love for Jesus drove him to pursue vigorously the most valuable prize of all: life in heaven with Jesus.

What was there about Jesus that so radically changed Paul's outlook? He did not see Jesus's miracles or listen to his teachings. He did not witness the cross and the empty tomb. But he did see the resurrected Christ who called him to account for persecuting him. Paul had imprisoned Christians, and Jesus told him that was the same as persecuting him. That was enough for Paul.

Later Paul went off to Arabia for three years to learn all he could about Jesus and his gospel. Whatever he saw and heard there, Paul was compelled to match love with action. He had been overwhelmed by Christ's glory, majesty, and power. From that time forward, everything about him was brand-new. Not only had Jesus saved him, he had become the focal point of his life and work. Only the incomparable greatness of Christ could achieve such a transformation.

To think about

- Describe Paul before and after he met Jesus.
- What changes has Jesus wrought in your life? What is your level of passion for him?

  Lord Jesus, you are supreme. You alone are worthy of my total affection and zeal. I confess my coldness and disobedience at times. Keep me pressing ahead toward the prize of your upward call. Thank you.

Jesus, Our Total Sufficiency

Colossians 2:6–15

I knelt in the pew of a small, rural church in Pennsylvania. A handful of the faithful had gathered to pray on Wednesday night. In this church I had spent my youth and college years.

My soul had been scraped as bare as the hard bench on which I propped my elbows and buried my face. My wife of seven years had died suddenly of a brain aneurysm, leaving me with an infant son and a two-year-old daughter. They had gone to live with their grandparents. I prayed with old friends but I was alone in this world.

In the abyss God spoke Colossians 2:10 to me. Despite my desolate grief, by the miracle of God's grace in Christ, I was complete in Jesus. I needed nothing to be complete, because I had Jesus. I didn't even need a wife and children. Thank you, Jesus.

Such is the Spirit's power and the Father's love that the apostle Paul's theology became refreshing water and nourishing food for my soul. At that moment my chief concern was not to decipher Paul's irrefutable logic. It was enough that Jesus had become my total sufficiency.

Of course my experience barely approximated what Paul had suffered for Jesus. You can meditate on his narrow escapes from stoning and drowning, plus the threats of mobs, beatings, imprisonments, riots, lack of food, lack of sleep, and what he summarized as carrying around the death of Jesus (2 Cor. 4:7–12; 6:3–10). Think about that when you read his assertion that Christians are brought to completion in Jesus. Paul's primary idea of our total sufficiency in Christ is that in Jesus we have everything needed for our salvation. The complete being of the Godhead lives in Jesus, and because we are in Christ, there is absolutely nothing we lack.

Colossians 2:9–15 resembles a JumboTron display of everything believers possess in Jesus. We are divested of our lower nature by a spiritual circumcision, buried with him and raised to new life. We have been made alive in Christ. He has forgiven us and has wiped out the indictment against us, nailing it to the cross. Triumphantly, on that cross, for our sake, Jesus threw off the cosmic powers of darkness like so much dirty laundry and made a public spectacle of them in his victory parade.

When we are falling low, we look to his cross and to his parade. We tell ourselves we are totally free and 100 percent forgiven. Therefore, whenever we think we need something or someone to make our lives happy and fulfilled, we recognize this as the devil's trick to draw us away from our completeness in Christ.

The hymn says it so beautifully:

> Jesus Christ is made to me all I need, all I need;
> He alone is all my plea; he is all I need.
> Wisdom, righteousness and power, holiness
>   forevermore,
> My redemption full and sure, he is all I need.
>
> Charles P. Jones
> "All I Need"

To think about

- What spiritual assets in Christ did Paul add up, finding they make believers "complete"?
- What have you sometimes felt you needed for your life to be complete? Why? How does Jesus satisfy those needs?

O God, the magnificence and magnitude of what you have done for me in Christ overwhelms me. Yet sometimes I feel dissatisfied with my life. Help me to remember my more-than-sufficient wealth in Christ every time I feel I lack something.

261

Jesus, the World's Arsonist

Luke 12:49–53; Matthew 10:34–39

Is the title "Jesus, the World's Arsonist" too strong a title for this meditation? Does it put you off? Does it destroy your image of Jesus? How then shall we account for Jesus declaring, "I have come to bring fire on the earth" (Luke 12:49)?

The angels celebrated Christ's birth, singing, "Peace on earth." But Jesus said that he did not come to bring peace but a sword, division. What gives? What can we learn about Jesus from this that will help us grow in his grace and knowledge?

First, we can appreciate our Lord's candor and forthrightness when recruiting followers. He was embroiled in a cosmic struggle for truth and righteousness. The forces at his disposal appeared to be meager indeed. True, crowds flocked after him, but Jesus wasn't interested in crowds and popularity. He sought tough, committed followers who would lay aside everything for his sake. He offered no cheap grace, no easy shortcuts to his kingdom. Quite the contrary. He made his terms of enlistment as clear and as tough as possible. What inducements did he offer? The kingdom of God, forgiveness, eternal life, satisfaction, and fulfillment, but he warned of the way of the cross, self-denial, and the possible loss of what is most precious of all—one's own family. Therefore, when Jesus tells us not to be surprised by what's coming, he does us a huge favor. He prepares us for painful spiritual warfare.

Second, Jesus did not demand anything of his followers that he was not prepared to endure himself. The arson he was about to commit centered on the cross, what he called his personal ordeal. His death ignited a blaze that burns two thousand years later. Metaphorically, of course, Jesus kindles flames of both obedience and hatred. Fire symbolizes the intensity and devotion of disciples who have gone to the martyr's stake for Jesus. Fire also represents the unbelievably cruel and bloody hatred that has been poured out on Christians and the church.

When tongues of flame lick at the basic unit of society, our family, the conflagration reflects the larger worldwide battle between truth and error, between righteousness and godlessness, and between Jesus and Satan. The grievous truth of Jesus on the cross separates believers and unbelievers right down to our most intimate relationships. He is the issue. What we believe about him determines not only our eternal destiny but also our human relationships here and now.

How can we admire and emulate Jesus in his role as world arsonist? We are called to adhere at all costs, with love and grace, to the truth about him. However, we do not set fires over secondary issues. We allow Jesus to be our guide so that we can discern the issues that are so critical we cannot stand idly by as though they don't matter, even at the risk of hard feelings. Peace at any price is not the Jesus way. If truth in love causes sparks, we pray that truth in love will prevail in the person of Christ. He, not us, must always be the issue.

To think about

- What purposes did Jesus serve by saying he came to cause divisions?
- How does your stand for truth in Christ affect your family circle? How can you be tactful and not obnoxious about your faith?

Heavenly Father, I confess how hard it is for me to see Jesus in the role of arsonist. I much prefer peace to division. I pray that my life will so speak of Jesus that others will want to follow him.

Jesus, Fully Human and Fully Divine

Philippians 2:5–11

In this short meditation I do not intend to try to unravel the profound mystery of how one person could be at the same time fully human and fully divine. But that's the truth about Jesus. Virtually from the beginning, theologians have wrestled with how to explain this truth.

Very simply, New Testament writers described Jesus as a unique person, the preexistent second person of the Trinity, who took on human flesh.

Jesus was with God from eternity past. He was the Godhead's agent of creation. The divine Word was and is God. Deity was his from the first. "Jesus is Lord" became the triumphant battle cry of the early Christians. It was the touchstone of their confession. "Jesus is Lord" delineates and distinguishes his followers today.

When the time was right, God the Son became the Son of Man. In his flesh, Jesus of Nazareth displayed the authentic credentials of deity. He suppressed a violent storm. He liberated captives from demons. He healed victims of diseases, blindness, and paralysis. He raised the dead. He defeated Satan. He exposed phony religionists and stood down earthly powers. The wisdom and grace of his teachings confounded his critics and blessed his followers.

So genuine were the hallmarks of his deity that Jesus could say that anyone who saw him saw the Father in heaven. He claimed to be the light of the world, the bread of life, the water of life, the resurrection and the life, and the only way to God. Jesus offered life to the full; freedom from oppression, worry, and fear; forgiveness of sins; and eternal life.

The New Testament writers did not explain how all of this came to be, only that it did and why it did. The apostle

Paul's terse paragraph in Philippians 2 about Jesus's divesting himself of his divine nature to become a human slave is not a theological treatise but an object lesson of what it means to be humble.

All we need to know is locked in this paragraph. The fully divine Jesus became the fully human Jesus to die on the cross and to be raised above all others in the universe. Fully restored to his supremacy, Jesus will be the object of universal worship. His name will be above all names.

This is all because God loved his fallen humanity so much that he gave his Son to be the world's Savior. Rather than stumble over the seeming physical impossibility of one person being both God and man, we are called to receive God's intervention with joyful gratitude and loving obedience.

Paul explained in one sentence that on the human level Jesus was born of David's stock, but on the level of the Holy Spirit, he was declared God's Son by his resurrection from the dead (Rom. 1:3–4). All we have and are we owe to Jesus our Lord. He was made like us, except for our sin, so that he fully empathizes with us and so that we find our needed grace and mercy in him. He died on the cross for our sins, and because he was fully human and fully divine, his sacrifice guarantees our forgiveness and our acceptance with God.

To think about

- How do you understand the humanity and deity of Jesus?
- What aspects of his humanity and of his deity are most meaningful to you? Why?

Lord Jesus, you are my human and divine Lord and Savior. I confess with praise and adoration the mystery of your being. May your power and your humility stamp themselves indelibly on my spirit and life, to the praise of your glory.

Jesus, Showcase of God's Grace

Ephesians 2:1–10

What is it like to receive grace? Insurance companies give us a thirty-day "grace" period to pay our premiums. That's a month beyond our due date. A small thing, perhaps, but sometimes we need it.

In college I worked long into the night trying to finish a paper, but my feverish attempts to meet the deadline fell short and I was doomed. My professor, however, extended grace to me and gave me additional time to turn it in. Whew!

The central theme of the Bible proves conclusively that all of us need grace from God. Not one person has ever achieved the levels of holiness that God requires. None of us is fit to stand in his presence and claim righteousness. When we are honest with ourselves, we admit we have failed to do good all of the time and many times we have done the opposite. We have been selfish, unkind, pushy, lustful, and greedy—if not worse.

God did something to bail us out of our predicament. Though we were rightly condemned and judged by God, he nevertheless offered us grace and forgiveness. During our so-called grace period, we have the incomparable opportunity to respond to his offer by saying yes to Jesus Christ.

Accepting God's grace in Jesus means saying no to all other efforts to please God and gain his favor. Jesus stands before us, as it were, and says, "It's me or nothing."

Jesus proves God's grace. When we focus on Jesus, we lose sight of our impoverished, sickly, insulting ways of trying to earn credit with God. When we focus on Jesus, we confess that even our pious thoughts and deeds—our churchy religion—fall far short of making it with God.

Jesus is God's grace in action. By sacrificing himself for us, Jesus cleared away all human obstacles to forgiveness and eternal life. His grace smashes our pride. His grace exalts our humility and confession of our sins.

In Jesus, God's grace is strong enough not only to forgive us, but also to make us good enough for heaven and good enough to represent him on earth. The grace of Jesus makes us fit subjects for God's workmanship. His grace puts us on display for the angels (1 Peter 1:12).

God's grace brings the dead to life and enthrones them with Jesus in heaven. How foolish we are then, when our pride suggests that we can add something to what Jesus has done for us by doing good works to earn his favor. Or even worse how foolish to think we don't need him.

We celebrate God's grace in Jesus not just because it satisfies a theological need. We celebrate it because it liberates us, it fills us, and it inspires and motivates us. "Wonderful the matchless grace of Jesus" rings the old gospel chorus. We want to achieve all that God invested in us when in his grace he gave his Son for us.

"My grace is all you need," God told the apostle Paul as he agonized over his sharp pain (see 2 Cor. 12:7–10). Paul needed grace for his salvation; he also needed it for his pain. So do we. It's all there in Jesus.

To think about

- How do you explain grace to someone struggling with how to please God?
- In what circumstances have you found grace in Jesus to be all you needed? How did this come about?

O God, I confess I have often tried to placate you with my own goodness. Forgive me for rejecting your grace. Fill me with an overwhelming sense of your grace in Jesus and how he meets all my needs.

Jesus, God's Way to Make Us Righteous

Romans 3:21–28

French painter Paul Gauguin struggled to put on canvas life's fundamental questions. His 1897–98 work *Where Do We Come From? Where Are We? Where Are We Going?* portrays happiness at birth but ends in idolatry and death. He found no satisfying answers.

The apostle Paul grappled with the thorny question of how to find God in the face of mankind's monumental failures and sins. He considered law keeping as a way to please God, but depending on our own righteousness only deepens our moral morass. If we're honest with ourselves, we know we can't possibly satisfy God. As Gauguin's figures testify, young and old alike go down to the grave without hope.

Enter God's solution: our Lord and Savior Jesus Christ. God's way of righting wrong and making sinners righteous changes everything radically. His way liberates us from the frustration of trying to make it on our own, because it works through our faith in Jesus.

From our standpoint, righteousness is free through a person—Jesus. It cannot be attained by trying to be good enough to satisfy God's holy requirements. We can receive God's pleasure only by trusting Jesus.

The apostle Paul examined the deep theology of God's way of making sinners righteous because he knew that somehow our sins had to be wiped off our indictments. All of us are guilty and deserve judgment. God's holiness cannot tolerate sin. What's our appeal in God's court of law? What hope do we have, not only to be acquitted of all charges, but also to be pronounced righteous?

Paul knew that Jesus's sacrificial death met and satisfied God's holiness and justice. God designed Jesus's mission as the only way to turn aside his wrath, taking away our sins and the judgment we deserve. In this way not only is God just, but he justifies, or makes righteous, all those who put their faith in Jesus.

Our pride and self-righteousness dissolve in the face of the magnificent, powerful figure of Jesus dying on the cross. As Martin Luther so aptly put it: "Did we in our own strength confide, our striving would be losing." To answer Gauguin: we came from God, we are here by his mercy, and we are going to him because of Jesus. Tragically for Gauguin, Jesus on the cross does not appear on his huge landscape.

Likewise, Jesus may not figure prominently on the landscape of our life, if we try to go through life nonchalantly. When guilt and frustration strike, we flee to Jesus. When we're not sure about eternity, we cling to him. We count unreservedly on God's promise that when he makes us righteous, we have peace with him and we rejoice in our hope of glory.

To think about

- Express Paul's theological problem in your own words.
- On a typical day, what difference does it make that God has made you righteous? Why is this important?

O God, you have given me everything I need in Jesus. I worship and praise you for sending Jesus to die for my sins and to make me good. May your righteousness flow from me and bless many others.

Jesus, a Servant's Heart

Isaiah 52:13–15; 53:1–12; Luke 22:7–27

Isaiah's prophecy indicated clearly the servanthood of Jesus, the promised Messiah. This major theme somehow eluded the men Jesus picked to work with him. While he conducted himself according to the prophetic picture, they fell into squabbling about personal greatness. Despite the repeated rebukes of Jesus, they continued to argue at their final meal with Jesus in the upper room.

That Passover meal provided a most graphic backdrop for Jesus's last demonstration of his servant's heart. Earlier, of course, he had warned them of the perils of trying to be first. In addition, for three years Jesus had served people, caring for their emotional, physical, and spiritual needs. Somehow, his disciples had missed the driving spirit behind his work, which was not to be great but to be a servant. Even when they had fulfilled their duties, they were still unworthy servants.

Gathered around the table with his shaken men, one of whom had just been identified as a traitor, Jesus took visible physical symbols to show precisely what his servant's heart would cost him. The traditional Passover meal was thus transformed into a sacred moment that plunged to the horror and depths of sacrifice.

Jesus took ordinary bread and said, "This is my body." He took wine and said, "This is my blood." Previously, he had driven would-be followers away by insisting that they had to eat his flesh and drink his blood (John 6:53–58). Now his disciples faced their critical hour. They had declared their allegiance and loyalty, but now their theories about discipleship would be thrust into the refiner's fire.

If they were to serve as Jesus did, it would mean much more than healing the sick and teaching them the news about God's kingdom. It would mean much more even than washing one another's feet. The ultimate demonstration of service was willingness to take the bread and the cup. The servant must be willing to die.

The bread and the cup, symbols of Jesus's body and blood, spoke of his impending death on the cross. The servant's heart had to be pierced. When we take the bread and the cup, we participate in the gruesome picture of Isaiah 53. The communion elements take us to Calvary. Walking the Jesus walk means not only taking up the servant's basin and towel, but also taking up the servant's cross.

We may not face death for Jesus, but we are required to die to our own comforts and agendas. Servants are called to be available, obedient, and humble. They anticipate their master's wishes and are totally at his disposal.

To think about

- Why did the disciples miss Jesus's point about servant-hood?
- What does it cost you to be a servant? How does Jesus, your prototype, motivate and guide your servanthood?

Thank you, Lord Jesus, that your servant's heart
took you to Calvary at the cost of your own life.
I confess I have not served to the point of dying
for someone else, or even being willing to do so.
Infuse me with the fullness of your servanthood.

Jesus, Praying under Intense Pressure

Matthew 26:36–46; Hebrews 5:7

Persistent, disciplined prayer saturated the daily life and ministry of Jesus. So when he entered Gethsemane's pressure cooker, he fell to his knees in prayer. Actually the whole night had been permeated with prayer.

The writers give us snatches of prayer in the upper room. Knowing what was to come, and having exposed the traitorous plot of Judas, Jesus gave thanks, nevertheless, to his heavenly Father. The worst agony lay ahead, of course, but we must consider the excruciating moral and spiritual pain Jesus felt as he gathered with his men for the last time.

Prayer was his only recourse. Not only did Jesus pray in the upper room, he told his disciples to pray (John 14:13–14; 16:23–24). Faced with impending doom and the shattering of their hopes, they were supposed to ask God for big things.

Sometime after he passed the bread and the cup and gave extensive teaching, Jesus declared that it was time to leave the secret place. He had to expose himself and his disciples to the worst possible outcome. Armed with prayer, he committed himself to his duty of obedience to God.

Perhaps on his way out of Jerusalem, Jesus talked to his Father, not about his own safety but about the spiritual safety, integrity, unity, and perseverance of his disciples (John 17). This mighty prayer was the prelude to his agonizing prayer—peppered with drops of blood—that he uttered in the garden, while his disciples slept.

The awful consequences of bearing the world's sins loomed before Jesus like an onrushing tornado. There was no time or place for shelter. The armed crowd and Judas were on their way. Jesus told Peter, James, and John that he felt as though he were dying from sorrow. There was time only for one last cry to his Father: "Spare me, if you will!" Jesus refused the sword and prayed instead. He refused to call in his angels and prayed instead.

Three times Jesus poured out his heart as time ran out. His prayer was simple and clear. He gave no long introductions, no sanctimonious preludes, just the sharp, bitter cry of despair. The prospect of the cup of suffering was about to overwhelm him. Yet even in the midst of his sorrow and agony, Jesus told his men to pray.

The heart of his prayer was twofold: "May this cup be taken from me. Yet not as I will, but as you will" (Matt. 26:39). Under this kind of pressure, the likes of which we will never know, Jesus yielded completely to his Father's will in prayer. As we follow Jesus, we must discover the intensity and spirit of his prayers.

To think about

- How do you picture Jesus at prayer? What aspects most impress you? Why?
- How do you evaluate the effectiveness of your prayer life? How does the Jesus way of prayer help you?

Heavenly Father, I want to pray as Jesus did in the Garden of Gethsemane. I confess I have a long way to go. Give me the courage and faith to lay my life totally on the line for you when the heat is turned on high.

Jesus, the One Who Refused to Retaliate

Matthew 26:47–68; Mark 15:1–20; 1 Peter 2:21–23

Retaliation and revenge are so deeply embedded in our human nature that it is hard to conceive that Jesus refused to take any action against his tormentors, especially when his trial was illegal and unfair. Our normal response to unfair accusations and injustice is to scream for our rights. Jesus did nothing like that.

When Jesus staked out the lifestyle of his new kingdom, he reversed completely the accepted order and declared that we should receive persecution and insults with rejoicing not revenge. In fact he announced that it was a blessing to be stomped on and humiliated. Going further he said that not only do his people refuse to retaliate against their enemies, they actually love them (Matt. 5:10–12, 43–44). This was a shocking reversal of common wisdom.

It was one thing for Jesus to state these principles in the peaceful Galilean countryside; it was quite another to put them into practice when his own freedom and life were jeopardized. Accosted by Judas and his armed thugs, Jesus stood quietly and refused to allow his men to jump to his defense. Even in the face of betrayal, he did not scream accusations at Judas.

Having been arrested, Jesus was dragged before his hypocritical religious accusers. They conspired to charge him with blasphemy, which was a capital offense. Jesus did not lash out at them, nor did he rebuke the perjurers at his trial.

Since the Roman subjects could not carry out his execution, they hauled Jesus before Pilate and Herod, who represented godless power. Jesus told them who he was, but his claim to deity befuddled them. Faced with such colossal misunderstanding, Jesus did not take the low road.

Meanwhile, Peter's faith collapsed as Jesus had predicted it would. Jesus did not have to retaliate for Peter's defection. The crowing rooster took care of that (Mark 14:72).

Throughout this story we see one chance after another for Jesus to rise up in self-defense. He answered questions honestly and did nothing physical or verbal that smacked of revenge. Rather, according to Isaiah's prophecy, he was like a lamb led to its slaughter (Isa. 53:1–7).

How hard it is for us to suffer unfairly without striking back! Perhaps nothing demonstrates so powerfully the uniqueness of Christian love as our refusal to retaliate. Love for Jesus means taking the tough stuff as he did. It's much easier to lash out than it is to leave revenge to God, much easier to hate than to love.

To think about

- Which provocative acts could have caused Jesus to retaliate?
- On what occasions have you been tempted to retaliate? How did you react? Why?

Lord Jesus, forgive me when I've attacked people in my own defense. Grant me the courage and grace to take hard knocks and hard words without retaliating in kind. Help me to know when I should confront others in your spirit, because I want to be like you.

Jesus, Liberator from Sin

Revelation 1:1–6

J esus freed us from our sins with his life's blood because he loves us. He set us free, not to live as we please, but to serve as royal priests of God. Our emancipation presupposes that we were slaves to sin. That is the bedrock fact of all Scripture. Nothing adds up apart from the fact of our slavery to sin. If sin did not hold us in bondage, Jesus shed his blood in vain.

Our freedom came at an outrageous cost—the blood of Jesus. His sacrifice was the core of his mission. Jesus gave us many wonderful teachings and he performed stupendous miracles, but, as John declared, Jesus came to this world as the Lamb of God to be killed for our sins (John 1:29). In God's view of things, there was no other way to secure our pardon and our release. That's how it looks in God's eternally fixed and true court of law. God's law reigns in the moral universe.

God gave clear signs of this principle when he prescribed an elaborate sacrificial system for his people Israel. The blood of sacrificial animals atoned for the sins of his people. This fact was so firmly embedded in God's law that the New Testament explained, "Without the shedding of blood there is no forgiveness" (Heb. 9:22).

In fact the blood of Jesus speaks through the entire redemption story, from Jesus's institution of the Lord's Supper to the consummation of his triumph in Revelation. We are justified by his blood, we have redemption through his blood, his blood cleanses us from all sin, and we triumph over evil by his blood.

The King James Version of Revelation 1:5 inspired the old gospel hymn that asks, "Are you washed in the blood of the

Lamb?" Reference to blood may turn off some moderns, but it speaks powerfully to what Jesus did for us on the cross. It also finds an echo in 1 John 1:9.

Christians rest in the assurance of God's love in Christ. His love brought Jesus to earth to die, to take the death penalty for our sins. Consequently we are washed clean; we are set free to achieve the highest possible purpose in life—to serve as royal priests in God's house.

Our freedom is a gift of inestimable value. It speaks of our eternal destiny. Freedom to serve is the highest possible purpose to which we can aspire. Freedom in Christ brings dignity and purpose. Freedom in Christ brings self-image that is not destroyed by our weaknesses, failures, and sins. Nothing changes our position as royal priests of God.

When we claim the blood of Jesus as our passport to heaven, we also claim it as our passport to meaning here and now. God has us here for a purpose, a highly significant purpose vouchsafed by his Son's bleeding body on the cross of Calvary. No wonder we shout with John, "To him be glory and power for ever and ever!" (Rev. 1:6).

To think about

- What was the cost of your liberation from sin? Why was this necessary?
- In what dirty places in your life do you need freedom and cleansing? In what roles can you be God's royal priest? How?

Lord Jesus, I fall before you in worship because you loved me so much that you shed your life's blood for me. Forgive me when I've been casual about your blood. May my freedom motivate me powerfully to live a life fitting to a royal priest.

Jesus, the Door to God's Grace

Romans 5:1–11

Romans 5:1–11 is a superbly effective marinade for the soul. This chapter draws us appreciatively to Jesus like the tantalizing smells from a slab of ribs on the grill. Instead of ribs, however, we discover deeply satisfying Christian theology centered on Jesus.

The apostle Paul went to great pains to explain the foundations of our faith. Each sentence of this passage requires our intense concentration, if we are to receive the fully adequate food for our souls.

The recipients of Paul's letter needed this foundation because Jesus was news to them. They had been nursed and fed on the Jewish law, giving them superiority to everyone else. Moses had the final answers; they were in the laws he had received from God.

When Jesus came along, according to Paul, he was God's way of making us righteous. However, for the Jews, a huge blockade stood in the way. They had to admit with Paul that the whole world was guilty before God, even the Jews. Nobody was righteous. God had introduced a new way to attain righteousness—faith in Jesus Christ his Son, the Galilean prophet who had been executed by the Romans in Jerusalem.

Righteousness by faith, exemplified by father Abraham, had replaced righteousness that came by keeping the law (Romans 4). Christians stand in the sphere of God's grace because Jesus opened the door. He did so by dying for us, the wicked, while we were yet sinners.

Paul used some big words—*justification* and *reconciliation*—to describe our benefits in Christ. This is not the place to expound them. Bible dictionaries are a great help. *Justification* presumes that unrighteous people have to be made

278

right with God. *Reconciliation* presumes that our sins lead to enmity with God, the perfectly holy one, and we need to make peace with him. Entirely because of Jesus, and without a shred of anything good we do, we can stand righteous before God and be at peace with him. What we have gained is totally attributable to Christ's sacrificial death.

The picture that emerges from Romans 5 is of Jesus giving us permission, as it were, to stand before God simply on his say-so. We have absolutely no credentials of our own to merit forgiveness and salvation. Everything depends on Jesus. "Simply to thy cross I cling."

When entering the sphere of God's grace gripping our souls, we understand how it is possible to continue at peace with him. His overwhelming grace in Jesus more than matches our needs for hope and endurance when suffering strikes us.

Here God's court of law, so to speak, addresses not just our legal need for righteousness and reconciliation, but his justice goes beyond that and covers our deepest pain and suffering. We can endure with hope because God's love floods our heart.

The door Jesus opens beckons us to stand in God's grace and to apply the healing ointment of his grace to every laceration of our soul. Jesus saves and Jesus heals for all eternity.

To think about

- How would you put Paul's train of theological logic in your own words?
- What difference does it make in your life to understand, believe, and act on the doctrines of Romans 5? How can these truths help you find peace, endurance, and hope?

Oh God, the majesty of your grace overwhelms me. Help me to focus not just on doctrine but on Jesus who brings all these truths to life in me. May I never grow tired of praising Jesus for dying for me while I was yet a sinner.

Jesus, Our Great High Priest

Hebrews 2:14–18; 4:14–16

The Jewish priesthood did not beckon Jesus. He never assumed that office and never performed that role. The priesthood was a carefully regulated office, handed down along tribal lines. From Israel's earliest days, the priests offered sacrifices and performed other specified rituals. On the Day of Atonement the high priest entered the Holy of Holies to be sure that Israel's sins were covered.

Jesus did none of these things. Instead of offering sacrifices for sin, he became the one sacrifice for sin that forever settled the matter. That's why the writer of Hebrews, looking back on the tumultuous events of Christ's death and resurrection, called Jesus the Christian's great High Priest.

He wrote with great passion and detail about how the sacrifice of Jesus far surpassed the sacrifices of the Jewish priests (Hebrews 8–10). He noted that Jesus did not even belong to the priestly line but traced his priesthood to that of the mysterious Melchizedek (Hebrews 7).

But in his opening chapters, the writer was more concerned about how his readers—most of them former adherents of Judaism—could link with Jesus in personal, practical ways. These people had suffered mightily for their commitment to Jesus and some of them were ready to quit the Christian faith. In effect, the writer was saying, "Don't quit now, because Jesus your great High Priest can more than take care of you."

For one thing, Jesus understands all about our pain and suffering because he was made exactly like us and can show us mercy, whatever our hurts. By his death on the cross, Jesus atoned for our sins, so that takes care of our most worrisome issue of all. We are freed and forgiven.

Jesus knew what it was like to suffer temptation, so he understands and helps us in our crises of faith. He is totally adequate for whatever circumstances may arise, so we hang in there no matter what.

Jesus conquered temptation, sin, and death. He is not a dead hero whom we venerate for his good deeds and wise teachings. He lives in heaven at his Father's right hand and, from his powerful position there, Jesus looks after every detail of every believer's life.

Just knowing these facts of the Jesus story doesn't do us much good. Of course we have to know the facts about Jesus and we have to rehearse them in our mind when the going gets rough and we want to resign. These facts drive us to Jesus and to prayer—what the writer called "the throne of grace" (4:16).

"Our time of need" covers every imaginable experience. We have daily needs and we have special needs when we are blindsided or disappointed. Jesus says, "Bring all your needs to me. I understand; I sympathize; I went through everything you are going through now. Come to me with full confidence and faith and I will give you my grace and my mercy."

To think about

- Why didn't Jesus take the role of a Jewish priest? In what sense is he our priest?
- Recall how God has met your needs when you have gone to the throne of grace. Why is it sometimes hard to turn everything over to Jesus?

Lord Jesus, I praise you for being my great High Priest. I praise you for dying for my sins. I praise you for being patient, sympathetic, understanding, and merciful, in spite of my failures and lack of faith.

Jesus, the Faithful Witness

Revelation 1:1–6

A faithful witness is one who speaks the truth. Jesus spoke the truth at all times, on all occasions, in a variety of circumstances. He never shaded the truth. He never hid the truth to gain acceptance. Jesus spoke the truth even when the truth condemned him to death. He is truth personified.

To what and to whom did Jesus witness? He confessed boldly in public that he had come from God on a mission to reveal God's truth about salvation and heaven. Jesus never backtracked on his claim of having come from heaven.

Jesus witnessed to God's standard of holiness and to the internal values of God's laws. Jesus revealed the true meaning of God's commands. He witnessed to the heart issues of obedience and faith.

Jesus spoke the truth about life and death, about sin and the devil. He thwarted Satan's attacks by witnessing to the power of God's Word. His faithful witness sent Satan fleeing and routed the demons who infested people all around him.

Jesus witnessed the truth to his friends and his disciples. He neither tricked anyone into following him nor appealed to their baser motives. He did not give them false promises or hopes but, instead, promised them suffering for his sake.

Jesus witnessed to the incomparable values of God's kingdom, denouncing materialism, pride, and hypocrisy. The simple power of his truth and courage drove the religious authorities to seek his execution.

To be faithful demands extraordinary courage, which Jesus had in dimensions that no one else has ever approached. His truth prevailed in the face of religious and political threats. Jesus never compromised the truth to save his own skin or to gain followers. Because his witness was so true and faithful, some people actually turned away from following him. At the same time his truth frees people from bondage to sin and selfishness.

Jesus was faithful to his own even when it hurt, exposing the treachery of Judas and the presumption of Peter. He witnessed to the coming persecution of his disciples and promised that in the end his truth alone would prove victorious by the indwelling power of the Holy Spirit.

Our Lord's faithful witness was nourished and instructed by constant communion with his heavenly Father. His daily prayers kept him in line with God's truth and the purpose of his mission. Jesus was so genuinely true that, though his cross was ever before him, he did not waver.

Our English word *witness* has its roots in the Greek word for "martyr." In one sense, Jesus was a martyr for truth. Often martyrdom awaits faithful witnesses to the truth, but martyrdom fails to suppress the truth.

Jesus rose from the dead and ascended into heaven. His truth marches on because he was, he is, and he always will be the only one, true, and authentic witness to God's eternal truth.

To think about

- In what ways is Jesus a faithful witness?
- What is there about his life as a witness that you can capture? What are the essential qualities of a faithful witness?

Thank you, Lord Jesus, that through the worst the world and Satan could hurl at you, you never caved in to falsehood or insincerity. You never ducked the truth. May my faithful witness help others find the truth you possess.

Jesus and Jerusalem

Luke 19:28-48

Rarely did Jesus set foot in Jerusalem, so perhaps we can assume that he didn't care much for the big city. He had grown up in a small town and spent most of his life in Nazareth. During his ministry, he hiked the hills of Galilee, Judea, Perea, and Samaria.

Jerusalem, of course, was the hub of national political, religious, cultural, and social life. It also served as the focal point of the Roman occupation. Religion and politics constantly erupted into furious conflicts in Jerusalem.

During his early Judean ministry, Jesus cleansed the temple in Jerusalem and granted Nicodemus a nighttime interview (John 2:12–3:21). Two years later he returned and offered himself as the water of life during the Feast of Tabernacles. He encountered trouble with the Pharisees, healed a blind man, and said he was the good shepherd. Then he withdrew.

En route back to Jerusalem, he healed a blind man near Jericho and brought salvation to Zacchaeus (Luke 18:35–19:10). He made his headquarters in Bethany, from where he entered Jerusalem to the wild acclamations of the crowds. With loud voices they broke into shouts because they had seen his mighty works, for which they praised God. Their collective enthusiasm reflected heightened messianic hopes throughout Israel (19:28–38). Jesus had said that his words and his works gave ample evidence that he had come from God (John 14:8–11).

Voicing the hopes of Psalms 113–18, these people from the city and pilgrims from Galilee accepted Jesus as God's envoy. When the Pharisees tried to rain on their praise parade, Jesus rebuked them and said the stones could praise him, if necessary (Luke 19:39–40).

Later the sight of Jerusalem caused Jesus to weep (vv. 41–42). He had shed silent tears at the grave of Lazarus. Here the word means loud wailing and sobbing, like the weeping of the widow of Nain and the mourners in the house of Jairus. Jesus was profoundly affected by what could have been. Because the city failed to grasp what God was doing in the person of Jesus, it would suffer horrendous destruction in AD 70.

For the second time Jesus drove merchants and money changers from the temple (vv. 45–46). He continued to teach every day with such effectiveness that the people all hung on his words. This drove the religious leaders of various parties together, along with the civic leaders, determined to throttle him.

Jesus, the God-man, fully merited Jerusalem's praise, and the city fully deserved his judgment. Nevertheless, it hurts us to see him weeping so profusely because of the city's spiritual blindness. How remarkable and challenging is this combination of attributes in our Savior!

To think about

- What do you learn about Jesus in these episodes? What impresses you most? Why?
- What is there in your life that might bring tears to Jesus's eyes? What is your emotional response to entire communities or pockets of people who reject Jesus?

Lord Jesus, because of my sin and pride, I'm not sure what camp I would have been in when you came to Jerusalem. Help me to see clearly into my own heart. Fill me with your compassion and your truth.

Acquitted and Made Righteous
in Jesus

Romans 5:12–21

OJ Simpson's 1995 murder trial gripped the nation. Millions of people were glued to their TV sets awaiting the jury's verdict. Attorney Johnny Cochran had mounted a successful defense of his famous pro football client, and the jury acquitted OJ of all charges. However, neither Cochran nor the jury pronounced Simpson a good man. That was far beyond the scope of their assignment and ability. Simpson may have escaped a possible death sentence, but he was never proclaimed righteous.

Let us change the scene for a moment. Let's pretend we are on trial, charged with not only breaking God's holy and just laws but also our failure always to do the good, the right, the true, and the beautiful. What are our chances before the bar of God? Ours is a bench trial. The verdict is solely in the hands of our Judge. Listen to the court records:

"Your wrongdoing has caused much harm. However, the effects of your offenses have been greatly exceeded by God's grace and his gift to you through Jesus Christ. The judicial action merited by your offenses resulted in a verdict of condemnation, but by the act of God's grace—even after so many sins—you are acquitted. You deserve death even for one sin, but you have received God's grace in far greater measure—plus he has given you his gift of righteousness—so that you might live through Jesus Christ.

"Just one sin brings your condemnation, but one act of God has acquitted you and given you life. One sin made you a sinner, but you have been made righteous by Christ's obedience. Even when you multiplied your sins, God's grace immeasurably surpassed them. Sin brings you death, but God's grace brings you righteousness and eternal life through Jesus Christ."

You will recognize this as my personalized version of the apostle Paul's profound description of how God's extraordinary grace in Jesus Christ overcame the universal effects of Adam's sin (Rom. 5:12–21). This is one of those classic behind-the-scenes revelations in Scripture that explains the whole story of mankind's fall into sin, the disastrous consequences of Adam's sin, and the overpowering of those dreadful consequences in the person of our Lord and Savior Jesus Christ.

In summary, God not only acquits guilty sinners who fully deserve his wrath, but also makes them good people, righteous in his sight, when they confess and claim Jesus as their only hope of redemption and forgiveness. To more fully appreciate all that Jesus has done for us, we simply put our name in place of Adam's and underline Jesus Christ each time his name appears in this passage.

Such meditation drives us to our knees in confession and repentance before God. It also drives us to claim Jesus as our only hope. We see in Jesus the outcome of God's incomparable program to save us. We see our total unworthiness but we also see Christ's love in giving us his righteousness.

To think about

- How does Paul's argument help you understand both sin and its effects and God's grace and its effects?
- How does God's grace help you live and reign through Christ? What do you need to do to grow in his grace?

Thank you, Lord Jesus, for your obedience on the cross to remove my guilty verdict and to make me righteous. I want your love and grace to motivate and empower me. I need your grace to remind me that I have been absolved from sin, fear, guilt, and shame.

Jesus, Man of Many Emotions

Matthew 9:36; 14:14; 15:32; 20:34; Mark 1:41;
10:17–22; Luke 7:11–15; 19:41–44; 22:39–46;
John 2:13–17; 11:4–6, 33–38; 13:1; Isaiah 53:3

We subtract nothing from the impressiveness of Jesus as the Son of Man when we ascribe many emotions to him. While our emotional swings often bring us trouble, his were never blackened by sin of any kind.

When the Bible tells us that Jesus shared our humanity, and was willing to be made like us in every way (Heb. 2:14–18), this includes our emotions. Looking at his emotional responses enables us to find both instruction and inspiration for our lives. Jesus wants to make us like himself by living in us.

Compassion was Jesus's most often cited emotional attribute. Closely related qualities include mercy and pity. Of course the depths of emotional feelings aroused by compassion vary with the circumstances.

In many cases, Jesus healed people because of his compassion for them. He seems to have been particularly moved by the plight of the blind. On the other hand, the spiritual destitution Jesus saw in the crowds and in individuals also brought forth his compassion. He fell into loud cries of mourning when he contemplated Jerusalem's stubborn refusal to receive him (Luke 19:41–44). Because Jesus loved him, he hurt inwardly when the wealthy man could not meet his terms of discipleship (Mark 10:21).

On some occasions his compassion rebuked the coldness of his disciples. However, in spite of their indifference and failure to grasp all that his mission was about, Jesus loved these men and showed them the full extent of his love by washing their feet (John 13:1).

Jesus expressed his compassion, sympathy, and grief for the unnamed widow of Nain (Luke 7:11–15) and for Mary and Martha, sisters of Lazarus. He wept silently at his friend's grave (John 11:35–38).

Hypocrisy among the self-righteous and corruption among the temple's dealers drove Jesus to anger. "Woe to you, teachers of the law and Pharisees, you hypocrites!" he remonstrated at least seven times during Passion Week (Matthew 23). On one occasion Jesus accosted the money changers with whips (John 2:14–16).

However, Jesus reached his emotional apex when he cried out to God again and again for release from his impending crucifixion. His overwhelming agony in Gethsemane brought sweat drops of blood to his brow (Luke 22:44).

Whatever emotional strains afflict us, we know that Jesus has been there. We worship him not because he was impervious to human feelings, but because he suffered them and conquered them. His compassion and love and the way he controlled his anger move us to emulate him. He grieves and sympathizes with us in our sorrows. He agonizes with our battles to follow God's will regardless of the cost.

To think about

- Why did the writers of the Jesus story reveal his emotions so clearly rather than hide them in an attempt to boost his reputation?
- Of what value is it to you to meditate on Jesus's emotional experiences?

Lord Jesus, I am touched by the depths of your feelings. I confess my lack of compassion. I want your love to fill me and motivate me, to the praise of your glory.

Jesus, the Greatest King of All

Ephesians 1:20–21; Philippians 2:9–11; Revelation 1:1–6; 5:11–14; 15:1–4

Jesus's reign as King of Kings and Lord of Lords was foreseen by the prophets, acclaimed by Jerusalem's crowd, challenged by Pilate, confessed by the apostles, and celebrated in the visions of John the apostle on the island of Patmos after Christ's resurrection. One cannot escape the biblical pervasiveness of God's rule in the affairs of human beings and nations.

Old Testament prophets and poets praised God for his rule. "My King and my God," they sang (Ps. 44:4). "The LORD is King for ever. . . . the kings of the earth will revere your glory" (Pss. 10:16; 102:15). Then Isaiah announced the coming of a king who will reign in righteousness. "Your eyes will see the king in his beauty," he promised (Isa. 33:17).

However, when the messianic King arrived, his people rejected him. Boldly and publicly Jesus told the Roman governor, Pilate, that he was indeed the King of the Jews. Pilate affixed this title to Jesus's cross, despite the howls of protest from the chief priests.

The glorious Christian affirmation of faith is that the crucified King lives and one day he will rule the kings of the earth. The apostle Paul defined Jesus's role with stunning clarity: right now and in the age to come, Jesus exerts full authority over all other powers and dominions. The day is coming when every knee will bow and every tongue will confess Jesus as Lord (Phil. 2:9–11). No wonder, at the height of his inspirational powers, Paul addressed and worshiped Jesus as "the King eternal, immortal, invisible, the only God. . . . the King of kings and Lord of lords" (1 Tim. 1:17; 6:15).

In his exalted vision of Jesus, John the apostle was transported to heaven's throne and there he saw the throngs of believers of all ages enthusiastically worshiping Jesus as the King of the ages. He saw all nations paying homage to Jesus (Rev. 5:11–14; 15:1–4).

"King of my life, I crown Thee now," we sing. Christ's rule is intensely personal as well as universal. Because he is King, he poses the question of authority to would-be followers. Therefore Christians worship and offer him obeisance, with complete and enduring confidence that Jesus rules completely every supposed authority in God's universe.

Knowing Jesus as our King sustains our faith as we confront both personal and international challenges to his rule. Our hope rests completely in his loving wisdom, grace, and power. "Who will not fear you, O Lord, and bring glory to your name?" (15:4).

To think about

- Describe the reign of Jesus in both Old and New Testament frameworks.
- How is your faith buttressed by the fact that Jesus rules in heaven now and one day will rule on earth as well?

Lord Jesus, you are indeed King of my life. Thank you that all earthly powers are subject to you. Build your church today to confess your rule in all areas of life.

Our Union with Jesus

Romans 6:1–11

The concept of a personal union with Jesus Christ blossomed in the upper room—"remain in me and I will remain in you" (John 15:4)—and fully occupied Jesus's mind on his way to Gethsemane. Before Jesus came it was not considered possible to be one with God. Old Testament worthies confessed their faith in a personal, knowable God who cared for them, but no one dared to suggest that they were united with him.

Jesus used many metaphors to picture his union with his faithful ones: he is their bread, their water, their life. They have to eat his flesh and drink his blood. Believers are as intimately united with Jesus as branches are to the vine.

After Christ's resurrection and ascension, Peter and Paul inaugurated a new way of considering believers' status: they are "in Christ." This became their favorite way of identifying Christians universally. The churches are "in Christ Jesus." This union is so dynamic for Christians that they are one with Jesus in his death, burial, and resurrection. When Jesus died, we died; when he was buried, we were buried; when he rose again, we were also raised to new life. The practical outcome of this marvelous mystical union can be summarized this way: we are dead to sin and alive to God in union with Jesus.

Our union with Jesus is not primarily emotional, although our feelings surely are influenced by it. Some days we can accurately confess, "I don't feel like I'm united with Jesus." Our feelings are notoriously unreliable. Our feelings do not change the fact of our incorporation with Jesus. All the benefits of our eternal union with him remain ours, no matter how we may feel.

But what if I stray? What if sin, to which I must regard myself as dead, pops up? Because I am one with Jesus, I go to him and confess both my sins and my wretched feelings. He does not, as a result, cancel my union with him. Obviously my sins disrupt the passion I feel for Jesus, but the door to restoration and joy is always open because he lives in me and I live in him.

Even the happiest and most successful marriage partnerships sometimes hit the shoals, but because two people love and respect each other, they confess their faults to one another, they forgive one another, and their union grows stronger in the process. And just as marriages must be fed to grow, so must our union with Jesus. Continually feeding on Jesus and drinking his water bring needed vitality and sparkle to our union. His love for us stays on course. Our love may waver from time to time, but not his for us.

> Oh, this full and perfect peace!
> Oh, this transport all divine!
> In a love which cannot cease,
> I am His, and He is mine.
>
> George Wade Robinson
> "I Am His, and He Is Mine"

To think about

- Why did Paul so strongly emphasize the believer's union with Christ?
- What steps can you take to grow in your relationship with Jesus?

Thank you, Lord Jesus, for living in me. Thank you for giving me such a rock solid foundation for my life. May I come to know you more deeply by listening to you and trusting and obeying you.

Jesus, Our Hope of Glory

Colossians 1:24–29

False teachers preyed on new Christians in the ancient churches, undermining the supremacy of Jesus with their various arguments. God assigned the apostles the formidable task of holding the churches firmly to Christ. They visited churches and wrote letters, some of which we study for our benefit as we go deeper with Jesus.

Vigorously Paul defended and promoted Jesus in his letter to the church at Colosse. He reminded his readers that Jesus is God's exact likeness. Jesus created everything, seen and unseen. As the leader of God's new creation, Jesus rules the new body of believers, the church. Jesus stands at the apex of God's plan to save the world. Because of humanity's alienation from and hostility toward God, Jesus died to make possible our peace with God. It's astonishing that Jesus makes us holy and spotless in God's sight, liberated from all charges against us (Col. 1:15–23).

In view of these dynamic facts, Paul urged the new Christians to stay the course, to hold firmly to the gospel, and not to be lured away from Christ. Our only sure way to salvation is claiming Jesus and following him.

At the same time, Paul's rehearsal of these truly awesome facts about Jesus moved him to recite the privileges of his life's work for him. He applied Christ's greatness to himself. When we are moved by, and perhaps saved by, someone's extreme act of generosity, kindness, or sacrifice, our lives take on a brighter sheen. When an army captain intervened for me and gave me an assignment totally fitting my gifts and interests, I left his office walking on air. This was a major turning point in my career.

That's what Jesus did for Paul, and he does the same for us. Paul rejoiced in spite of the fact that his obedience to Jesus brought him incredible suffering (v. 24). Paul responded by preaching "the word of God in its fullness" (v. 25).

God used Paul to unveil a truth previously hidden to the entire world. He unlocked a treasure chest overflowing with riches, the choicest gem of which was "Christ in you, the hope of glory" (v. 27). Whatever happens now, we stand securely because Jesus dwells in us. We do not hope for glory as though there is some doubt about it. Our Christian hope means absolute certainty, because it is anchored in Jesus.

Hope in the glory to come sustains us, not only in the face of false teachings but also in the face of disappointments, hurts, illness, and estrangements, or, for some Christians, persecution, homelessness, and hunger.

Jesus in us stabilizes our soul when sudden difficulties strike. He helps us keep our future glory as our main focus. He tells us to relegate everything else to secondary status. Jesus is in us now and forever. His ultimate triumph guarantees our place in glory.

To think about

- How would you defend Christ's supremacy to someone who has not yet acknowledged him as Lord and Savior?
- What stresses in your life tend to sully your pure enjoyment of all that Jesus has done and will do for you? How can you knock them out of your way?

Oh God, I am stunned by the total supremacy of Jesus. Teach me to rise above any deterrents to my growth in Christ. May my hope of glory in Jesus send a strong message to others.

Jesus Obeyed God's Will Implicitly

Matthew 26:39–44; Hebrews 5:7–9; 12:1–3

By age twelve Jesus knew what it meant to obey his Father's will. We do not know how or when he first sensed his calling, but one detail gives us a clue. As Jesus grew up, he was filled with divine wisdom and grace. When he was thirty, he obeyed God's will and received baptism at the hands of John, after which God's divine approbation roared from heaven.

God's will came first as Jesus did carpentry work, worshiped with his family, prayed, and studied the Scriptures. Surely it was a test of his obedience to see the years drift by without any significant career advancement. Why was God waiting so long to call him into action?

Suddenly, when his call came, his commitment was severely tested by Satan. After forty days without food, he could have turned stones to bread, but he refused. God's will was more important than bread. He could have accepted all the world's kingdoms from Satan, but again he refused, desiring to follow God's will. Also he refused to disobey God by jumping off the temple to prove his deity (Matt. 4:1–10).

Of course Satan hounded him continually by various means. "He's out of his mind," the critics said. "He's possessed and empowered by the prince of demons." His own family became a stumbling block to his obedience to his Father. And what can be said of the obtuseness of his disciples? Of the mobs demanding food and healing? Of the relentless pressure to find food and lodging? Of the people's plan to take him by force and make him king? Of his own brothers' not-so-subtle hint that he improve his public profile by performing miracles in Jerusalem? Of their refusal to believe him? Of the betrayal by one of his inner circle? Of the desertion by all of the disciples after his arrest? Any one of these could have caused him to swerve from the path of obedience.

These were all part of the three-year course in obedience for Jesus. He learned obedience by these tests, trials, and temptations (Heb. 5:8). Supremely, however, he learned the cost of obedience in Gethsemane and at Calvary. In Gethsemane we hear his mournful cry for release from his commitment to die for the world's sins. This is where the agony of obedience reached its most intense pitch. The cross before him was a pass-fail exam for Jesus.

We might ask how Jesus passed. What made the difference for him? Never having a moment to relax, nevertheless he insisted on time alone with his Father. Day by day he met God in worship, prayer, and commitment. Day by day he received new infusions of heavenly power to maintain a steady course, even though it led to his arrest, trial, and crucifixion.

Those moments of intense prayer, spotlighted in Gethsemane, gave Jesus the inner resolve to endure and persevere. Even as he pleaded for some way to avoid Calvary, he acknowledged that God's will must be done. To follow Jesus means putting God's will first in everything.

To think about

- What were the keys to Jesus's obedience?
- How have you been tested in regard to doing what you know God wanted you to do? How can you strengthen your resolve to obey?

Thank you, Lord Jesus, for your perfect obedience.
Give me the same unflagging desire to do my
Father's will in all things.

Jesus Faced Danger
and Death Courageously

Mark 14:43–65; John 18:28–40; 19:1–16

In the Garden of Gethsemane, after his Passover meal, his extended teaching, and his agonizing prayer, Jesus confronted danger in the form of Judas, his betrayer, and an armed band. His hour had come; his prayer had been answered. Obviously, in his heavenly Father's wise and loving will, there was no other path to follow except to die on the cross for the world's sins.

How did Jesus face this reality? With unspeakable courage and bravery. Consider his choices. He could have fled with his disciples, hoping to escape into the woods in the darkness. He could have taken up weapons and fought alongside his disciples, as one of them tried to do. He could have called in a legion of angels to rescue him and his men. But Jesus stood firmly in the face of Judas and his gang. He punctured their power and their weapons with well-chosen words of stern rebuke. He did not cower and grovel before them. He did not beg for mercy. He did not explain that he was the wrong man.

Remarkable courage at his arrest was followed by extraordinary courage at his various trials. Before the religious and the political leaders, Jesus stood his ground. He refused to appeal for time. Even though his religious trial was a put-up job with paid liars, Jesus did not buckle before his accusers. His calmness rebuked their anger and rage. His self-control confounded Pilate. Anyone who stood before the Roman governor was supposed to cave in to fear and anxiety. Not Jesus.

Jesus knew his fate was sealed, yet this did not diminish his courage. He knew what the prelude to death would cost him, but he stood tall through the worst his executioners threw at him. Incredibly, he maintained amazing composure under intense duress. Because Jesus knew who he was, where he had come from, and where he was going, he rose above the vicious attacks on his person and his body.

Facing danger and death is never easy. Does Jesus expect us to handle mortal threats with the same courage that he did? In one sense yes, in another way no. When we walk with him in the valley of the shadow of death, he gives us extraordinary courage. Of course we are afraid because we are human. Fear is nothing to be ashamed of or to feel guilty about, unless it paralyzes us and causes us to deny our confession of faith in Jesus as Lord.

Thousands of martyrs have gone to their crosses with the same courage Jesus demonstrated. In our day many more are called to do the same. Some make the news headlines, but most die unheralded. Persecution of Christians thrives unchecked around the world. Living as Jesus did in the face of danger and death means confessing and recognizing that he walks with us. We ask him to give us the courage and faith that he knows we need, even to die for him if necessary.

To think about

- Review the sequence of Jesus's arrest and trials. What stands out? Why?
- In what settings have you been forced to choose between Jesus or something else? How did you decide? What was the outcome?

Heavenly Father, you know my weakness and fear in the face of danger and death. Give me the courage and composure that Jesus had. Do that for Christians under the gun around the world. Because Jesus lives in me, I want to follow his example.

Jesus, the Perfect Husband

Ephesians 5:22–33

Jesus was not married, despite what *The Da Vinci Code* alleges. But he is the perfect husband for his bride, the church. The apostle Paul says the "profound mystery" of husband and wife becoming "one flesh" is a figure of Jesus and his church (Eph. 5:32). He says, in effect, that Jesus is the perfect husband in several powerfully vivid ways. Sometimes, in our efforts to apply God's guidelines to our marriages, we tend to overlook what Jesus offers his followers.

Jesus's all-encompassing, overwhelming love secures the foundation for both marriage and our walk with him. Just as husbands and wives never outgrow the need to hear, "I love you," so Christians, as the bride of Christ, revel in the daily reminder from Jesus: "I love you." When in our weaker, troubled moments, our heart and mind drift from his assurance, Jesus whispers, "Remember, I gave my life for you. Look to the cross and you will not doubt my love."

Knowing that our marriages, and our union with him, become sullied by sin, Jesus takes us aside to remind us: "I love you so much that I made you holy and clean. You can straighten out your issues with me and be restored to purity."

Jesus, our wise and loving husband, staggers us with a humanly impossible promise. Sometimes men get carried away and make rash promises to their wives, but Jesus keeps his word. He pictures his children as a wedding gift to himself—a gift so outrageous that as we look at ourselves, we say, "Impossible!" Why? Because we know we are stained, wrinkled, blemished material.

Jesus steps in and says, "But wait just a minute. I have not completed my intentions for my bride. Yes, you are quite flawed material now, but one day you will be perfect, so perfect in fact that you will be holy and blameless, and no one will ever find the evidence of any sin whatsoever in you."

In the meantime, however, we struggle to be strong in faith and obedience. We know what Jesus, our husband, expects of us, but some days we slip into spiritual thirst and hunger. Jesus is our water and bread of life, but there are times when we fail to eat and drink of him. However, because we belong to him, he "cherishes and nourishes" us (v. 29 KJV). Because he cares for us, he provides for us according to his unerring wisdom and unfailing, never diminishing love and grace. These words soothe my heart and restore my soul.

In Jesus alone all our emotional and spiritual needs are met. He is our extreme Lover. We lack nothing in our marriage union with him.

To think about

- In what ways is Jesus your perfect husband?
- How can you build a stronger, more satisfying marriage with him?

Thank you, Lord Jesus, for loving me in spite of who I am. Thank you for promising to make me your perfect bride.

Jesus, Our Conqueror

Romans 8:31–39

I have conquered cancer twice. Two times Jesus has conquered my disappointment, fear, and hopelessness in the face of the disease. He has not only extended my physical life, but enriched substantially my spiritual life and my walk with him. Jesus has done for me everything the apostle Paul promised he would.

Paul wrapped up his deep theology of our salvation in Christ with a dramatic "so what?" question. What difference does it really make that God gives us salvation, requiring only our faith in Jesus? Few statements in Scripture drive to the heart of our experience as does his conclusion of Romans 8.

God did not spare his own Son, so we can trust him for everything we might possibly ever need. Whatever our circumstances, we focus entirely on God's gift of Jesus. Jesus died for us, rose again, sits at God's right hand, and pleads our cause, so what do we have to fear—from cancer or anything else?

These facts about Jesus compel us to flee to him again and again. We confess him as Lord and Savior. So begins our spiritual journey with Jesus. We learn more and more about him as we worship, join others in Bible study, and dig into the Bible for ourselves, continually searching for those facts that address our specific needs at the moment. Such is our lifelong adventure.

I had been a believer for more than fifty years before I encountered Jesus while battling cancer. My wife and I fell to our knees and we prayed. I took long walks, talking to Jesus. Of course my desire for healing jumped to the top of my prayer concerns.

One day as I was returning from a walk, Jesus spoke to me and said, "Wait a minute. What worries you? What do you need? Do you not realize that you are completely secure in me? I have taken care of your most critical need, your eternal salvation. No condemnation awaits you. I died for you. That's the main thing, isn't it?"

What could I say? Of course I knew all these facts were true, but somehow at that moment Jesus became my conqueror in an authentic, fresh way. Tears welled in my eyes—tears of gratitude, because Jesus reminded me of what was most important, not his healing of my body but his healing of my soul and spirit. He conquered my fears and liberated me so that healing did not dominate my thoughts.

Jesus is our conqueror because he loves us and because he is stronger than anything in life or death. Nothing can ever cut us off from his all-powerful love.

Thank God for all the doctrines of salvation. Thank God that those facts keep us anchored in Jesus when we are rocked by threats to our peace and security.

To think about

- What big truths did Paul have in mind when he asked, "What shall we say in response to *this*" (Rom. 5:31)?
- What steps can you take to be sure that the crucial gospel truths make a difference when circumstances threaten to overwhelm you?

Thank you, heavenly Father, for the powerful assurances of your all-encompassing love in Jesus. May I apply your love to my deepest fears and concerns. I want Jesus to be my conqueror in all things, to the praise of his glory.

Jesus Endured Incredible Pain

Mark 14:65; 15:15–25

Incredible pain was the hallmark of the 2004 movie *The Passion of the Christ*. That graphic depiction of our Lord's suffering was too much for some people. However, long before films were made, followers of Christ have tried to duplicate the pain he suffered. Some flagellate themselves, while others have actually been crucified. In many churches, vivid crucifixes are a steady reminder of Christ's pain.

The truth is, the writers of the original Jesus story did not elaborate on his incredible suffering. We have to fill in the details ourselves as we realize what a horrible death crucifixion actually was. The entire drama was suffused with physical, emotional, and spiritual abuse and pain.

What is utterly amazing is that Jesus knew all this beforehand. He knew he had come to earth to suffer excruciating pain. That was the cost of our redemption. He taught his disciples that he would be arrested and abused by the religious authorities. Succinctly, he said he would "suffer many things."

What that meant is sketched briefly by the four New Testament historians. Other secular writers of the Roman era are much more explicit about the nature of crucifixion. In most cases, the release that death brought was delayed during hours of terrible pain on the cross. We can only imagine what it was like to hang there dying of shock and dehydration. Jesus did not suffer as long as might be expected.

Of course, before the actual crucifixion, Jesus suffered the pain of humiliation, mockery, and scourging—a terrible, bloody whipping. His executioners drew blood long before they arrived at the Place of the Skull.

The stories shield us from the worst of the physical details. Later on, Peter simply used the word *suffering* to describe what happened to Jesus. He said we must "arm ourselves" with the same attitude Jesus had (1 Peter 4:1). Paul confessed a strong desire to know "the fellowship of sharing" Christ's sufferings (Phil. 3:10).

Their approach to Christ's incredible pain points the way for all of us who would walk in his steps. We shall never replicate what happened to Jesus and we are not called to do so. How much we dwell on his pain is a personal matter. To follow Jesus means we must accept pain and suffering as part and parcel of our commitment to him. Not only must we accept it, but we can also anticipate the glory to follow.

To think about

- Why do you think the Gospel writers did not dwell on Christ's physical sufferings?
- How does Jesus's suffering affect your attitude toward suffering?

Lord Jesus, how can I ever thank you enough for suffering incredible pain for me? Draw me closer and closer to the same attitude you had. Forgive me for complaining.

Jesus Forgave His Executioners

Matthew 18:21–22; Luke 23:32–34; Ephesians 4:32

One day Peter asked Jesus a hypothetical question about forgiveness. For some reason he recalled what Jesus had taught on this subject. Seeking to set a high standard for himself, Peter proposed forgiving someone seven times for a personal offense, going well beyond the customary three times that the rabbis taught. Imagine his shock when Jesus told him the answer was seventy times seven. Such hyperbole demonstrated that there should be no limit to one's forgiveness.

The Jesus stories show that again and again Jesus offered forgiveness to people. When he claimed to have authority to forgive their sins, the religious leaders accused him of blasphemy. Clearly they understood that by his telling people their sins were forgiven, Jesus was taking a divine prerogative.

He taught that because God is a forgiving God, his people are also to be forgivers, regardless of the intensity and duration of the offense. Just as there is no limit to God's forgiveness, so ours is to be limitless as well.

While this lesson saturated the teachings of Jesus, he also had to model what it meant under the stupendous pressure and pain that his enemies inflicted. That pressure mounted steadily from the upper room to the Garden of Gethsemane to the various trials and finally to his conviction, beating, humiliation, and crucifixion.

Normally such suffering increases hatred for one's antagonists. When the boiling point is reached emotionally, we cry out for relief and for judgment on our tormentors. We wish them the worst. In some cases, we vilify them. Even some Old Testament heroes cried out for vengeance.

That's the reason the words of Jesus, while he hung in the throes of death on the cross, are so stunning and so contrary to what we might expect. From out of nowhere, Jesus prayed that God would forgive his persecutors.

Typically, in those days people would expect to hear the dying criminal say something like, "May my death atone for all my sins." In this case, Jesus had no sins to atone for. He had done nothing to deserve execution. He was completely guiltless before God and humanity. That's another reason his prayer was so extraordinary.

When we trust Jesus and face brutally tough treatment as he did, we remember his words from the cross. With him, we must say, "Father, forgive them."

To think about

- How did Jesus summon strength and courage to ask God to forgive his executioners?
- In what circumstances have you been pressed to the limit to forgive? How did you react? What was the outcome?

Father, I confess my unforgiving spirit. I find it hard to forgive even small slights. Change my attitude. Make me more like Jesus, so I can forgive others as he did.

Jesus Defeated Death

Matthew 28:1–15; Romans 6:1–10; Hebrews 2:14–15

If we were reading the life of Jesus as a novel, we might hope against hope that he would be saved at the end. There might be some dramatic intervention, some appeal to a higher court that would acquit him of the crimes charged against him. We would know that he was innocent and that the charges were blatant lies. So with considerable distress we would put the book down when Jesus died on the cross, thinking that it was too bad such a wonderful life had to end that way.

But the story did not end when Jesus expired at the Place of the Skull. After he was certified dead, friends buried him. Three days later other friends went to check on his tomb and they could not find his body. His tomb was empty.

Fear and excitement gripped the tiny band of Jesus's loyalists. Of course Jesus had told them he would be killed and that he would come back from the grave alive. Perhaps they thought such talk was meant to inspire and encourage them when they entered the lions' den of Jerusalem. Regardless, they could not grasp the fact—and who can blame them for this?—that Jesus was alive, that he had indeed defeated death as he said he would. Not until Jesus stood before them did they realize the stunning truth of his resurrection. One of them, Thomas, demanded proof from the nail prints and the spear wound before he would believe (John 20:26–28).

Under a variety of circumstances, and before different groups, Jesus gave irrefutable evidence that he had come back from the grave. This fact turned his frightened, defeated disciples into lions. They turned Jerusalem and the world upside down with their fearless testimonies to Christ's resurrection.

Nothing so confirmed that Jesus was God as his defeat of death. Here at last was deliverance from the bondage of the fear of dying, for his resurrection power was made available to all who believe. Again and again the apostles appealed to his resurrection as the valid reason for faith in Jesus and for liberation from sin's power.

So our novel has no ending. The life of Jesus goes on and on. He is alive in heaven. He rules from his Father's right hand. He is not a dead, misguided revolutionary hero, as some people suggest. And someday he will come back in great power and glory because he defeated death and the powers of darkness.

Because Jesus lives in us, death and its sting cannot conquer us. We enjoy a living partnership with a living person. His victory over death brings deliverance now and glory to come. Because he defeated death, we live in Jesus and he lives in us. In the end we too shall rise from the grave and enjoy eternity with him.

To think about

- Why did Jesus's disciples miss the point of his teaching about rising from the dead?
- What difference does the power of his resurrection make in your life?

Lord Jesus, thank you for defeating death and overcoming the powers of evil. Thank you that you are my living God and Savior, that you are not dead like the founders of other religions. My desire is to know your resurrection power in my life.

Jesus, Source of Hope and Purpose

John 14–17; 20:19–31; Acts 1:1–11

Before he departed from the upper room and headed for the Garden of Gethsemane with his disciples, Jesus taught them extensively about how to relate to him and the Holy Spirit after he was gone. All of it was predicated on the fact that he would die and rise from the grave.

Certainty about his death seemed to grip his team at last. With great fear about what might happen to them, the twelve disciples met with Jesus in a secret place. If his enemies were going to kill Jesus, what would they do to his followers? Adding to their sense of loss and distress was the disturbing betrayal of Judas.

When Jesus said they could not follow him, Peter rashly declared that he would go with Jesus, even if it meant death. Jesus wisely disabused him of that notion and called his disciples to a life of peace and freedom from worry. How strange that he would tell them not to be afraid! How could they not worry about their future when he was gone?

He told them that he alone is the way to God, eternal life, heaven, and genuine security in the midst of terrible fear. Since they knew Jesus, they knew the Father.

In desperation, their questions flooded the room. How could they know the Father? Where was he going? What would happen to them? Jesus forced them to look back over three years and he rehearsed what he had done. Stripped to its essence, their future hinged on believing him, trusting him, hoping in him, loving and obeying him, and enjoying the presence of Father, Son, and Holy Spirit. He was their vine and they were his branches. They would bear much fruit for him.

Certain fearful prospects lay ahead. Those who hated Jesus would think that they were doing God a favor by killing his people. Jesus acknowledged his team's grief at the prospect of losing him, but he assured them they would find joy. He told his men to pray as they had never prayed before. Jesus was candid with them: "You will face tribulation, but be cheerful because I have defeated your enemies" (see John 16:33).

After his resurrection, Jesus met them again, not just to prove that he really was alive but to offer them a profound purpose for living. His disciples still longed for a kingdom of this world, but Jesus told them his kingdom was to be advanced by their faithful proclamation of the gospel under the Holy Spirit's power.

Following Jesus means facing our troubles with confidence, and enjoying joy and peace because he is with us. He gave us the Holy Spirit to instruct us and to be everything we would want Jesus to be if he were with us in the flesh. Hope is the most precious commodity we own, thanks to Jesus. Finding life's purpose in doing what Jesus wants us to do is the most satisfying part of life's adventure.

To think about

- Summarize how Jesus gave his team hope for the future.
- How do you face the future with confidence in Jesus? How has he met your need to defeat doubt and discouragement?

Lord Jesus, thank you for your patience with me,
for giving me your lessons again and again. I want
to love and obey you and enjoy your presence,
even in dark hours. Use me in ways small and large
to tell your Good News to many others.

Jesus's Worldwide Vision

Matthew 28:16–20; Acts 1:8; 2:1–47

After Jesus ascended into heaven, the disciples did as they were told and waited in Jerusalem. Probably they talked incessantly about recent events and the implications of Jesus's teaching about the worldwide scope of his salvation plan. They went over the upper room session again and again. They puzzled over what Jesus had meant when he charged them with the task of teaching all nations.

How could this slim band of eleven possibly accomplish such an awesome task? Jesus had said that he possessed full authority. Was that enough? He also had said that he would be with them. Was that sufficient? Finally, he had said the promised Holy Spirit would fall on them for their worldwide mission.

That was all they had to go on. Could they do it? Would they do it? They faced what appeared to be insurmountable obstacles. They had no political or religious power base, no money, little education, and no experience. Besides all of that, they feared persecution and death.

But when the Holy Spirit arrived, all of those impossibilities were shattered. The Jesus team taught the Good News in a multitude of languages to people from all over the Mediterranean world. Eventually their experience on the Day of Pentecost reverberated around the globe.

The disciples trusted Jesus and obeyed his commission, even though they did not have all the answers and had no strategic plan to follow. The only plan Jesus gave them was: "Love and obey me and my Father and I will live in you. That's how the world will know the truth about me."

Everything that Jesus had promised was fulfilled in these unqualified men. They had been with Jesus and that experience was enough for them to take on Jerusalem and the world. Persecution and death came, as Jesus had promised, but they never flinched. We enjoy the presence, peace, and forgiveness of Christ because they listened to him and did what he said.

As followers of Christ, we obey his command to teach people everywhere the Good News about the forgiveness and eternal life available only in him. It does not necessarily mean becoming a professional evangelist or missionary. It does mean keeping his worldwide perspective foremost in our prayers, our sacrifices of time and money, and our willingness to do as much as we can to spread the gospel.

To think about

- How do you think the disciples felt about their impossible assignment? Why?
- Have you discovered your place in Christ's mission? What is it? If you have not yet discovered it, what steps can you take to do so?

Heavenly Father, thank you that in Jesus I can find an overriding purpose for my life. Help me to focus supremely on his worldwide plan. Make me aware of needs near and far, so that I can be part of his saving mission for the world.

The Cross of Jesus, Our Pride

1 Corinthians 1:18–31

How difficult it must have been for the extremely proud, self-righteous Saul of Tarsus to confess pride in the crucified Christ! In the midst of his vicious campaign to exterminate Christians, Saul had been struck down by Jesus. So dramatically powerful was their confrontation that Saul completely repudiated his confidence in his traditional religion.

Jesus gave Saul a new mission in life, and he became Paul the flaming apostolic evangelist. Instead of demanding rigid conformity to the laws of his old faith, Paul held high the cross of Jesus and declared that salvation was possible only through faith in him.

Exactly how Jesus performed this radical change in Saul we are not told. Not only did Jesus change his life's direction, he totally altered his theological perspective. The man who previously abhorred the thought of a crucified Messiah now clearly perceived the utter necessity of Christ's death on the cross.

Paul rejected the arguments of human philosophy so that the fact of Jesus on the cross might achieve maximum impact. He did so knowing full well that educated, cultured Greeks would reject his message as ignorant stupidity. Likewise, the Jews would rebel at the idea of Jesus, who claimed to be God, allowing pagan Romans to crucify him.

Nevertheless, in what can be called history's ultimate paradox, this Jesus on the cross speaks to us most emphatically of God's wisdom and power. Since he suffered there, the cross towers over everything else as our only hope of salvation. It stands as a permanent rebuke to human pride and self-righteousness. Thus Christians have erected crosses over their places of worship and they adorn themselves with crosses as jewelry. The honor that we now give to this symbol

314

of Christ's suffering may in fact subvert the truth that God chose something weak and contemptible to overthrow the world's wisdom and power.

So when we proclaim our pride in Jesus on the cross, we are confessing our total unworthiness. His cross makes us admit, as Paul did, that we are the worst of sinners. His cross reveals the terrible consequence of our sins. We are so bad that it cost God his Son to redeem us and restore us to fellowship with him.

There is no place for human pride in God's presence. If we boast in anything, it is of Jesus our Lord and Savior. Our desire to be number one gives way to making Jesus number one. We do so because of our deep gratitude for what he has accomplished for us.

Paul gave a neat summary of what the cross of Jesus means for us: he is our wisdom, righteousness, holiness, and redemption (1 Cor. 1:26–31). If we are to achieve any progress at all in our walk with Jesus, we must spend hours of significant thought and meditation on these theologically charged affirmations. They prime the pump of our praise. They constitute the substance of our pride in Jesus on the cross.

Whatever our needs, we look to Jesus on the cross and find that he is abundantly loving, wise, and powerful to meet them.

To think about

- Why was Paul so adamant about the centrality of Jesus on the cross?
- What spiritual disciplines draw you to the cross? How do you keep the cross fresh in your mind and heart?

Lord Jesus, your cross completely humbles me. I confess my pride, which makes it hard to take up my cross and follow you. Fill me with praise, hope, and confidence in the light of the cross.

315

"For to Me, to Live Is Christ"

Galatians 2:17–21; Philippians 1:19–26

For to me, to live is . . ." How do you complete this statement? Even for followers of Christ, our answers differ according to where we are in our spiritual pilgrimage. Our answers also reflect our changing circumstances: our age, health, family, career, wealth, and so on. But regardless of where we stand, somehow we must orient ourselves toward Jesus. He is the North Star on our life compass. At the starting point of our journey, Jesus occupies center stage. For some, this brings a radical reorientation in their life; for others, Jesus comes into sharper focus more gradually, and they can't recall a time when they did not know him.

Right now it does not so much matter how we started, but where we stand today. It would be easier if we could chart our love affair with Jesus on a graph, which would move up and down. The dips do not bother us as long as the long-term trend is upward.

Followers of Jesus confess that "for me to live" sometimes means something or someone other than Jesus. In his revelation to John, Jesus acknowledged this condition among the churches. Among them were Christians whose first love for Jesus had cooled off. Others were lukewarm. The apostle Paul wrote bitterly about defectors, who no longer lived for Jesus (1 Tim. 1:20; 2 Tim. 2:17–18; 4:14–16). Such warning signals tell us how important and necessary it is to ask ourselves often whether we are living primarily for Jesus.

Because I've had two bouts with cancer, I visit my oncologist every two months. I could easily say, "For me to live is to avoid another round of cancer." Each time I leave his office with a good report, I thank God. He reminds me that each day is his gift to me, not just of health but also of knowing

316

and trusting his Son. For me to live must mean much more than physical survival.

Just as important as those checkups are, even more important are the times I spend checking on my walk with Jesus. We cannot say, "For me to live is Christ," unless we take steps to keep our relationship with him sound, wholesome, and healthy.

Jesus saves us from our past sins, he saves us now, and he will save us for eternity. Now is our opportunity to bring all our dreams, hopes, and fears under the scope of his love and wisdom.

Three times the writer of Hebrews commanded, "Today, if you hear his voice, do not harden your hearts" (3:7–8, 15; 4:7). Jesus becomes our North Star when we hear him through our prayer, Bible reading, worship, and fellowship. He speaks in our varied circumstances, sweet and bitter.

> Thou only art true Life,
> To know Thee is to live
> The more abundant life
> That earth can never give:
> O risen Lord! We live in Thee,
> And Thou in us eternally.
>
> E. Margaret Clarkson
> "We Come, O Christ, to Thee"

To think about

- What factors inspired Paul to declare that Jesus was his life?
- Graph your spiritual journey. Where are you in your walk with Jesus? How can you keep moving onward and upward?

Lord Jesus, I want everything in my life to center on you, but I confess that at times other affections get in the way. Keep me listening closely and obediently to you, so that your place in my life will become larger and larger. Thank you.

Jesus Died That I Might Live for Him

2 Corinthians 5:11–15

I fell in love with Jesus when I was a teenager. Two doses of John 1:12 administered by evangelist Percy Crawford brought me to my knees. I rose from the communion rail at the front of the church, liberated from the weight of sin. Jesus had accepted me and forgiven me and I was satisfied.

No spiritual disciplines shaped my relationship with Jesus until I arrived on the college campus. A tiny "Christ Died for Our Sins" placard on the rear bumper of my 1931 Chevrolet caught the attention of a Christian student. He invited me to a student Bible study and prayer group. There my love affair with Jesus blossomed like early spring daffodils.

The ramifications of my commitment to Jesus gradually took hold of me. One night a speaker in Philadelphia nailed me with 2 Corinthians 5:15. Could I really stop living for myself and live for Jesus instead? Like ancient Jacob wrestling with an angel, I grappled with Jesus for some time before I surrendered.

Jesus died to achieve much more than our forgiveness. He died to unfold for us an entirely new purpose for living. Successful Christian living demands that we be fully occupied with Jesus. Whatever other "secrets" of success in Christian living we may discover, none will ever surpass the beauty, power, and simplicity of living for Jesus, who died and rose again.

The apostle Paul draws us to Jesus with superb logic. "I have been crucified with Christ and I no longer live, but Christ lives in me" (Gal. 2:20). "We were therefore buried with him [Jesus] through baptism into death in order that, just as Christ was raised from the dead . . . we too may live a new life" (Rom. 6:4). "Since, then, you have been raised with Christ,

318

set your hearts on things above, where Christ is seated at the right hand of God" (Col. 3:1).

Such discoveries propelled me into that "new creation." The old was departing and the new was arriving. Newness gave birth to joy as I submitted everything to Jesus. Of course sometimes I resisted when Jesus prescribed some tough medicine, and I rebelled when I should have obeyed.

But Jesus never quit on me. He rebuked me for living for myself. He reminded me, "He who did not spare his own Son, but gave him up for us all—how will he not also, along with him, graciously give us all things?" (Rom. 8:32).

Can we trust him to do that for us? Can we pray, "Yes, Jesus, your way is the best way for me"? Can we ask him to make us cease living for ourselves? Absolutely, provided we "fix our eyes on Jesus, the author and perfecter of our faith" (Heb. 12:2).

One way or another, everything hinges on Jesus: who he is, why he came, why he died for us and rose again, and what he loves to do for us now. As we marinate ourselves in Jesus, the desire to live for ourselves diminishes and we are liberated to love and serve the best Friend we will ever know.

To think about

- What did Paul mean when he declared, "Christ's love compels us" (2 Cor. 5:14)?
- In what aspects of your life are you living for yourself? How can you be set free to live for Jesus?

Thank you, heavenly Father, for the compelling love of Jesus. May his love conquer my fears and reservations about living for him. Thank you for your patience with me. Exalt Jesus in me. Thank you.

The Lamb's Wedding Feast

Revelation 19:6–9

No banquet has ever been held, or ever will be held, that matches the magnificence of the Lamb's wedding feast. For one thing, shouts of a great multitude, like the roar of rushing waters and peals of loud thunder, announce the feast. Imagine, if you can, the biggest, loudest band you ever heard and a crowd of more than one hundred thousand football fans wildly cheering the winning touchdown. Well, the heralds of the Lamb's wedding banquet far surpass anything like that.

This universal outburst erupts because "our Lord God Almighty reigns" and Jesus has arrived to meet his bride (Rev. 19:6). God invites only his church to come to the wedding. His church, the bride of Christ, wears bright, spotless, fine linen. The bride's gown represents the righteousness of believers in Christ.

"Give glory to God," the multitude cries. "Rejoice and be glad." The appropriateness of this response matches the occasion. The wedding of the Lamb signals the climax of history, the culmination of God's saving plan for the universe. The battle against the forces of evil is over and God's victory must be celebrated through the union of Christ and his bride.

The apostle John, who received this vision from Jesus, uses language that we can grasp to tell us what Christ's triumph will be like. Since our human weddings deserve to be celebrated, how much more does the wedding of Jesus and the church call for the greatest feast and celebration of all time!

The angel added this postscript to the wedding invitation, which can be considered a major understatement: "Blessed are those who are invited to the wedding supper of the Lamb!"

(v. 9). Blessed indeed! The blessing is both personal and universal.

The whole world's redemption must be celebrated. Jesus has won the cosmic struggle for control of the universe. Good has overcome evil at last. The supplication in the Lord's Prayer: "your kingdom come . . . on earth" (Matt. 6:10) has been answered. Creation has been liberated from its bondage to decay. The seemingly endless days of groaning for redemption are over (Rom. 8:21–22).

People who have entrusted their lives to Jesus have at last achieved the full benefits of their redemption that he promised and the apostles preached. Isaiah's prophecy, "Death has been swallowed up in victory" (1 Cor. 15:54), has been fulfilled. Those who have loved Jesus through years of tribulation have been vindicated. Their emotional release is appropriately compared to rushing waters and loud thunder.

Until we celebrate the great wedding feast, we follow Jesus with determination, regardless of the cost. We know that one day we will receive the most glorious invitation ever posted: "Come and celebrate with Jesus, your bridegroom. The wedding feast has been prepared for you. This is your reward."

To think about

- Why do you think the inauguration of Christ's reign must be compared to a wedding celebration?
- What steps can you take to prepare for Christ's wedding supper?

O God, I cannot possibly take in the magnificence and meaning of everything in this wedding scene. Help me to grasp its glory, joy, and power. May this scene give me hope and joy when I suffer doubts, fears, and troubles.

Jesus's Invitations and Promises

Ten minutes' meditation on each of Jesus's invitations and promises will bring incomparable encouragement, instruction, and hope. Jesus is on call 24/7. Whenever and however you need him, flee to him and he will rush to your aid and comfort.

"Come, follow me" (Matt. 4:19).

"Whoever loses his life for my sake will find it" (Matt. 10:39).

"Come to me, all you who are weary and burdened, and I will give you rest" (Matt. 11:28).

"If anyone would come after me, he must deny himself and take up his cross and follow me" (Matt. 16:24).

"Unless you change and become like little children, you will never enter the kingdom of God" (Matt. 18:3).

"If two of you on earth agree about anything you ask for, it will be done for you by my Father in heaven" (Matt. 18:19).

"If you believe, you will receive whatever you ask for in prayer" (Matt. 21:22).

"Take and eat; this is my body. . . . Drink from it, all of you. This is my blood of the covenant . . ." (Matt. 26:26–28).

"Repent and believe the Good News" (Mark 1:15).

"Don't be afraid; just believe" (Mark 5:36).

"Come with me by yourselves to a quiet place and get some rest" (Mark 6:31).

"Everything is possible for him who believes" (Mark 9:23).

"Whoever welcomes me does not welcome me but the one who sent me" (Mark 9:37).

"What I say to you, I say to everyone: 'Watch!'" (Mark 13:37).

"Your faith has saved you; go in peace" (Luke 7:50).

"Ask and it will be given to you; seek and you will find; knock and the door will be opened to you. For everyone who asks receives; he who seeks finds; and to him who knocks, the door will be opened" (Luke 11:9–10).

"Blessed rather are those who hear the word of God and obey it" (Luke 11:28).

"Seek his kingdom and these things will be given to you as well" (Luke 12:31).

"Unless you repent, you too will all perish" (Luke 13:5).

"He who humbles himself will be exalted" (Luke 14:11).

"The tax collector . . . said, 'God have mercy on me, a sinner.' I tell you that this man . . . went home justified before God" (Luke 18:13–14).

"Zacchaeus, come down immediately. I must stay at your house today." So he came down at once and welcomed him gladly (Luke 19:5–6).

"Get up and pray so that you will not fall into temptation" (Luke 22:46).

To all who received him, to those who believed in his name, he gave the right to become children of God (John 1:12).

"You must be born again" (John 3:7).

"Whoever believes in him shall not perish but have eternal life" (John 3:16).

"Whoever drinks the water I give him will never thirst" (John 4:14).

"Whoever hears my word and believes him who sent me has eternal life" (John 5:24).

"I am the bread of life. He who comes to me will never go hungry" (John 6:35).

"Whoever comes to me I will never drive away" (John 6:37).

"Everyone who looks to the Son and believes in him shall have eternal life" (John 6:40).

"The one who feeds on me will live because of me" (John 6:57).

"If anyone is thirsty, let him come to me and drink" (John 7:37).

"I am the light of the world. Whoever follows me will never walk in darkness" (John 8:12).

"I am the good shepherd. . . . My sheep listen to my voice; I know them and they follow me" (John 10:11, 27).

"I am the resurrection and the life. He who believes in me will live, even though he dies" (John 11:25).

"Put your trust in the light while you have it" (John 12:36).

"Do not let your hearts be troubled. Trust in God; trust also in me" (John 14:1).

"Believe me when I say that I am in the Father and the Father is in me; or at least believe on the evidence of the miracles themselves" (John 14:11).

"I will do whatever you ask in my name, so the Son may bring glory to the Father" (John 14:13).

"He who loves me will be loved by my Father, and I too will love him and show myself to him. . . . If anyone loves me, he will obey my teaching" (John 14:21, 23).

"I am the true vine. . . . Remain in me, and I will remain in you. . . . If a man remains in me and I in him, he will bear much fruit" (John 15:1, 4–5).

"If you remain in me and my words remain in you, ask whatever you wish, and it will be given you" (John 15:7).

"If you obey my commands, you will remain in my love" (John 15:10).

"Until now you have not asked for anything in my name. Ask and you will receive, and your joy will be complete" (John 16:24).

"Here I am! I stand at the door and knock. If anyone hears my voice and opens the door, I will come in and eat with him, and he with me" (Rev. 3:20).

Thank you, Lord Jesus, for the magnitude of your gracious, loving invitations and promises to me. I confess you as my Lord and Savior. I accept your invitation to believe, follow and obey—to the praise of your glorious grace. Amen.

Lord, I want to be like Jesus in my heart, in my heart.
Lord, I want to be like Jesus in my heart, in my heart, in my heart.
Lord, I want to be like Jesus in my heart.

Author unknown. African-American spiritual.

Apostolic Affirmations of Jesus

What did the leaders of the early church make of Jesus? How did they present him to the world? What stupendous, revolutionary claims did they make for him? The following apostolic affirmation of Jesus will strengthen your faith and your resolve to keep on worshiping, obeying, trusting, and hoping in Jesus. They validate heaven's incomparable accolade about Jesus: "Worthy is the Lamb who was slain, to receive power and wealth and wisdom and strength and honor and glory and praise!" (Rev. 5:12).

Due to copyright restrictions, we can't print out these verses. Please read them in your Bible.

Acts 2:22–24, 32–33, 36, 38; 3:13–16, 18–21; 4:10–12, 30; 5:30–31; 7:56; 10:36–43; 13:23–25, 27–33, 37–39; 15:11; 16:31; 17:2–3, 31; 18:28; 20:21; 26:17–18, 22–23; 28:23, 31

Romans 1:2–4; 3:22–25; 5:1–2, 6–8, 10–11, 17; 6:3–5, 8–11, 23; 8:1–3, 17, 29, 32, 34–35, 39; 10:4, 9; 12:5; 14:9; 15:3, 8

1 Corinthians 1:4–9, 17–18, 23–24, 30; 2:2, 16; 3:11, 21–23; 4:5, 10, 15; 5:4, 7; 6:11, 15, 20; 7:23; 8:6, 12; 10:3–4,

16; 11:1, 3, 23–27, 29; 12:12, 27; 15:3–8, 14–28, 57; 16:23–24

2 Corinthians 1:5, 19–22; 2:14–15; 3:3, 14; 4:4–6, 10–11; 5:10, 14–21; 8:9; 9:15; 10:5; 11:2–3; 12:9; 13:3–5, 14

Galatians 1:3–5, 12, 15–16; 2:4, 14–16, 20–21; 3:1, 13–14, 16, 22, 26–29; 4:4–7, 19; 5:1, 6, 24; 6:14, 18

Ephesians 1:3–12, 19–23; 2:4–7, 10, 13–18, 20–22; 3:4, 6, 8, 12, 16–19; 4:13, 15–16; 5:2, 23, 25–27, 29

Philippians 1:10–11, 18, 20–21, 29; 2:5–11; 3:7–12, 14, 20–21; 4:7, 13, 19

Colossians 1:13–20, 22, 27–28; 2:2–3, 6, 9–15, 17, 19–20; 3:1–4, 11, 15–17

1 Thessalonians 1:10; 2:19; 3:13; 4:14, 16–17; 5:9–10, 23–24

2 Thessalonians 1:7–10; 2:8, 14; 3:5

1 Timothy 1:14–17; 2:5–6; 3:16; 6:14–15

2 Timothy 1:1, 9–10, 12; 2:1, 8, 11–13; 3:15; 4:1

Titus 2:13–14; 3:4–7

Hebrews 1:1–4; 2:9–11, 17–18; 3:1–3, 6; 4:14–15; 5:5–10; 7:21–28; 8:1–2, 6; 9:11–15, 24–28; 10:5–7, 10, 12–14, 19–22; 12:2; 13:8, 12, 20–21

1 Peter 1:3–4, 13, 18–21; 2:4, 6–8, 21–25; 3:18–19, 21–22; 4:1; 5:4

2 Peter 1:11, 17; 3:18

1 John 1:1–2, 7, 9; 2:1–2, 22, 28; 3:2–3, 8, 16, 23–24; 4:2–3, 9–10, 14–15; 5:1, 5–6, 11–12, 20

Jude 24–25

Revelation 1:5–8, 13–18; 3:20–21; 4:3, 10–11; 5:5–6, 8–10, 12–13; 11:15; 12:11; 13:8; 14:1, 4; 15:3–4; 17:14; 19:6–7, 11–16; 20:4–6; 21:6, 9–10, 22–23, 27; 22:3–5, 12–13, 16, 20

Lord Jesus, you alone merit my total worship and commitment to all you were, are, and will be. I stand with the apostles in declaring my allegiance to you and to all the truth about you, who alone are the way, the truth, and the life.

Jim Reapsome, a retired editor, pastor, and teacher, lives in Downers Grove, Illinois. He edited *Evangelical Missions Quarterly* for more than thirty years and pastored churches in Pennsylvania and Illinois. He has written numerous Bible study guides.